Penguin Books

Poverty and the Planet

Ben Jackson has been the World Development Movement's Campaigns Officer for the last three years. He studied geography at St John's College, Oxford, and has worked in a Ugandan village, researched with Ethiopian refugees in Sudan and travelled widely in Africa. He has researched and written many articles and campaign publications on the Third World, recently contributing to two reports on environment and development, *Britain and the Brundtland Report* (1988) and *Brundtland in the Balance* (1989), co-editing the latter.
He is married and lives in London.

The World Development Movement is Britain's main pressure group winning changes for the world's poor on issues like environment and development, trade, debt and aid. WDM is cross-party and backed by the major aid agencies and the churches. You can support WDM as a Friend or Member from £10 a year by completing the form at the back of the book.

World Development Movement
21–25 Beehive Place
London SW9 7QR

POVERTY AND THE PLANET

A Question of Survival

Ben Jackson

World Development Movement

PENGUIN BOOKS

PENGUIN BOOKS

Published by the Penguin Group
Penguin Books Ltd, 27 Wrights Lane, London W8 5TZ, England
Viking Penguin, a division of Penguin Books USA Inc.
375 Hudson Street, New York, New York 10014, USA
Penguin Books Australia Ltd, Ringwood, Victoria, Australia
Penguin Books Canada Ltd, 2801 John Street, Markham, Ontario, Canada L3R 1B4
Penguin Books (NZ) Ltd, 182–190 Wairau Road, Auckland 10, New Zealand

Penguin Books Ltd, Registered Offices: Harmondsworth, Middlesex, England

First published 1990
10 9 8 7 6 5 4 3 2

Copyright © World Development Movement, 1990
All rights reserved

The moral right of the author has been asserted

Filmset in 10 on 12 Photina

Printed in England by Clays Ltd, St Ives plc

Three exist where three are not:

Commoner exists where there is no king,
   but a kingdom cannot exist where there are no
   commoners;
Grass exists where there is nothing that eats grass,
   but what eats grass cannot exist where no grass is;
Water exists where there is nothing that drinks water,
   but what drinks water cannot exist where no water is.

Fulani poem, Nigeria

Contents

List of Figures

List of Tables

Introduction

This book is about global causes of the poverty and ecological degradation which daily blight the lives of at least a billion people on our earth. Like the World Development Movement (WDM) for which it is written, the book aims to stimulate people in the rich countries to play an informed part in ending these outrageously preventable problems in a world of plenty and sophisticated technical know-how.

It is written in the belief, born of both WDM's and my own experience of public and political campaigning, that one of the greatest obstacles to ending world poverty is a lack of clear understanding of its causes. It is not so much that there is a lack of knowledge of the detailed technical issues, but more often that the wrong questions are asked of the wrong people. The detailed contours of surface symptoms are repeatedly scrutinized, while the deeper causes go unexamined.

It is WDM's experience that in setting out to tackle the immediate, pressing problems of poverty, you are often drawn far away to unexpected places to find their cause. The paradoxical truth is that to find the most effective answers to the problems, you do not necessarily start with the most obvious and direct solution. The best way of helping the hungry, for example, may seem to be to send food from the food stores of the rich countries, but in the long run it may only add to the problem. This can be equally true in trying to tackle environmental problems in the Third World. You may start in a burning rainforest, but end up in the boardroom of a high-street bank.

The best efforts of Western aid charities to alleviate the daily problems faced by the poor – whether soil erosion or lack of food –

are often undermined as the deeper causes of poverty and environmental degradation recurrently rear their heads. Many of the agencies themselves concede this and try to channel their efforts into long-term development projects. But even this more long-term help can only be on a localized scale. Relying on a continual treatment of only the symptoms still means that the patient – whether people or land – is likely to die in the end. Tackling these root causes is the concern of this book. It is also the logic of WDM, which exists solely to campaign for the political changes needed to end world poverty and put people-centred and environmentally sustainable development in its place. It is, too, why WDM is supported in its work by all of Britain's main aid charities and churches.

The book also emerged from the growing moves towards Third World development groups and environmental organizations working together at international, national and local levels. It was in fact partly my own experience in working for WDM on joint campaigns with environmental pressure groups which led to the writing of the book. Such alliances are to some extent a matter of practical politics. Pressure on national and international institutions dealing with the Third World from different quarters is likely to be more effective if it is unified. But the growing alliances are more than marriages of convenience. There is a deepening understanding of the fundamental links between underdevelopment and the environment, between poverty and the planet.

However, this dialogue has necessarily thrown up some complex issues, cases of clashing priorities and the need for people to unlearn entrenched ideas. Both lack of genuine development and inappropriate forms of development threaten the poor and the environment. It is no longer adequate simply to oppose existing forms of development; we must begin to say what should take their place. The book also tries to point to some of these possible future paths, based where possible on present success stories.

The book also arose from WDM's own particular recent experience. After twenty years of political campaigning on world poverty, it took some while to take stock. Those active in WDM took time to look back over the successes and failures of those years. Such a review involved not only new ways of working, but also a look at the agenda for future action. The book reflects this and will form part of a major ongoing campaign of public discussion and political action in which, we hope, some of those reading it will be able to play a part.

The book has been purged as far as possible of technical jargon, on the assumption that those reading it will not have specialist knowledge of the issues discussed. However, I do not believe that keeping things simple or writing something that it is hoped will equip some of its readers for political campaigning necessarily means simplistically glossing over the debates, dilemmas and difficult questions.

By the year 2000, *on present trends*, there will be more people in Africa who cannot read and write than at the start of the decade of the continent's independence. By the same year, it is also estimated that four out of five of the countries presently exporting tropical timber will no longer even be self-sufficient, such is the rate of deforestation. World events at the beginning of the 1990s, however, were a reminder that long-established trends and structures, which many thought immutable, can be changed by the combination of people's action from within countries and the enabling actions of those outside. The issues dealt with in this book are also deep-rooted, but it is written in the firm belief that they are similarly not unchangeable.

Acknowledgements

Writing this book has been far from a solitary endeavour. I have received great support from many of WDM's present members, Council, volunteers and staff – as well as drawing on WDM's experience and knowledge, accumulated over twenty years of Third World campaigning. I would especially like to thank Edward Mayo, WDM's Campaigns Co-ordinator, for his support throughout the project and his substantial input to the text, especially in chapters 3 and 4. I am indebted to the members of WDM's Campaigns Committee who commented on drafts and to its chairperson, Shelagh Diplock, for her support. Many other people from WDM, other development and environmental organizations and friends have helped me greatly by contributing their ideas, providing information and commenting on drafts of the book or chapters. I would particularly like to thank Rachel Ayling, Michael Barratt-Brown, Elaine Barry, Czech Conroy, David Cooper, Tim Crabtree, Rebecca Francis, Jo Graham, Earlene Horne, Jo McGregor, Charlotte Mbali, John Mitchell, Ivan Nutbrown, Atiq Rahman, Milan Rai, Geoff Tansey and Pauline Tiffen. Paul Goodwin and Peter Madden generously donated time in research. Neville Dack, James Leith and Robert Wilkinson carefully proofread the book.

Tom Aston put in a lot of work making the English clearer and more readable. Julia Casson, Paul Dwyer, Jean Walton and Gill Peace all helped in the final stages, processing and incorporating the amendments. My father, George Jackson, kindly lent me the computer on which the book was written. Finally I would like to thank Gill Anderson, my wife, for her comments on the book, support and forbearance as the piles of reports, boxes of papers and wordprocessors invaded. None of the above people or any of the organizations with which they are associated is responsible for the opinions or any errors contained in this book.

Figure 2.1 is reproduced with the permission of Gemini News Service.

'Three exist where three are not' was originally published in *Oral Literature in Africa*, edited by Ruth Finnegan (1967), and is reproduced by kind permission of Oxford University Press.

Note: Throughout the book 'dollars' means US dollars, unless otherwise stated. 'Billion' means a thousand million.

Selected List of Abbreviations

AMC	Agricultural Marketing Corporation (Ethiopia)
ANC	African National Congress (South Africa)
ANTA	National Association of Farmworkers (El Salvador)
ATP	Aid-Trade Provision
CAP	Common Agricultural Policy
CIA	Central Intelligence Agency
CIIR	Catholic Institute for International Relations
DAC	Development Assistance Committee
DTI	Department of Trade and Industry (UK)
EC	European Community
ECA	United Nations Economic Commission for Africa
ECOWAS	Economic Community of West African States
FAO	Food and Agriculture Organisation (UN)
GATT	General Agreement on Trade and Tariffs
GNP	Gross National Product
HFCS	High Fructose Corn Syrup
IDA	International Development Association
IFAD	International Fund for Agricultural Development
IIED	International Institute for Environment and Development
ILO	International Labour Organisation
IMF	International Monetary Fund
IUCN	International Union for the Conservation of Nature
JFHQ	Joint Forces Headquarters (UK)
NAO	National Audit Office
NGO	Non-Governmental Organization
NIC	Newly Industrializing Country

ODA	Overseas Development Administration (UK)
ODI	Overseas Development Institute
OECD	Organisation for Economic Co-operation and Development
OPEC	Organisation of Petroleum Exporting Countries
PAMSCAD	Programme of Action to Mitigate the Social Costs of Adjustment
RADI	Réseau Africain pour le Développement Intégré (Senegal)
REST	Relief Society of Tigray
RRC	Relief and Rehabilitation Commission (Ethiopia)
SAARC	South Asian Association for Regional Co-operation
SADCC	Southern African Development Co-ordination Conference
SAP	Structural Adjustment Programme
UDR	União Democratica Ruralista (Brazil)
UN	United Nations
UNCTAD	United Nations Conference on Trade and Development
UNEP	United Nations Environment Programme
UNICEF	United Nations Children's Fund
USAID	United States Agency for International Development
VER	Voluntary Export Restraint
WCED	World Commission on Environment and Development
WDM	World Development Movement
WFP	World Food Programme
WHO	World Health Organisation
WWF	World-wide Fund for Nature

1 A Question of Survival

We have not had the same past, you and ourselves, but
we shall surely have the same future. The era of separate
destinies has run its course.

Cheika Hamidou Kane, Senegal

In February 1989, hundreds of Indians and other local people
gathered for a remarkable meeting in the remote town of Altamira
in the northern Brazilian Amazon. They had come to protest at the
government's plans to flood – with Western financial backing –
more than 7,000 square kilometres of rainforest and with it the
lands of some 70,000 people by building the Altamira hydro-
electric dam complex.[1]

The demonstration was spectacular, noisy and defiant. As José
Antonio Muñoz Lopez, planning director of the Brazilian power
company Electronorte, began his defence of the scheme, a tribes-
woman called Toia rushed forward wielding a machete at him. Her
symbolic though none the less frightening attack ended with her
delivering him a light slap on each cheek with her giant knife. 'We
have not come to hear about new studies; we want the project
cancelled here and now,' said a local Xante Indian leader defiantly.
'We are the real Brazilians and we have been here for centuries
and centuries. You must respect us.'[2]

In the face of the common threat posed by the dam to their forest
environment and livelihoods, *seringueiros* (small-time rubber-
tappers) and forest Indians, fisherfolk and poor local town dwellers,
who in the past had fought over dwindling forest resources, protested together in an unprecedented display of unity. As the Xante
chief pointed out:

There are poor people all over Brazil, but the country gets foreign
money, not to help the poor, but to build dams that will benefit the big
companies far away.[3]

All this was enacted in front of the world's television cameras and 500 foreign journalists, environmentalists and politicians. They were drawn to Altamira as it provided a focus for growing worldwide concern over the destruction of the tropical rainforest. Suddenly, around the world, everyone from pop stars to conservative Western politicians seemed to be rushing to save the rainforest. But Brazilian leaders were angry. 'Ecological extremists – Indians and foreign groups interested in manipulating the Amazon – want to see Brazilians without lights. They are anti-progress,' thundered one government minister.[4] Brazil accuses environmentalists of keeping the country poor by trying to stop people from developing their own land, the Amazon, to grow food, dig out minerals and generate electric power. In the global war of words over the environment and economic development in the Third World, little appeared to have changed since 1972 when Brazil's leaders defiantly declared to an international conference on the environment that 'smoke is a sign of progress'.

PANDAS OR PEOPLE?

To many in the slums and villages of Asia, Africa and Latin America, environmentalism seems like an expensive luxury. So, too, for their rulers, the immediate need to provide food, water, health services and education has overshadowed any long-term consideration for the environment. Add to this the volatility of the world economy, erratic commodity prices and the treadmill of huge debts, and it is not hard to see why the environment has been a low priority for poor countries. In fact, many – both in the Third World and outside – believe that Western environmentalism is an excuse to freeze the existing world order, by causing a diversion from the real issues of economic injustice and exploitation of the poor by the rich. In short, environmentalists put pandas before people.

Thinking on both sides is now changing. But only in the last few years has nurturing the environment been widely recognized as central to tackling poverty. By observing environmental destruction in the Third World, many came to realize the folly of ignoring environmental issues. The transformation of forests into deserts, of fertile earth into sunbaked concrete, of running rivers into silted floodwaters, all proved that only by care of the environment could the livelihoods of those most dependent on it – the poor – be sustained.

The alternative was to allow the vicious circle of poverty and destruction of the earth to continue. It promised a slow death for millions from malnutrition and related diseases, the break-up of communities and cultures, the migration of millions more to the already overcrowded and squalid cities, and sporadic outbreaks of famine. For every television image of twig-like children, victims of famine and natural disasters in Bangladesh, Sudan or Ethiopia, there was an environmental disaster to match – deforestation, erosion, silted rivers. And behind every environmental drama there were, in turn, the harsh realities of rural poverty, of landless villagers destroying nature simply to eat and drink, and of governments pursuing economic growth at any cost to the environment, encouraged by Western companies, governments and financial institutions.

GROWING GREENS

Historically, economic booms have nourished 'green' movements and this may partly explain Third World suspicion of Western environmentalists. The modern environmental movement grew out of the seemingly unstoppable Western economic growth of the 1950s and 1960s. Despite the prosperity of the 'never-had-it-so-good' consumer society, unease was growing about pollution and the wasteful destruction of nature which was a hallmark of Western industrial development. An agenda of concern emerged which centred on pollution (acid rain, lead in petrol, pesticides); waste (nuclear and toxic); preservation of nature and the countryside (disappearing species of wildlife, habitats and beautiful scenery); and the conservation of natural resources and energy.

Rachel Carson was one writer who shaped the embryonic environmental movement in the United States of America. In 1962 her classic book, *Silent Spring*, was one of the first to awaken a wide audience to the damage wrought to wildlife by the 'chemical barrage' of agricultural pesticides:

> Over increasingly large areas of the United States, spring now comes unheralded by the return of the birds, and the early mornings are strangely silent where once they were filled with the beauty of bird song.[5]

In North America and Europe, local and national campaigns rapidly spread to conserve the natural habitats of endangered species before they were flattened by burgeoning cities and spreading motorways in the search for more wealth regardless of the expense to nature.

More radical critics turned some of the basic principles of Western economics on their head: 'small is beautiful' instead of faith in large-scale technology and industry; 'limits to growth' instead of the ceaseless search for higher levels of economic growth and use of natural resources; holistic thinking instead of the infinite specialities of modern science. In return, Western political leaders and business people accused environmentalists of naivety and of trying to turn the clock back.

As the movement gathered pace, so did the diversity of its shades of 'green-ness'. 'There are almost as many shades of opinion within the environment movement as there are within politics itself,' says former Friends of the Earth Director and Green Party activist Jonathan Porritt.[6] On one side are those who totally reject the consumer society and the individualism of the Western way of life in favour of a back-to-nature, communal lifestyle. But on the other are the smart country set and squires who read *Country Life* magazine, along with green-belt commuters, spurred on by their desire to escape the city for a nostalgic rural idyll and vehemently defensive of their privileged access to the countryside. Despite the differences, environmentalists carry a broad conviction that the growth of industrial and technological society is what threatens the environment and quality of life.

Seen from the Third World, however, these were purely Western preoccupations. From this perspective, concern for the environment became associated with affluent Westerners absorbed by their problems of 'overdevelopment'. People in the Third World were concerned with poverty and underdevelopment – not pollution and preserving the countryside. Some environmentalists became suspect in the eyes of Third World activists who said they neglected the problems of poverty or, worse, hid their real causes. Debates about the limits to world resources, for example, diverted attention from the question of who got what in the grossly unjust world economy. At the same time, leaders of Third World countries such as Brazil were adamant that environmental problems could only be tackled when poor countries had achieved a certain level of prosperity – as had happened in rich countries.

A NEW ALLIANCE

The either/or style of debate over environment and development has not disappeared, but increasingly there is a meeting of minds. Many involved in Third World development now recognize that, contrary to the old idea of environment as a luxury, it is poor people in the Third World who face the most pressing environmental crisis. The environment can no longer be the preserve of middle-class Westerners. In addition, national economic development will be 'development' only for the short term if it ignores the destruction of the natural resources upon which any kind of lasting development must be based. At the same time, environmentalists now concede that the rape of the planet cannot be halted simply by imposing environmental conservation on the Third World, because the seedbed of ecological destruction is the global divisions between rich and poor. A series of 'keep out' signs around the world's forests and environmental hot-spots would not only be morally unacceptable, with the poor still hungry outside; it just would not work.

One landmark in this new thinking was the publication in 1987 of *Our Common Future*, the report of the World Commission on Environment and Development, chaired by the former Norwegian Prime Minister, Gro Harlem Brundtland. For over two years, a high-level international team of commissioners travelled the world holding public hearings and taking evidence. Time and again they found this evidence pointed to the close links between poverty, inequality and environmental degradation. They called for 'sustainable development': 'development that meets the needs of the present without com promising the ability of future generations to meet their own needs . . . in particular, the essential needs of the world's poor'.[7]

In recognition of these links, people are forming new alliances concerned for the environment, world poverty, human rights and peace. In Britain, for example, groups as diverse as Friends of the Earth, World-wide Fund for Nature, World Development Movement, Survival International and Quaker Peace and Service have joined forces to push the British government to take concrete action to promote sustainable global development.[8] In 1988, 50,000 people from all walks of life took to the streets of Berlin to protest against the impact of the International Monetary Fund and World Bank on poor countries and the environment, as the world's two major financial institutions met for their annual meetings in the city's plush International Congress Centre.[9] These new alliances reflect the day-to-day experience of the poor in the Third World.

In the countryside, where most of the world's poor live, people's lives are bound up with the land and environment because they directly supply their daily necessities. The land gives food and pasture. Trees provide fuelwood, fruits, medicine and building materials. Water is collected from the local well or river. Some communities, such as those on the shores of Lake Malawi or the coast and islands of Bangladesh, depend upon the waters which yield the fish they trade and eat. Increasingly, life-sustaining local resources – soil, trees, water – are under attack from the rich First World and the rich in the Third World, and are being over-exploited by the poorest people in their desperate struggle to make ends meet. In the Third World, as Anil Agarwal, Director of the Indian Centre for Science and the Environment, says, 'environmental destruction is not an issue of quality of life but is a question of survival'.[10]

SCORCHED EARTH

Throughout the Third World land is dying, or, to put it more accurately, being killed. Human action rooted in poverty and the pressures of the world economy is degrading the land. When disasters like drought or flood strike, it no longer returns to full productivity.

Land degradation comes in many forms: bare slopes left without topsoil or scarred by deep gullies after protecting trees have been cut down; skeleton soils whose fertility has been leached out by water; dry but once productive land turned into barren desert, exposed to the ravages of wind and blown thousands of miles into the ocean and atmosphere; ground poisoned by pesticides and other toxic chemicals; land invaded by plants unpalatable to livestock, after natural vegetation has been removed. The results can be devastating. The Sahel drought of the early 1970s was a deadly trigger for starvation only because for years the land had been bankrupted through human misuse and over-exploitation – a process which has become known as 'desertification'. As many as a quarter of a million people died in the disaster on the southern fringe of the Sahara, as well as three and a half million cattle, sheep and goats. In the ensuing social and political turmoil every government in the region fell. Nearly a million 'environmental refugees' – a sixth of the population – fled from Burkino Faso (then Upper Volta), and half a million from neighbouring Mali.[11]

Desertification may also be changing the world climate. Climate experts Jule Charney of the Massachusetts Institute of Technology and William Quirk at NASA's Goddard Institute for Space Studies argue that human destruction of vegetation in the Sahel may have set up a vicious circle in which the 'desert enhances its own dryness, i.e. it feeds back on itself'. As trees and vegetation are destroyed the soil is exposed, so making the land surface more reflective; this has the effect of preventing clouds from forming, so reducing rainfall, and in turn preventing vegetation growth. Thus the cycle continues.[12]

Less dramatic soil erosion and land degradation can be just as disastrous. Of the 850 million people living in the world's drylands, 230 million live on land affected by severe desertification. The United Nations Environment Programme describes how the poor are affected as their ecosystem slowly breaks down:

As crops fail, domestic animals die, water sources dry up and fuelwood becomes more and more difficult to obtain, the prospects for survival dwindle. Often they do so slowly, almost imperceptibly. Nutritious grasses are replaced by less palatable ones, forcing livestock to search larger areas for food; farmers are forced to move on to steep hillside land or areas previously considered too infertile to warrant cultivation. Water sources become polluted with silt and salt. And the trees on which rural families throughout the developing world depend . . . become virtually unobtainable.[13]

Sudan, hard hit by famine in the 1980s, has lost vast tracts of once productive land through desertification. Yields of the staple food crops, sorghum and millet, have steadily declined since the 1960s, even excluding drought years.[14] Travelling eastwards out of the capital, Khartoum, one soon reaches stony, flat expanses of virtual desert. In the dry season the horizon turns to an orange-brown haze as the exhausted, dusty soil blows away in the wind. All that interrupts the landscape is an isolated tree or the occasional cluster of nomads' black tents and their camels gathered around a murky water-hole. Life is becoming an increasingly hard struggle for these wandering herders as pastures become fewer and further between.

Many Sudanese can remember the same area two decades ago when it was generously scattered with trees and used as prime seasonal grazing. During the 1960s and 1970s between five and nine million acres of this ecologically sensitive land were cleared of trees to make way for large-scale mechanized sorghum farms, with the purpose of turning Sudan into a 'breadbasket' from which the product could be exported to the booming Middle East.[15] Businessmen from the cities, with the backing of the Nimieri government and finance from Arab bankers and the World Bank, 'mined' the soil for quick profits before it gave out from over-use and erosion. In this 'suitcase farming', land was exhausted after only five to seven years on average by large farmers who would then simply move on to new areas. Nomads were pushed off their traditional pastures on to ecologically marginal land or into small farming areas (not without bloody confrontations), so increasing the rate of desertification.

TROUBLED WATERS

Together with the sun, water sustains life on Earth. It is constantly recycled by nature. From the ocean, land and plants, water is drawn into the atmosphere to form cloud. It returns to the land as rain and to the sea via rivers, lakes and the ground. As it passes through this cycle it touches all parts of the environment – land, soil, vegetation, atmosphere – and this affects people.

Three out of five rural people in poor countries have no easy access to clean drinking water. Three out of four do not have even the most basic sanitation. About 10,000 children die each day from diarrhoea alone, largely caused by dirty water.[16] Four out of five deaths in the Third World are due to water-related diseases. In recognition of the fact that clean water is the best medicine, the 1980s were officially named the International Drinking Water Supply and Sanitation Decade by the United Nations. But domestic water remains a low political priority compared with meeting other demands for water for large-scale irrigation projects, industry and power generation.

In the Third World as a whole, irrigation swallows up the largest quantity of water. In Asia's 'Green Revolution' of the 1960s and 1970s the aim was to grow more food by using high-yielding varieties of crops(HYVs), fertilizers and pesticides, but water was the catalyst for increased productivity. In countries like India and Pakistan, overall food production increased as a result. However, as much research since has shown, gains were concentrated in particular crops (wheat and rice), in areas already physically favoured, and amongst rich farmers who could afford the technical package and had the political muscle to get at water pumps.[17]

Water pumps can have not only a political impact, but also an environmental one. To make best use of the seeds and chemicals provided during the Green Revolution, farmers sank hundreds of tubewells and used diesel and electric pumps to tap underground water. What seemed like a limitless free gift of nature was used up much faster than it was being replenished. The water table dropped by as much as twenty-five to thirty metres in only ten years in parts of Tamil Nadu in south India, as vast quantities of groundwater were drawn to the surface for irrigation.[18] Village wells and traditional irrigation systems were left high and dry. Lower groundwater levels, caused by both pumping and deforestation, have deprived 23,000 Indian villages of water, according to Nalni Jayal,

Senior Adviser to India's Planning Commission.[19] Two thousand people died in one incident in West Bengal after a village water source dried up and people were forced to drink dirty pond-water.

DAM THE PEOPLE

India's first Prime Minister, Pandit Nehru, described large dams as the 'temples of modern India' and saw them as a symbol of national pride. Built to provide irrigation and, more often, power for industrialization, they seemed to offer newly independent countries a means of catching up with the West. They remain temples to the 'think-big' school of development. But to the 'people-and-their-environment-first' school, they have become symbols of all that is wrong with that approach.

Big dams are found wanting, even by the standards of orthodox economic cost-benefit analysis (which takes no account of 'unquantifiable variables' like the eviction of local people or long-term environmental problems). The long-term cash costs are becoming clearer as environmental chickens come home to roost in the form of lost land, lower soil fertility, disrupted fisheries and inefficient power production. Irrigation from large dams was meant to make the desert bloom and so bring wealth from poor land; but badly managed irrigation is worse than none at all. The wrong balance between input and output of water creates an expensive and salty or waterlogged wasteland. In other instances, in the rush to produce hydro-electric power, fertile land and forests have been lost beneath the rising waters of the dam. And when the Egyptians, with Soviet assistance, built the Aswan High Dam, farms downstream were deprived of the richly fertile Nile silt deposited by the annual floods since biblical times. Silt is now building up around the dam, while replacement fertilizers cost an estimated billion dollars a year.[20]

In the Amazon, dams have flooded thousands of square miles of rainforest, of which little has first been used for timber. Instead, the decaying trees have starved the water of oxygen, killing off fish and other aquatic life. Rotting vegetation and dissolved minerals from the tropical soils have produced lakes so acidic as to damage the dam's turbines.[21] Even so, none of this has cured the thirst for mega-dams. Under Brazil's '2010 Plan' some 136 new hydro-electric dams are planned, including the Altamira dam complex on the Xingu River, which has drawn such powerful public protest. The Babaquara dam, part of the Altamira complex, will create the world's largest artificial lake. There have been persistent worldwide protests against the involvement of the World Bank and other Western financiers in these schemes.

WHO PAYS?

Developers have justified the building of large dams using limited national resources as providing poor countries with the means of harnessing nature for boosting industrial output and food production. However, the long-term return on investment in major dams has been patchy and the benefits of increased electricity supplies or irrigation for cash crops have largely gone to industry and to those in the cities who are rich and westernized. Big dams have been paid for by people who are already a low priority for foreign experts and government planners – the poor. They are the people living in remote areas whose environment is destroyed by dams. As a result, thousands of peasant farmers and tribal people have been forced to move to poor, erosion-prone land with little compensation. Fishing communities have been devastated and local people have become the victims of water-borne killer diseases like malaria and schistosomiasis or river blindness.

TREES OF LIFE

Trees sustain life for millions of rural people across the world. They protect the fragile soil cultivated by farmers, regulate local climate and water, and supply a host of daily needs. Whether in the form of large forests or as trees scattered across the countryside, it is hard to exaggerate their vital importance for rural people and the serious implications of their loss.

Woodfuel is by far the largest source of household energy in poor countries, yet supplies are diminishing throughout the Third World, especially in Africa. In 1981, about 1.3 billion people lived in areas short of woodfuel.[22] If there is a shortage, people either have to use other fuels, like cow dung or crop stems which deprive the soil of vital nutrients, or they simply go without. Such is the shortage of fuelwood in the high Peruvian Sierra that families can only heat their homes when a fire is lit for cooking, despite the bitter mountain air, and workers can only have one cooked meal a day.[23] Poor city-dwellers are also hard hit by rising wood and charcoal prices. In cities such as Addis Ababa in Ethiopia and Maputo in Mozambique, families may have to spend as much as a third to a half of their income on fuel.[24]

The growing scarcity of woodfuel has been called the 'real energy crisis'. For local people, however, this is only one of the consequences of the dwindling numbers of trees. In Zimbabwe, for example, villagers know that many more live trees are beginning to be cut for fuel, instead of just dead branches; cattle and goats can no longer supplement their sparse dry-season diet by eating the leaves of trees and bushes; streams and paths on hills turn into earth-gobbling gullies with no trees to bind the soil; crops unprotected by thorny fences are eaten by goats; wild fruits – like the mupfura, which is rich in vitamin C – are harder to come by; medicinal types of berry and bark become scarce; special woods for house-building, utensils or ox yokes are difficult to find – as are the slow-burning varieties used to bake bricks.[25] The loss of trees puts pressure on all areas of daily life in rural Africa.

WOMEN AND WOOD

Women suffer these pressures more directly than men. They are usually responsible for collecting firewood in rural areas of the Third World. As trees are cut down, women have to walk further to find it, and steadily have to devote more time to searching for the family's firewood. In the foothills of the Himalaya, just a generation ago it took local women and girls no more than two hours to gather the family's regular supply of firewood and fodder.[26] Now it takes a whole day of steep mountain walking to gather the same amount, because the only trees left – outside commercial tree reserves – are in distant or inaccessible places.

More time spent on collecting wood adds to the backbreaking burden of women who endure the double workload of farming (in Africa they grow 80 per cent of the food) and household chores ranging from collecting water to pounding flour and caring for children and relatives. The impact of deforestation on women's workloads is even more acute in countries like South Africa or Zimbabwe where, since colonial times, the men have had to find work in the mines, commercial farms and factories many miles away from the family farmstead.

It is hardly surprising that women are now mobilizing communities to plant and protect trees. In Kenya, hundreds of local women's groups have started tree nurseries and helped more than sixty communities to become self-sufficient in wood as part of the national Green Belt Movement, started in 1977 by activist and academic, Professor Wangari Maathai.[27] Women of the Indian Chipko movement have organized themselves to 'hug' trees to form a human barrier against the axes of commercial contractors trying to cut down forests in the Himalaya – a response to the life-and-death threat of deforestation to poor women in the Third World.

HOLDING THE EARTH IN PLACE

The local struggle of Himalayan women to save trees is also a battle to protect people hundreds of miles away from the very different threats of disastrous flooding and silted rivers. This illustrates the intimate connections between different parts of the natural world and between them and human existence – the essence of ecology. The destruction of forests in the Himalaya, where the great rivers of the Indian subcontinent – the Ganges, Brahmaputra, Indus – rise, increases flooding downstream in Pakistan, the Indian plains and, most disastrously, Bangladesh. The destruction of Himalayan forest and downstream flooding are connected in three ways.[28] First, the roots of trees hold soil on the steep slopes and the leaves shield it from the direct impact of rain. Without them, the monsoon raindrops batter the bare earth and make quick work of washing soil into the river. As the silt settles further downstream, the level of the river bed rises, making flooding likely.

Second, deep, loose forest soils and the roots and trunks of the trees act as a sponge, helping rain to soak into the ground, which then releases water into the river gradually and evenly. On a slope with no trees, water runs straight over the surface and reaches the river all at once. The flow of the river rises quickly to a peak and there is sudden flooding when rain falls. When the rain stops the river rapidly runs dry.

Third, trees draw water up from the ground through their trunks and branches and 'sweat' it into the atmosphere through their leaves (a process known as 'evapotranspiration'). When trees are cut down this process stops, increasing the amount of water going into the rivers and making floods more likely.

The people of Bangladesh have been devastated by this ecological progression. In September 1988, the grossly swollen banks of the Brahmaputra in the east and the Ganges in the west engulfed as much as three-quarters of the whole country in its worst-ever floods.[29] Nurrudin Mian, a boatman whose house was submerged, said, 'The river is my life but Allah knows why it suddenly chose to devour us like this.' To find an answer he would have to look to the cumulative pressure of commercial timber exploitation dating back to the British Raj, the lack of planning between the countries of the region, and the search of the poor for land and firewood in the distant Himalaya, all of which have conspired to turn the river from a life-giver into a life-taker.

One observer described the scene from the air:

> The entire landscape looked as if it had been hit by a brown snowstorm, with just a few village houses and some trees rising above it. One whole bank of the Ganges was completely submerged, which made the other side of the river appear to be the coastline.[30]

Twenty-five million people were left homeless, more than a thousand died as a direct result of the floods, and three million tons of rice were lost. One villager, who had taken refuge on his roof, described other hardships: 'I stay awake through the nights to protect my children from deadly snakes which often climb on to the roofs.'[31] As Atiq Rahman of Bangladesh's Centre for Advanced Studies says, 'The poorest are the worst affected by any environmental hazard and often are the least able to overcome its consequences.'[32] The root cause of this kind of environmental disaster is a profoundly twisted ecological and economic logic which turns the earth against its people, and which we now explore further.

2 Why Are the Forests Disappearing?

It is rare to find a case in which environmental destruction does not go hand in hand with social injustice, almost like two sides of the same coin.

Anil Agarwal, Director of the Centre for
Science and the Environment, India

The destruction of the tropical rainforests is now one of the world's best-known environmental problems; many believe it is the most serious. Every day more than 150 square miles of tropical rainforest are wiped out or seriously degraded. An area the size of the British Isles is lost every year, and the rate of destruction is increasing.[1] Forests are being laid waste for commercial profit and land speculation, to earn foreign currency to pay off debt and to meet the needs of large-scale industrial development. They are logged for timber, burnt to make way for cattle ranches and big farms growing cash crops like pineapples or rubber, and turned into dams, roads and mines in the name of 'development'. The forests are also being lost because, for the poor majority, they offer a last chance for them to feed themselves and their families. The poorest move into the forest to clear land and eke out a living, even if only for a few years, before the soil is exhausted.

THE CHAINSAW MASSACRE

In South-east Asia, logging is the main cause of deforestation. If you want to make big money as a tropical logger, speed is of the essence. Expensive heavy machinery must be made to pay for itself as soon as possible and is often operated on short-term government timber concessions with no obligation to replant. In their rush to turn hardwood into hard cash, loggers treat the rainforest as a one-off bonanza rather than a continuing resource to be nurtured for the future. But the bonanza will not last long.

In the once forested Philippines, local plywood manufacturers are pushing the government to allow imports of tropical woods, which used to be abundant, because local supplies are exhausted.[2] In a last-ditch attempt to preserve supplies Thailand actually banned timber exports in January 1989; but it was too late, as imports were already coming in. According to a study by the World Resources Institute, World Bank and UN Development Programme:

> By the end of the century, the thirty-three developing countries that are now net exporters of forest products will be reduced to fewer than ten, and total developing country exports of industrial forest products are predicted to drop from their current level of more than seven billion dollars to less than two billion dollars.[3]

Hasty extraction is not only destroying a future economic resource, but also the fertile homelands of local people. Sixty per cent of the land area of Sarawak in Malaysia, where the Penan people live, is leased to logging concerns.[4] In 1987, after repeated appeals to the Malaysian government had failed, the Penan mounted blockades and sit-ins on logging roads to prevent logging machines encroaching on their land. They were forced to repeat their action the following year after the government reneged on its promise of protection.

Encik Asik Nyelit, a Penan community leader, explained to a Malaysian newspaper why they took their action:

> If logging happens on our land, it is the end of our community. We Penan of Sungai Ubong have seen and heard that it is extremely difficult for people in those areas where logging has taken place, to look to their needs. They have to go hunting very very far as the animals they hunted before have died or run away. They cannot use the water of the rivers for 'palo' [the local staple food], because the sago flour gets mixed with mud and sand. They cannot catch fish because how can the fish live in muddy water? . . . The Sungai Ubong is our home. Our ancestors have chosen this place as their home . . . and they have told us this is our land and our home.[5]

But, according to Terence Mallinson, President of the Timber Traders Association in the United Kingdom, 'the effect of logging

Source: GAIA & GEMINI NEWS

Figure 2.1   Map of the distribution of the world's remaining tropical rainforests.

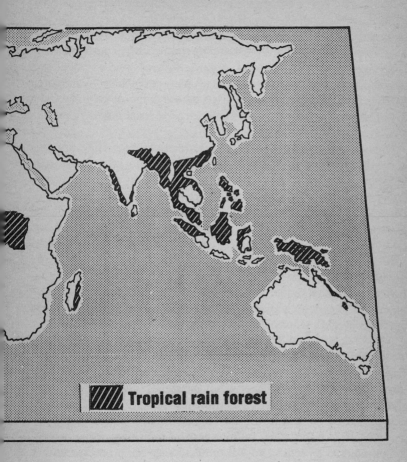

Tropical rain forest

is grossly exaggerated in the general public's mind as a cause of forest depletion compared with the inroads of agriculture and other influences'.[6] Timber companies say that the amount of tropical timber traded is small compared with the total number of trees lost.

Even so, the impact of logging goes far beyond the relatively few trees actually taken away from the forest to be sold. First, because loggers take out only the most valuable species, but in doing so leave large areas devastated. Second, because they provide a bridgehead into the forest for hundreds of povery-stricken colonists by building roads into some of the remotest areas where the most valuable trees are to be found. Third, roads tend to escalate local land values and hence heighten speculation.

Once the most lucrative trees in an area have been felled and the surrounding forest decimated, loggers move on to a new area; replanting is rare. One report estimated that in a typical forest concession in South-east Asia, 55 per cent of the remaining forest was destroyed or seriously damaged, although only 10 per cent of the trees were actually harvested.[7] 'The people who exploit the forests take only a small proportion, leaving the rest with no economic value,' says Julio Cesar Cenatano, the director of the Latin American Forestry Institute.[8] In addition, as much as a hundred million cubic metres of tropical timber is wasted in South-east Asia alone in the grossly inefficient logging and milling process; nearly twice as much as all the world's tropical hardwood exports put together.[9]

The force behind the timber boom is the Japanese, European and American demand for cheap tropical timber for everything from disposable chopsticks to building materials and mahogany toilet-seats. The real money-spinner is not the rough logs themselves, but the process of turning them into these finished products; a business dominated by companies in the rich countries. Despite their lip-service to free trade, these nations protect their own wood-processing industries by setting import tariffs to keep out processed timber products (like furniture or plywood) from poor countries. Poor exporting countries can make a small profit by exporting un-processed logs, giving little chance for investment in replanting and long-term forest management.[10] The constant knock of the debt-collectors of Western banks and governments on the doors of timber exporters like Brazil, Indonesia or the Ivory Coast increases the pressure on them to cash in their forests now for whatever hard currency they can earn.

Even in exporting rough logs, poor countries get a raw deal. Big foreign timber companies try to avoid paying for all the timber they cut down, or evade the taxes and duties levied on shipping it out. These are the only ways in which poor countries can make any money from the process. Companies use a selection of methods to pay as little as possible for the logs, ranging from the devious to the illegal, and often with local corruption easing the way,

Papua New Guinea (PNG) has suffered at the hands of Japanese companies which, according to an official Commission of Enquiry, were evading export duty by stating the prices of logs to be an average of 10 to 20 per cent below those actually paid by foreign buyers.[11] In one case, the PNG government received much lower tax revenues than expected on a timber concession in the Gogol Valley in the region of Madang. The Japanese company, Jant, sold wood chips from trees it felled in Gogol to its parent company, the Honshu Paper Company in Japan (itself part of the Mitsui empire), at an artificially low – and therefore low-tax – price, knowing that Honshu would then reap higher overall profits (a technique often employed by transnational companies and known as 'transfer pricing').[12]

A recent report summed up the Jant operation:

> The local environment has already suffered degradation, and the long-term impact of the project is still unknown. Replanting did not take place at the planned pace and agricultural developments have not even remotely proceeded as hoped. Logged-over areas have been left bare or, more precisely, covered in debris, to regenerate themselves. The new growth is poor ... Waterlogging and compaction have occurred, and grasses have invaded logged-over areas ... Local people have not received what they were promised and they have benefited little from the operation. The sums received as royalties have been negligible.[13]

FAST-FOOD FOREST

In other countries, those racing to turn the forest into profit have not even bothered to exploit the timber first. Instead, vast areas of rainforest have simply been burnt to make way for big commercial farms. In Central America, beef production has more than doubled, from 153,000 tonnes a year in the early 1960s to 350,000 in 1980, at the expense of turning large areas of the region's rain-forests into cattle ranches. Costa Rica lost nearly a third (7,370 square kilometres) of its forests between 1970 and 1980.[14] According to one report, three-quarters of all newly-cleared farmland in the country is used for cattle pasture.[15]

Losing forests might originally have been an acceptable price to pay if this new beef had gone to feed hungry Central Americans; but it hasn't. In fact, people in El Salvador and Guatemala now eat *less* beef on average than they did in 1960. Taking the region as a whole, beef consumption per head was only slightly higher in 1980 than 1960.[16] The extra beef was exported, often destined for American supermarkets and burger-bars.

Cheap beef from Central America was brought on stream as US farmers moved into more profitable but more expensive grain-fed beef. Unlike beef from the rest of Latin America, Central American beef can be freely imported to the United States as frozen carcasses, since it is free of foot-and-mouth disease. It is then processed by US companies to provide cheap beef for hamburgers, hot dogs, TV dinners, baby foods and pet foods for the hungry American market.

Cheap imports have helped to keep American hamburger prices down by as much as five cents per pound.[17] It is not surprising, therefore, that the US government and US-dominated development banks have poured in aid on a massive scale to foster the Central American beef business, despite its responsibility for destroying forests and pushing out peasant farmers. Foreign aid and local government subsidies have boosted the profits of the rich, though highly inefficient, cattle barons, who are also the chief supporters of US-backed regimes governing most Central American countries.

There has been little support for local people trying to grow their own food, and the big ranches provide very few jobs. People are being excluded from fertile land and have little option but to clear yet more forest, often from inaccessible steep slopes with the most fragile soils. As the human and ecological toll of the grossly unequal access to land mounts, so the social conflict and armed uprisings which scar the whole region are bound to increase.[18]

BIG IS BEAUTIFUL

Rainforests are also being felled to create large-scale industrial wealth in the name of encouraging national progress and tackling poverty. In reality, many of these schemes benefit the rich at the expense of the rural poor and damage the environment so much that any sustainable development for the future is undermined.

Brazil's Grande Carajas Programme is a giant among 'mega-projects'. At an estimated cost of $62 billion, it is one of the largest development schemes in the world. It aims to convert an area of eastern Amazonia the size of Britain and France put together into a complex of mines, iron and aluminium smelters, dams, railways, timber industries, food-processing plants, cement works, ranches and plantations.[19] Half the area covered by the programme is rainforest and its completion could destroy some 16 per cent of Brazil's Amazon rainforest, according to one report.[20] Despite the now infamous remark of Greater Carajas Council Chairman, João Sayad, 'Unless I am mistaken there are no Indians in the Greater Carajas region,'[21] the project also threatens the lands of 13,000 of them.

Western finance has given its backing to this destructive plan by funding the Carajas Iron Ore Project, a key part of the overall scheme. In 1982 the World Bank approved a loan of $304.5 million for the project, towards a total cost put at the time at about $5 billion.[22] Others providing funds included the European Coal and Steel Community (ECSC) (now subsumed in the European Community), which promised $600 million, and the Japanese, who were to contribute a further $336 million.[23] In return for funding, the European Community (EC) receives a steady supply of high-grade iron ore at a knock-down price. In one EC Commissioner's diplomatic language, 'the EC will get favourable pricing conditions [on the iron ore] which will contribute to preserving the competitiveness of the European steel industry'.[24]

The World Bank has provided a pithy description of the scheme: 'Iron ore from the vast iron ore deposits in Para state will be developed, exploited and exported.'[25] The aim was to earn foreign exchange and so ease Brazil's 'balance of payments constraints' by generating about seventeen billion dollars' worth of annual exports by the 1990s. As Brazil has been the Third World's biggest debtor

since the debt crisis broke in 1983, the largest of these constraints is clear.

Western money has gone to the Brazilian state mining company,
Companhia Vale do Rio Doce (CVRD), to construct the massive
Carajas iron ore mine, a 560-mile railway to the sea and a new
deep-water port on the north-coast island of São Luis. The mine and
railway have been working since 1985, and twelve fully loaded
trains, each of them a mile long, make a daily journey from the
Carajas mountains to São Luis through the forest lands of the
Guajaja and Gavioes Indians.

The funding agencies have come under fire for the devastation
wrought on the forest and its people by the project. The EC has
tried to distance itself from the iron ore project and the World Bank
has attempted to reassure critics by saying that:

> The Carajas Iron Ore Project is distinct from the Grande Carajas Pro-
> gramme, which is coordinated out of the Ministry of Planning [of the
> Brazilian government] and has not received World Bank financing.[26]

But in reality the distinction of the iron ore project from the Grande
Carajas Programme is fairly theoretical, for it plays a key role in
providing the wider programme with transportation and an economic nucleus. In addition, even the World Bank's own undertakings
on the iron ore project, to ensure that the government respects the
rights of indigenous people and protects the environment, have
been broken.

According to Survival International, no consultation of the indigenous community in the Carajas region took place, let alone
any attempt to gain their consent to the iron ore project:

> Nor was there any serious effort to demarcate Indian lands in advance
> of the construction of the railway, the mining complex or the Tucurui
> hydro-electric scheme. Although the Bank made its loan conditional on the
> provision of an Amerindian Sub-Project to be funded by the CVRD and
> administered by FUNAI [the Brazilian government Indian agency], no
> specific budget for the land question was required . . . with the result that
> it has been left wholly to the underfinanced and incompetent organs of the
> Brazilian state.[27]

The railway and the port have also made possible the building of
about twenty pig-iron smelters, using charcoal made from native

tropical forest (instead of the normal coking coal). The inefficiency of the process is staggering: one ton of charcoal requires four tons of tropical forest wood and will fuel an iron smelter for only five minutes.[28] The accounting method used to value the smelters regards the trees as having no value – a free subsidy from nature.

Any other plans to establish large-scale plantations of quick-growing eucalyptus trees to fuel the smelters seem wholly unrealistic, both by making the iron prohibitively expensive to produce and in the light of the catalogue of past failed attempts to establish plantations in Amazonia's unsuitable environment. Many believe that the potentially massive demand for charcoal is now the biggest threat to the Brazilian rainforest. Officials at Brazil's Amazon research institute, INPA, estimate that to fuel the plants will require the felling of 450 square miles of Amazon forest a year.[29]

'A LAND WITHOUT PEOPLE, FOR A PEOPLE WITHOUT LAND'

Loggers and big projects are literally paving the way for an army of desperate settlers fleeing landlessness and poverty to go to the forests as a last resort. The poor and dispossessed flow along roads and railways built to service big development schemes and logging operations that have done nothing to benefit them. These people merely seek enough land to grow food for their families, or opportunities to earn a little money.

Global estimates of how much rainforest is cleared by small farmers range from seven to twenty million hectares a year.[30] Despite the bad connotations it has in the West, 'slash and burn' agriculture was originally developed by forest people over centuries as an agricultural system in tune with the local ecology. In traditional slash and burn a plot of forest is cleared and burnt, and food is grown using the nutrients left behind in the ash. After a few harvests the fertility of the ash and the soil is exhausted and pests and weeds start to take over. The land is then left to recover, perhaps for up to a century, before being used again. The system has sustained the land for generations, but the huge scale of today's forest colonization means that land is not allowed to lie fallow long enough for the forest, soil and nutrients to regenerate naturally.

Deforestation in the Amazon is not a result of there being too many people, or of simple population pressures. The Amazon makes up 60 per cent of Brazil's territory, but only twelve million people live there, of whom over half live in cities.[31] It is the style of settlement fostered by the government that has done the damage, inequalities rather than sheer numbers that are destroying the forest. To blame the settlers directly for forest destruction, as many official accounts do, avoids the underlying question of why they are poor. Poverty forces them to clear the forest in the first place. Huge government resettlement schemes, often with Western finance, promote rainforest colonization as the solution to problems of poverty and landlessness; the more important but politically sensitive option of sharing out land more fairly is not tackled.

Just 2 per cent of Brazil's landowners control 60 per cent of the nation's arable land. At least half of this land lies idle,[32] since landowners often regard land more as a status symbol than a source of crop production. Brazil's notorious World Bank-supported Polonoroeste colonization project seemed to offer landlords and politicians a way of tackling landlessness by 'removing some of the rural poor from the regions where they were born and dumping them in the Amazon', in the words of Brazilian Environment Minister Jose Lutzenberger.[33]

The scheme promoted the myth of a land of opportunity waiting for settlers. It was proudly presented as 'a land without people for a people without land', thus disregarding the thousands of tribal people, rubber-tappers and others already living in the forest. The new settlers gained only short-lived returns from their plots of infertile soil amid the cleared forest, and after years often had to sell up to large cattle-farmers.

In another scheme, the Indonesian government, with money from the World Bank and the Asian Development Bank, has moved three and a half million peasants from the crowded inner islands of Java and Bali to the sparsely settled islands of Kalimantan (Borneo), Sulawesi, Irian Jaya and Timor. The resettlement scheme in Indonesia has degraded forty-eight million hectares of forest.[34] The original plan for Indonesian transmigration was massive: to move sixty-five million people over twenty years; but this had to be scaled down because a drop in oil prices left the government short of funds.

As existing settlement sites have deteriorated ecologically, so the economic returns have fallen. In response, the World Bank is switching its policy to encouraging the planting of palm oil, rubber and tree crops which it believes will fare better. But this will leave settlers victim to fluctuations in international commodity prices, which have been spiralling downwards for years. WALHI, an organization representing 400 Indonesian non-governmental organizations (NGOs), says:

This move to turn transmigration sites into mono-culture cash-crop production farms could prove to have even worse economic and environmental consequences than transmigration as it was originally conceived.[35]

Added to the problems of landlessness, the tightening external economic squeeze on poor countries has also helped force the poor to exploit the diminishing forest. The stark reality of the 1980s, the decade of debt, was a sharp increase in levels of poverty, particularly in Africa and Latin America. As the cost of servicing foreign debts has drained resources from poor countries, so their poor are being squeezed to pay their country's huge debts. According to official World Bank figures, in 1989 the poor world paid a staggering $52 billion more to the rich world in debt repayments than it received in aid and new loans.[36] IMF austerity programmes push up food prices, push down wages, and decimate already weak health and education programmes.

Against this background of mounting poverty and desperation, thousands of jobless poor are flooding into the Amazon in a series of Klondike-type gold rushes. By 1989, there were about 825,000 *garimpeiros* (small prospectors) panning or digging for gold in the Amazon – more than double the number four years earlier.[37] The mercury the miners use in gold panning is highly poisonous and is having devastating effects on human life, rivers and ecosystems. It is a 'Bhopal developing in the Amazon Basin', according to Amazon expert Susan Hecht.[38] At the Serra Pelada mine in eastern Amazonia, some 15,000 *garimpeiros* toil in hot and dangerous conditions, digging by hand to carry huge waste-sacks up from a pit 300 metres deep, hoping to strike lucky.[39]

THE COST: NEAR AND FAR

The hundred million inhabitants of the rainforest are in the front line of the battle to save their environment. Their way of life is directly threatened by the devastation of the forest. Piakan, a Kayapo Indian leader from Brazil, at a meeting in 1988 in the House of Commons, appealed for British support to save the rainforest:

> We just want to be respected and carry on living on our land. I'm not against the Brazilian government; I want to help them conserve the country; but if they are destroying the environment then I will demonstrate against it.[40]

Beyond the 200 million people who actually live in the rainforests, there are a further billion who rely on the rivers which flow from them.[41] There are millions more, both in the rich and poor world, whose environment depends on the mediating effects of the rainforest. Its destruction could have far-reaching effects on the ecology of the globe and on future economic development. Rainforests do not exist in isolation, for they are a key part of a much wider set of complex, interacting natural systems. Human survival and economic development depend on these systems to sustain the soils, rivers, and the local and global climates which are the basis of food production, health, energy and raw materials; in short, development.

The tropical rainforests are some of the most complex and abundant ecosystems in the world, but they are also fragile. The extraordinarily luxuriant vegetation of the rainforest hides the fact that it grows on soils from which most of the goodness has been washed downwards by centuries of the near constant warm rain in the tropical climate. Unlike northern forests, most of the nutrients are locked up in the vegetation itself and are taken up quickly by small organisms, particularly fungi, on the forest floor as leaves fall or plants die. These in turn release nutrients back into the roots of the trees and shrubs. The natural recycling of the rainforest works very quickly and efficiently – nutrients spend little time on the forest floor where they would quickly be lost. If the cycle is broken and the trees are destroyed, especially in hilly watershed areas, the soil is soon washed away by the rain and any nutrients leached out. The land is left barren or covered with tough grasses, such as *imperata*, which are unpalatable to animals. The increased sediment in the rivers causes trouble downstream by clogging up reservoirs, irrigation systems, canals and docks.

The rainforests are also a vital genetic storehouse, with potential benefits for all humanity. Half of the known species in the world are found in tropical forests. They have already provided many of the strains from which modern crops and medicines are derived. Half the doctors' prescriptions dispensed by chemists have their origins in wild organisms, worth around $14 billion in the United States alone. Other, as yet unexploited, species promise huge economic potential. The *fevilla* vine found in the western Amazonian rainforest bears seeds with such a high oil content that a hectare of such vines could produce more oil than a hectare of commercial palm-oil plantation.[42] Other potentially useful – even life-saving, in the case of medicinal plants – individual species are already being lost.

The loss of the rainforests is also linked to local, regional and global changes in climate. Climate experts now recognize that 'climate is not something imposed on the living earth from above'.[43] The forest plays a key part in regulating climate by its effects on the reflectivity of the land surface and by the way in which it recycles water from the earth back into the atmosphere. These interactions are complex and not yet fully understood. Human action in one area could have disastrous results in a very different area through a long chain-reaction and knock-on effects.

Global warming due to the greenhouse effect is the main climatic problem that has been linked to the destruction of the tropical rainforest (although most of the greenhouse gases are still produced in the rich countries). Destroying the forests increases the production of the key greenhouse gas, carbon dioxide (CO_2), in two ways. First, CO_2 is released when rainforests are burnt to clear land. Second, large amounts of vegetation are lost which would have absorbed carbon dioxide and turned it into oxygen through the natural process of photosynthesis. Increasing levels of atmospheric carbon dioxide (as well as other gases like CFCs and methane) cause global warming as they trap the heat of the sun within the atmosphere.[44]

The impact, both in rich and poor countries, could be severe. A warmer climate could directly affect farming and other human activities. The North American grain belt, supplier of much of the world's grain surplus, could be particularly hard hit, while African drought might become more frequent. As the water in the seas expands, the ice caps could start to melt. The warming could lead to the flooding of low-lying land and cities. There would be serious consequences for some rich countries like the Netherlands, or in London and south-east England; in low-lying poor countries like Bangladesh, disastrous floods could escalate and scarce fertile land be lost for good. More than 1,200 coral islands that make up the Maldives, of which none is more than two metres above sea level, might disappear beneath the waves.

THE LOGIC OF DESTRUCTION

Potentially, the consequences of the destruction of the rainforests could hit everyone. How, then, can it still be continuing? The reasons for the destruction of the rainforests show that Third World environments are squeezed from both sides. The powerful – the rich, businessmen, bureaucrats, politicians, Western banks, and development experts – steal and destroy the most basic inheritance of the poor, the Earth. At the same time the poorest people – the hungry, the landless, women and the urban unemployed – destroy their environment because they are powerless to look beyond tomorrow. They have to cut down trees or over-use land they know to be fragile, just to survive. From the point of view of powerful profit-makers and powerless livelihood seekers[45] there are strong economic incentives for destroying the environment, in the short term at least. There is a perverse logic in the global ecological destruction.

It follows that environmental destruction in the Third World cannot be prevented without challenging the economic and political pressures that underlie it: from unequal land distribution to international debt and unfair trade. Technical understanding of how cutting down trees leads to the soil being blown away, or to a drier climate, can help in finding solutions to the problems of rapid desertification. But it is not in itself enough. Flying in a Western forestry expert or setting up a project to plant lots of trees will be ineffective, even harmful, if the politically sensitive questions – why are the trees being cut down? by whom? for whose benefit? – go unanswered. Too often, environmental problems are labelled as purely scientific questions with technical answers, because they involve complex physical processes like the greenhouse effect or soil erosion. Accurate scientific understanding of how these processes work is vital, but this can too easily slip into the belief that 'if only we knew all the facts we could solve the problems', when political will is often what is most needed.

The British Prime Minister, Margaret Thatcher, has used lack of scientific data as a justification for not making regular progress reports to Parliament on government action to promote environmentally sustainable development internationally, saying that 'safeguarding the environment effectively presupposes the availability of accurate and reliable scientific data'. That is where the government's priorities lie.[46] For decision-makers this kind of reasoning provides a way of distancing environmental problems from the government policies, business interests and unequal world economy which have, in fact, been the key agents disrupting the natural workings of the Earth.

In short, greed and poverty, not ignorance or stupidity, kill people and planet alike. To show how vital soil or trees are to the poor, and thus how much environmental degradation threatens their livelihoods, is not to revive the old idea that the poor and hungry are the helpless victims of a hostile environment; the poor at the blind mercy of 'nature red in tooth and claw'.

Poor people find themselves and their local environment at the end of chains of cause and effect which start with the rich and powerful, both in the capital cities of the Third World and thousands of miles away in the boardrooms and government offices of London, Brussels, Washington and Tokyo. It is these causal chains which are shaping the destiny of both people and planet, and which the remaining chapters of this book need to explore.

3 Feeding the World

Why do the babies die when there's enough food to feed
the world?

Tracy Chapman, singer

The Khatimia Mountains form a small rocky island protruding
from the wide, level expanse of eastern Sudan. They are an advance
outpost for the vast Ethiopian highlands which lie just over the
border ten miles to the east. Their steep sides tower above the
rough road busy with trucks and Land Cruisers carrying relief
supplies for refugees. As the road turns past the last mountainous
wall, the Wad Sherife refugee camp comes into view.

Row upon row of khaki tents are spread out across the plain,
stretching into the distance. It looks like an army encampment, or
some giant Boy Scout jamboree that has been picked up and
dumped on the hot, dusty African plain. But the mirage does not
last long. As I arrived at the camp in July 1985, I saw painful
images of famine and refugee life: the grief of losing close relatives,
suppressed in the bid to carry on, but seen in a momentary
expression of pain; the sense of loss and shame at having to
abandon one's livelihood and home, to be reduced to living on
hand-outs in a foreign land; the constant queuing for ration cards,
food and water; the regimented lines of crowded tents; people
seeing their sick children having to be treated, not for any particular
disease, but for hunger.

But there was more than just desperation and despair. Children
showed their capacity to make the best of it, the determination to
laugh and play. One showed us the toy car he had made from
scraps of wire, complete with steering and wheels that worked. A

little later we heard a shout from a shelter we were passing. We turned to look, thinking our voyeuristic presence was resented; instead there was a smiling Eritrean woman beckoning us into her shack.

Inside, we were greeted by her family while she brewed up strong, sweet Ethiopian coffee laced with ginger on a makeshift charcoal stove. She offered us one of the tiny cups she was passing round. Once you have one cup, custom dictates you must stay until you have drunk the third and strongest. Although they spoke little English, we managed to communicate in gestures and a few broken words. The woman told of a son and daughter they had left behind, in the rebel army in Eritrea fighting against another onslaught by Ethiopian government forces. The family told us something of their arduous journey from war and famine.[1]

These burning flickers of humanity and humbling generosity made a deep impression. They made the injustice and pain that surrounded them more vivid. No longer were the war and famine affecting cardboard cut-out figures from a charity advertisement or TV news report; it was happening to real people.

There were a staggering 120,000 Ethiopian refugees in Wad Sherife when I visited it. An overlapping crisis of war, famine and environmental decay had driven them from their homes in the war-torn northern provinces of Eritrea and Tigray. The flow into the camp had fallen from its peak a few months earlier, when hundreds arrived every day, but a steady stream of frightened and hungry people were still making the long journey from their mountain homelands to the camp. There were not enough tents to go round; new arrivals – often the hungriest and weakest – had to set up ramshackle shelters of sticks, banana leaves and mats. The shacks gave little protection from the blistering midsummer sun and punishing dust storms that swept down from the mountains and across the open plain. Inside them were people who, in their homeland, had been poor – but tough – farmers and labourers.

Some of the refugees had taken several weeks to trek hundreds of miles. Many of the relatives and friends they had started out with had not made it. Some refugees could only travel at night to avoid being bombed by the MiG jets of the Ethiopian air force. Stripped of dignity and independence, their communities scattered, people now lay hungry and sick, trying to preserve what little energy they had left.

THE LAST RESORT

The refugees had reached the end, not only of the journey from conflict and famine, but of a long battle against hunger and deteriorating land. Only when their own survival strategies had been exhausted had they reluctantly left their villages. Even after they had fled, many refugees were trying to scratch out a living in exile in Sudan rather than simply rely on aid hand-outs in a vast camp. The Western notion that relief camps attract people because of the lure of free food is misplaced. The majority of African refugees (including many Ethiopians in Sudan) try to remain independent by surviving outside the camps without aid, either in the towns or by finding land in the countryside.[2] Faced with hunger, poor people do not just give up and start walking to a relief camp. They stay in their homes for as long as possible. Dessalegn Rahmato, of the Institute of Development Research at Addis Ababa University, shows that peasant farmers in Ethiopia's Wollo province marshalled all their resources and local agricultural techniques to ward off starvation. They were not passive victims. They anticipated famine and prepared for it. It was only when all their efforts had failed that they actually left their homes.[3]

As food becomes scarce, families carefully utilize all their resources. First, the mother spins out the food they have for as long as possible. She must make the painful decisions about who gets what. Community tradition dictates that the most vulnerable – children, old people, pregnant women – take priority, although it is not uncommon for the elderly to refuse food, insisting that their share is given to the children. Meals are less frequent and become monotonous. If the family is still short of food, they borrow it from any wealthier relatives or friends in the neighbourhood. They also exchange any less basic foods they may have, like spices or milk (if they have a cow), for the staple sorghum or *teff* (Ethiopian millet). Family members, particularly the men, may then start to migrate to search for any work available on the farms of better-off farmers or in the cities, to earn what they can to buy food.

Next, the family reluctantly starts to sell possessions which are often their only savings: tools, pots and pans, religious or marriage jewellery, and animals. In Tigray recently, according to one report, when everything else had been sold for food, people pulled down their own houses to sell the wooden door-frames as firewood on the roadside for a few coins. People are squeezed into hunger and destitution. Prices tumble as more and more poor peasants have to sell off their belongings and livestock, usually to richer farmers and merchants. At the same time food prices rise. In Ethiopia's Sidamo Province in 1984, nomadic cattle-herders could only sell bulls normally worth $200 for between $20 and $40.[4] The herders could not afford to buy food and went hungry.

It is only when all these options run out that the poor actually abandon homes and fields for the cities and feeding camps inside Ethiopia or across the border in Sudan. Dessalegn Rahmato concludes that:

Although relief and emergency food aid, most of which was provided by Western countries, was responsible for saving the lives of countless peasants in north-east Ethiopia, it is equally true that indigenous survival techniques and the collective efforts of the peasantry were instrumental in saving a far greater number of people from death.[5]

THE 'BIBLICAL' FAMINE

Looking at how Ethiopian peasants reacted to and coped with famine takes one beyond the stock images of helpless *victims* of famine to discover their deep resourcefulness. It also reveals who starves during famine and why. People more often starve because they are poor than because food is short. In contrast, the reaction to the famine by Western governments and international agencies was misconceived because of a fundamental misunderstanding of the causes of famine. The mistake, in the words of the World Bank, is that:

. . . by paying too much attention to changes in food availability, governments and relief organizations have sometimes failed to recognize other causes of famines. As a result, some relief has been misdirected. The loss of real income better explains why famines occur and who is hurt by them.[6]

Although in March 1984 the UN's World Food Programme (WFP) notified donors that Ethiopia needed 300,000 tonnes of food, it implied that this could be made up by food aid already pledged and by the grain stores of the government's Agricultural Marketing Corporation (AMC). An Oxfam internal report on the response to the famine concluded that: 'There could hardly have been a clearer way of saying that there was no need for further food aid.'[7]

Much of this food aid was in fact for longer-term projects rather than relief. The AMC's grain, bought from peasants in areas with better harvests, could only be sold, in line with AMC's role as a grain marketing board. It was not available for free famine relief. (In Ethiopia and throughout Africa, grain boards of this kind are constantly under pressure from Western governments to be more commercially-minded and are a prime target for all-out privatization under IMF economic adjustment programmes.) As the UN conceded months later, 'the government lacked the budgetary resources to finance the transfer of grain from the AMC to the RRC [the Government's Relief and Rehabilitation Commission]'.[8] Instead, the grain was sold to those who could afford it and those with greater political clout – people in the cities, and the army.

It could be argued that the government should have diverted money from other spending to buy grain for famine relief. But equally, donors could have bought grain, or swapped it for later replacements, as WFP in fact suggested to the donors. (The preference for donors to send their own food, as a way of getting rid of their own surpluses, is discussed later in the chapter.) The indigenous Relief Society of Tigray (REST) did in fact tackle famine in Tigray in this way in 1983 and 1984. Using outside funding, it bought excess grain on local markets in the west of the province for distribution among the hungry. During the famine emergency of 1989, at least 50,000 of the total 300,000 tonnes needed were readily available on markets within the province, but the starving were too poor to buy it.[9]

One reason why the international community was so slow in responding to the Ethiopian famine of 1984 was that the UN and Western governments still saw famine as a food-shortage problem, rather than as the inability of people to 'command' food. They therefore looked at the country's overall food stocks as the main measure of the threat of starvation. This blinded them to growing signs of famine in the countryside and so they lost precious months before the all-out aid effort was launched which could have reached people before they started to abandon their homes.

WHO STARVES?

The image of famine as a great leveller, sweeping all before it, is a myth. Famine is not indiscriminate. It hits people in some areas more than others (and not necessarily the areas with the worst crop failure), and people in the countryside more than those in the towns. Most significantly of all, famine kills the poor and not the rich.

The eminent Indian economist Amartya Sen investigated the facts behind major famines of recent history, including the Great Bengal Famine of 1942 and famines in Ethiopia and the Sahel in the 1970s. In his mould-breaking study, *Poverty and Famines*, he concludes that 'starvation is the characteristic of some people not *having* enough to eat. It is not the characteristic of there not *being* enough food to eat.'[10] He finds that explaining starvation in terms of food shortages is misleading, for this concentrates too much attention on production and not enough on people. Instead he stresses what he calls people's 'entitlements to food'. They get entitlements to food through growing their own, working for money so that they can buy food, trading (as herders trade their cattle for grain), or by being directly lent or given food. Famines happen when large numbers of people are deprived of entitlements and so starve to death. Sen argues that famine is much more often a case of Food Entitlement Decline (FED) than Food Availability Decline (FAD). Many more go hungry regularly because they lack entitlements (in the shape of land, jobs, or anything to trade) in the first place.

In Ethiopia, those who starved were, first, poor farmers who not only lost their direct entitlement to food because their crops failed and they had no food reserves, but also because they had no crops to sell and were too poor to buy food, even though it might have been available in the market. A second group to lose their entitlement to food were paid workers such as casual labourers, household servants, prostitutes and migrant labourers. They starved because their earnings dropped in relation to the price of food. Many people from destitute farming families trying to find work drove down wages, while the high demand for food pushed its price up. People providing small-scale services, like barbers, blacksmiths or shoe-repairers, lost trade because others were hard-up. Their earnings also fell, while food prices rose; many went hungry. Food shortage was only part of the overall picture. Those who starved were already the poorest and weakest, who had nothing to fall back on in hard times.

HUNGRY WORLD

As many as a million people died in the Ethiopian famine of 1984–5. Across Africa, tens of thousands more died. Famines continue to threaten. But devastating as they are, famines are, in three senses, just the tip of the hunger iceberg.

First, disasters like drought, flood or crop failure turn into famines only where poor people in poor countries are already living close to the margins of survival. In Ethiopia, bad weather led to famine because farmers and labourers were too poor to ride it out. The government also lacked adequate resources to act as a safety-net for the drought-stricken, and used what it did have for the army and for the lavish 300-million-dollar tenth anniversary celebration of the country's revolution.[11] In contrast, when drought hit the Midwest of the United States in 1988, although some farmers did go out of business, there was no starvation. The farmers, government and economy were strong enough to make famine impossible.

Second, famine tends to concentrate attention on an immediate natural catalyst, such as drought rather than on the long-term impact of environmental degradation on the poor. In Ethiopia's highlands, where 70 per cent of the people live, more than half the area shows signs of accelerated erosion, according to one report.[12] Forests covered 48 million hectares of the highlands at the turn of the century, but now this has declined to just 4.7 million hectares.[13] Soil erosion and the shortage of fuelwood have become chronic.

These problems hit the poorest people hardest, particularly the peasants. The land is further degraded by the poverty of the peasants. As in many African countries, they are taxed heavily and paid little for what they produce. Again reflecting an Africa-wide tendency, about 90 per cent of the government's agricultural budget goes into the large-scale farms (in Ethiopia state farms, and in other countries large-scale private farms).[14] Peasant farmers are left with little money, labour, time or incentive to improve land in the long term.

Third, most hungry people are not those affected by mass famines striking a particular area at one time. Most of those who die of starvation are victims of a quiet but ongoing 'famine' that continues day in, day out. Every few weeks this quiet hunger kills the same number of people in the Third World as the famine in Ethiopia in 1984–5. Fourteen million children every year, or 40,000 a day, die from malnutrition and common diseases – many of them hunger-related.[15] According to the World Bank, even in 1980 as many as 340 million people did not have enough food to prevent serious health risks and stunted growth in children.[16] The number may have doubled by now. One in three people in the Third World does not have enough to eat for an active working life.[17]

This starvation occurs in the midst of plenty. Statistics show there is more than enough food to go round. At a global level, the UN's Food and Agricultural Organisation (FAO) estimates that the world grows enough grain to provide every human being with 3,600 calories a day, well above the average 2,400 calories a day they need.[18] Neither is hunger a simple question of there being too many mouths to feed – of pressure of population on finite resources. Between 1950 and 1983, world population increased from 2.51 billion to 4.66 billion, but agricultural production increased from an average of 248 kilograms to 310 kilograms *per head*.[19] In a Third World country, the food that hungry people lack is usually equivalent to less than 5 per cent of the country's overall food supply, according to the World Bank. But as it points out:

. . . this does not mean, however, that a 5 per cent increase in food supplies would eliminate malnutrition. It means merely that in many countries the supply of food is not the only obstacle to food security.[20]

Yet economists continue to focus on inefficient production methods, while environmentalists analyse the physical constraints of soil, changing climate and growing population. The basic problem is still defined as shortage rather than entitlement. The economic, technical and environmental obstacles to growing more are indeed serious problems, but they have little meaning without asking *who* is affected by them.

PEASANTS, IGNORED LEFT AND RIGHT

Devastating famines in Ethiopia, Sudan, Mozambique and other countries in 1984–5, and the repeated threats of famines since, has firmly linked Africa with hunger in the public consciousness. But even in a 'normal' year, about 100 million people, or a quarter of Africa's population, get less than 80 per cent of the daily food the UN estimates they need.[21]

Africa is a continent dominated by peasant families tilling their own small farms, growing much of their own food in the form of maize, yams, sorghum or cassava. They may also grow cash crops, like cocoa, or extra food to sell in order to raise money for clothes, tools or children's schooling. A majority of families do have land. Unequal land distribution is not, in general, the major cause of hunger and environmental destruction in Africa; not, at least, in the way it is in Latin America and Asia.[22] (Although it is a major cause in countries heavily settled by white colonists, including Kenya, Malawi, South Africa, and, as we see below, Zimbabwe.)

Peasant farmers account for about seven out of every ten Africans. Although poor, they produce a large proportion of the continent's wealth and a significant proportion of the crops it trades abroad. They have also developed sophisticated ways of managing the various and sometimes delicate environments of Africa. And yet the peasant majority have been widely despised, ignored and exploited first by colonial rulers and then by African governments, aid donors and experts, who put their money on 'modernizing' Africa into development by setting up Western-style industries and big hi-tech farms. Many of these have turned into expensive and unproductive failures.

This antipathy towards the peasants has been shared by both

Western capitalist-orientated and 'socialist' African countries alike.[23] The former inherited it from colonial thinking and, for many years, the advice of the Western aid experts who regarded the peasant producer as backward and inefficient. They condemned the peasant as unresponsive to market incentives and undynamic, preferring never to take risks. Small-scale peasant agriculture had to be transformed into large-scale capitalist farms, using the most modern technology and machinery. This would, on the one hand, produce efficient big farms and, on the other hand, a ready supply of labourers for mining and industry. Africa was to repeat Europe's pattern of industrial revolution – held to be the 'natural' path for development. Peasant farmers had no place in that order.

But no radical alternative has been offered by most of the avowedly socialist governments of Africa, from Ethiopia to Mozambique.[24] Those who took their lead from the eastern bloc imposed an equally inappropriate model. It idolized the industrial worker, but talk of ending the oppression of the proletariat counted for little in countries where the vast majority of the people did not even live in the towns, let alone work in industry. Peasant producers have been squeezed in an attempt to provide cheap food for the urban workers. Even within agriculture the peasants have been seen as feudal remnants, not part of a new socialist future. There have been attempts to enforce collectivization. State farms have swallowed the bulk of government revenue.

Not only have both these strategies drained scarce resources away from the peasant majority, but their toil has been exploited to finance it, in two ways. First, governments extracted the foreign currency needed to buy in foreign technology and machinery from peasant-produced cash crops – like cocoa in Ghana, cotton in Nigeria, coffee in Uganda. The bulk of the profit from these crops has been creamed off by governments buying cheaply from peasants who are only allowed to sell to the government; the produce is then sold at higher prices on the world market. Second, peasant farmers had to supply cheap food for city bureaucrats and workers. Cheap food means workers can be paid less, and the prices of the goods they produce can be set at a lower level. It also helps to keep at bay the threat of food riots and political unrest in the cities, where governments know they are most vulnerable.

THE PRICE IS WRONG

In Africa, official farm marketing boards have controlled all buying and selling. They have paid peasants a pittance for both their food and cash crops. Many, although not all, have been wastefully inefficient and have been plundered by elite bureaucrats for personal gain, at the peasants' expense. Although some critics attack the marketing boards as attempts at socialist-inspired state intervention (while those on the other side of the political fence seek to defend them for the same reason), they were, in fact, first created by Africa's imperial rulers.

The colonialists did in some cases try to make money out of Africa by directly grabbing land. They set up plantations – for instance coffee in Kenya, rubber in Liberia – and large settler farms and ranches, as in Rhodesia (now Zimbabwe). In countries where this pattern was dominant, in Kenya for example, African farmers were not allowed to grow cash crops in competition with white farmers and were pushed into working as their low-paid farm workers.

But in many countries, the colonialists extracted farm wealth by controlling African farmers through taxes and, crucially, markets. Peasant farmers often had to grow cash crops to pay colonial taxes, while at the same time they wanted to earn some money for themselves. But the prices for cotton or cocoa were controlled by cartels of European companies, and increasingly by colonial governments themselves through marketing boards. During the Second World War in particular, the activities of the marketing boards were stepped up in order to obtain cheap crops and food, either for the war effort directly or to be sold for arms and munitions.

In 1940, for example, the British government bought up the whole of British West Africa's cocoa output (largely peasant-produced) through the new West Africa Cocoa Control Board.[25] In 1942, the organization was extended to become the West African Produce Control Board, buying up groundnuts, palm oil and other products. After the war a similar system was kept on, in the name of protecting farmers from uncertain world price fluctuations; but the boards paid farmers well below what they got on the world market, and the British Treasury pocketed the difference. Britain's post-war government, too, presented the boards as a means of protecting African farmers. In fact, they were a way of 'exploiting colonial producers to shore up the crumbling defences of sterling and the imperial economy', according to academic Gavin Williams.[26]

The marketing board system did not stop with the end of colonialism in West Africa – or elsewhere on the continent. In independent Nigeria new justifications were offered – the boards would protect the peasant from the vicious private middleman and from foreigners. But the exploitation of the peasants continued. They saw few of the benefits promised by bureaucrats and aid experts. The boards' funds (or, more accurately, the peasants' funds) were increasingly used outside agriculture to subsidize Western-style industrialization.

In Uganda, the Cotton Price Assistance Fund provided money to build the Owen Falls hydro-electric dam project.[27] In the 1960s it 'lent' 100 million Ugandan shillings to the central government budget. The boards simply became a way of taxing the peasants – sometimes for industrial development, but also for the private gain of individuals. In addition, many boards were very inefficient and their running costs had to be borne by the farmers. Boards also paid them late, and sometimes not at all. One study found that, in Africa:

Domestic prices offered to farmers for export crops rarely exceed 75 per cent, often lie below 50 per cent, and not infrequently lie below one-third the level of international prices.[28]

In Nigeria, even with price increases brought in through peasant protest in the late 1960s, the purchasing power of crops like cocoa and groundnuts was lower in the 1970s than in the depression years of the 1930s.

While rich countries have been paying less and less for commodities, peasant farmers growing crops like cocoa or cotton have seen their incomes decimated. At the same time, national economies have also suffered in the long term as overall production has declined and prices have plummeted.[29] Farmers have been growing fewer of the crops it is no longer worth their while growing and have tried to find other non-farm work, which is usually badly paid. They have thus become poorer, hungrier and more vulnerable to disasters like crop failures.

FOOD

The squeeze on cash crop prices would not have mattered so much if peasants had been supported in growing food and offered fair prices for food crops. But they weren't. In colonial Africa, peasant food production was regarded as 'backward' and the emphasis was on growing money-making crops. Peasant farmers were starved of credit, markets and inputs to grow food. After independence, little was done to change this and governments pressed peasants to supply food to them on the cheap, by controlling prices. In Kenya a typical control, the Maize Marketing Act, stipulates that:

> All maize grown in Kenya shall, subject to the provision of this Act, be purchased by and sold to the Board, and shall, *without prejudice to the Board's liability for the price payable* in accordance with section 18 of this Act, rest in the Board as soon as it has been harvested.[30]

A researcher working in southern Zaire noted in his field diary one occasion when

> . . . an elderly peasant complained that he had been fined by the agricultural monitor for refusing to sell maize at the decreed minimum price. Friends urged his silence: you never know who can be listening.[31]

While on another,

> . . . the local government secretary warned peasants at a public meeting that fines and jail sentences awaited those who sold at prices above the minimum. He also warned that barter is illegal.[32]

Farmers have little choice but to sell their crops at the set price. The alternatives are to sell on the black market – dodging the taxman, but running the risk of punishment – or simply not to sell crops at all, as many decide to do.

MOVING MOUNTAINS

Peasants were unable and unwilling to be exploited any longer for cheap food. The Sahelian famine of the early 1970s focused world attention on the growing African food crisis. This was perceived as hunger caused by food production not keeping pace with population growth, so leading to rising food imports. Since the problem was defined as one of production, the answer was seen as simply to grow more food with modern hi-tech methods of agriculture. But not only did this take little account of who was going hungry (a problem of some people's *entitlement* to food, not overall shortages); it concentrated too much on food sold in official markets (particularly in the towns), which did decline, and overall production, which probably did not.[33]

Just as the threat of urban food supplies started to make governments edgy, some wealthy knights in shining armour appeared to prop up their bankrupt food policies. The standard-bearers of this band were the European Community's Common Agricultural Policy (CAP) and the US Department of Agriculture; they came bearing food to relieve governments suffering the fallout from their food war with peasant farmers. Rich countries gave some food away as food aid. Between 1974 and 1985 cereal food aid to sub-Saharan Africa grew five-fold, reaching, 5,589,000 tonnes.[34] Although we tend to think of food aid being rushed to a famine emergency like that in Ethiopia, this is only a fraction of the total given. Most (90 per cent in the case of EC food aid) in fact goes to governments on a regular basis for them to sell to their own people. Aid officials say that funds raised can be used for development projects and that food aid saves governments from spending valuable foreign currency on imports.

Others argue that food aid can spearhead commercial imports from rich countries, helping to build up a taste for Western foods – like bread made from wheat, a crop very difficult to grow in most African countries. Commercial food imports to Africa from North America and Europe certainly did grow rapidly during the 1970s, much sold at knock-down prices. Given or sold, the food was not simply the expression of rich countries' goodwill to feed the starving that it seemed to be. Europe and the United States shipped food to Africa to shift the embarrassing food mountains – created by their own policies – in a way that appeared philanthropic.

The CAP may have originated in a post-war vision of Europe freeing itself from dependence on food imports (mostly from North America) and supporting Europe's small farmers, but it has become distorted by its own momentum. Self-sufficiency in Europe was achieved and then surpassed. The social arguments for the CAP, however, remain illusory. Eighty per cent of all CAP support goes to the richest 20 per cent of farmers. The drift from the land has not stopped, with the European agricultural workforce declining by a quarter since 1974.[35] Except where freak weather conditions have taken a hand, large doses of environmentally destructive chemicals and huge unrestricted subsidies have served to build up food surpluses. These surpluses grow as Europe and the US out-produce each other in a bid to dominate world farm trade – including the Third World market. The heroic knights turn out on closer inspection to be ruthless traders flogging off their grain mountains and milk lakes at rock-bottom prices.

Apart from disillusioning European voters, this might not have mattered. To many it seemed more important that food was going to hungry Africa than that the motives in sending it were pure. But the short-term respite offered by food aid and imports had disastrous long-term implications for Africa, for it has led to an unhealthy dependence on Western foods which are difficult and expensive to grow naturally.

Fundamentally, the import approach has been another nail in the peasant farmer's coffin. Already disadvantaged by government policy, the small farmer has been priced out by the subsidized dumping of EC and US food surpluses in the Third World. In the Sahel of Africa, for example, EC beef has been sold at 20 per cent less than the price of unsubsidized locally produced beef.[36] It has not been worth the small farmers' money or labour to struggle to grow food or sell livestock at government prices. Poor farmers have become poorer as they earn little from farming. The poorest have found themselves pushed further into a hand-to-mouth existence, unable to save food or money, and have therefore become more vulnerable to famine when drought strikes. The land has also suffered, because farmers have had little in-centive and no money or labour (since family members have had to find jobs in town to make ends meet) to invest in improving it by terracing, for instance. The weakened buying power of the poor rural majority has also undermined fledgling basic indus-tries, since they offered the main potential mass market within the country.

LEARNING TO LEARN

Mobilizing and building on local people's knowledge of farming and their immediate environment is crucial if enough food is to be grown for the hungry. There is a constant bias in government and aid-funded research and training in favour of the outside rather than indigenous, mechanical rather than human, chemical rather than organic, and marketed rather than consumed. The rich rather than the poor are set to benefit, men rather than women, and adults rather than children.[37]

Crop research, for example, concentrates on cash crops like cotton, coffee or palm oil rather than food crops – and especially food crops like cassava and millet, grown by the poorest in the harshest environments. Livestock researchers are more concerned with the problem of protecting European breeds of cattle used in commercial meat and milk production against the unfamiliar tropical environment, rather than those of the smaller but tougher indigenous breeds of cattle kept by poor rural people. They are even less likely to be interested in the other animals poor people keep, like goats (often despised by the experts.) Despite some moves to correct the bias in recent years, it remains deep-seated. According to a 1987 report, the International Livestock Centre for Africa decided to downgrade its emphasis on the problems faced by famine-vulnerable nomadic cattle-herders in dry areas in favour of 'progressive' dairy farmers in high-rainfall areas, producing for the cities.[38]

THE 'MAGIC OF THE MARKET': MAKING HUNGER DISAPPEAR?

During the 1980s African countries did, however, start to reverse the bias against agriculture and to increase prices paid to farmers. A number of countries abolished government controls holding down farm prices (including Mali, Niger, Nigeria, Somalia, Uganda and Zambia; also Madagascar and Cameroun) and some reformed or abolished their marketing boards (such as Nigeria, Senegal and Somalia).[39] Food crisis and agricultural decline, with few hopeful signs that industry would be able to compensate, had started to persuade some African governments that change was needed. But a second major push came from the IMF and World Bank who insisted that farm prices be freed and state control in agriculture cut as a major part of the free-market adjustment policies demanded of debt-strapped African countries.[40]

The World Bank says that 'taxes in many poor countries (not only Africa) discourage domestic food production and encourage food imports'.[41] In answer to the charge that their programmes hurt the poor, the Bank says that higher free-market crop prices help to 'raise the income of the rural poor, increase food security and generate foreign exchange'. The IMF and World Bank appear in this light not as the ogres of austerity bringing poverty in their wake, but as champions of the downtrodden peasant.

We have already seen how low farm prices, first imposed by colonial governments and maintained since, have deprived peasant farmers of a livelihood, undermined long-term management of the land and prevented Africa from feeding itself. Where IMF and World Bank adjustment policies have tried to reverse this discrimination they have created a welcome break for Africa's rural poor. But this has led many to assume that adjustment policies are always good for the peasant farmer. Some Western free-market crusaders propose the IMF policy of 'getting the prices right' as a panacea for hunger. It is not.

LARGE FARMERS STILL ON TOP

First, despite the World Bank/IMF rhetoric in support of the small farmer, adjustment has in practice been biased towards the big farmer. Prices have been increased more for the crops grown by the large-scale, hi-tech commercial farms which governments and the World Bank still seem to see as the ideal goal of African agriculture, even if their anti-peasant prejudice has been tempered to some extent.[42] For some farmers, what adjustment policies have given in better prices with one hand they have taken away with the other. For example, devaluing the currency and freeing price controls has made farm inputs, such as fertilizers and pesticides, cost more –

especially in the remoter areas where some of the poorest peasants live.

In Zambia, for instance, adjustment programmes increased producer prices for maize, sunflower, groundnut, soya bean, cotton and coffee. But peasants mainly grow cassava, millet and sorghum. None of the producer prices for these crops was increased. Furthermore, a subsidy to the marketing board, NAMBOARD, to help farmers transport their crops to market was cut as part of the policy package – and yet small farmers had few other ways of getting their crops to market.[43]

MARKET LOSERS

Furthermore, while farm price rises may leave some farmers winners, there are losers too. In particular, higher farm prices for food crops are passed on to customers, some of them poor, as more expensive food in the market. The exception is where governments step in to subsidize food. But most Third World, and particularly African, governments can ill afford to do this, and anyway IMF programmes usually specifically forbid them to do so.

Price rises affect different groups of poor people differently. Poor peasant farmers find themselves better off overall, because they gain from better prices for crops they sell in the market. At the same time, higher food prices do not affect them much since they grow most of what they eat and buy little from elsewhere. But other groups of poor people with little or no land, such as landless farm workers and the poor and unemployed in the cities, have to spend a large proportion of the little money they have on food. A price rise can mean starvation.

In Latin America, where a majority of the poor live in city slums or are farm workers on large farms, the higher farm and food prices of adjustment programmes have been devastating. Even in Africa, the problem of urban bias does not mean that all city-dwellers live a cushioned life of state-subsidized plenty; one has only to visit the slums of Lagos, Khartoum or Nairobi to see that. With unemployment often running at 40 per cent or more in African cities and no state provision for the poor, rising food prices push poor families deeper into hunger.⁴⁴ It is little wonder that IMF-imposed price rises have sparked off food riots in cities across the Third World.

Even in the countryside, higher food prices can bring disaster for poor people if they do not grow their own food. In Bangladesh and India, for example, the rural poor get about half their food energy from bought food.⁴⁵ If food prices go up, many cannot afford to eat. Furthermore, most poor people own little or no land and therefore cannot reap much benefit from higher farm prices. It is the big farmers who benefit from higher prices. In Bangladesh, more than three-quarters of the rice sold on the market is produced by only 15 per cent of the farms, mostly the large ones.⁴⁶ In Africa, where higher prices have been hailed as a boon for the poor, landlessness is on the increase – in Kenya, Zimbabwe, Malawi and elsewhere. Feeble attempts in Brazil, Kenya and Thailand to include an element of land reform in adjustment programmes have buckled under political pressure from big landlords. This is in stark contrast to the resolute response of the IMF when the poor have protested that adjustment programmes have pushed up their food prices.

PEASANTS AND THE ENVIRONMENT

Peasant farmers and the landless are often accused of destroying the environment. We have seen, for example, how poor farmers are blamed for deforestation in the Amazon. In Africa, peasants and nomadic herders are often said to cause erosion because they are ignorant and persist in their old ways. These kinds of attitudes have deep historical roots.

Enthusiasm for conservation in the Third World is not a new phenomenon. Following the creation of the American Dust Bowl in the 1930s, a wave of environmental concern spread out to Europe's colonies. Many colonial administrators and agricultural experts shared a concern over environmental degradation, but blamed local people's 'backward' techniques. In Rhodesia (now Zimbabwe), a colonial forester said:

. . . it is expecting too much of the uneducated African willingly to conserve the forests on hillsides and catchments in the interests of generations to come. His whole tendency in the past has been to destroy forests and he cannot understand the reasons for laws framed to preserve them.[47]

The Rhodesian authorities used forced labour to carry out conservation in the 'Native Reserves'. One old Zimbabwean recalls how these measures incited political resentment:

In the 1950s the introduction of soil conservation brought a lot of miseries to many people. They were asked to make contour ridges which took an awful lot of time and fined for not making them to standard. People were shifted from their original villages to be concentrated into lines and land was allocated into grazing and arable.[48]

Such enforced conservation took place right up to independence in 1980. The punitive approach to conservation persists in rules about which types of land may be planted with which crops, or in controls on 'overstocking' of cattle.

Whites did not perceive that the problem would have been less acute had they not taken the bulk of the prime agricultural land, leaving the African population struggling to live in areas with poor soils liable to erosion and unpredictable rainfall. Even in the Native Reserves, large numbers of trees were felled by white contractors for fuel and construction timber for the mines. Yet 'uneducated' African farmers were blamed for environmental damage.

GROUND KNOWLEDGE

The emphasis on large-scale commercial agriculture using modern technology undervalues a vast store of knowledge about the local environment and farming techniques which have evolved over generations to suit local soils, climate and vegetation. As Robert Chambers points out:

From rich-country professionals and urban-based professionals in Third World countries right down to the lowliest extension workers it is a common assumption that the modern scientific knowledge of the centre is sophisticated, advanced and valid and, conversely, that whatever rural people may know will be unsystematic, imprecise, superficial and often plain wrong. Development then entails disseminating this modern, scientific and sophisticated knowledge to inform and uplift the rural masses.[49]

Increasingly, small farmers' techniques are being recognized as environment-friendly and agriculturally beneficial, where once they were dismissed by experts as damaging, backward and inefficient.

In west Africa, many farmers practise some form of shifting cultivation – clearing and burning natural vegetation, growing crops for a season or two and then moving on to a new plot, leaving the old one to regenerate. For a long time (and, indeed, still today), this practice was condemned as wasting the natural fertility of the cleared vegetation in burning instead of returning the goodness to the soil by making the debris into compost.

Recent soil research shows that the major deficiency of forest and upland soils in west Africa is not too few nitrates, which the compost recommended by outsiders would have supplied, but high acidity and lack of phosphorus, which the ash from the local farmers' technique of burning *would* have remedied.[50] It is not a matter of chance that local farmers were correct and the outsiders were wrong. Researcher Paul Richards says that, in contrast, in nitrate-short savanna areas, 'techniques of composting, manuring, mulching and digging-in of straw and other plant residues, tend to be much more highly developed'.[51]

Mixed cropping is another technique widely used by small farmers in both west and east Africa. Several crops are grown together on the same land – say, a grain crop like maize or sorghum – along with a tree crop like coffee or bananas, with some beans or peas at ground level. This approach contrasts with the tidy fields of single crops, like wheat, cultivated by modern Western agriculture. Research has only been carried out on crops growing alone, not on mixed crops. Its misleading results led to farmers who continued to use mixed cropping being condemned as untidy, conservative and lazy.

Mixed cropping has now been shown to: increase crop yields (where, for example, nitrogen-fixing crops like cow peas fertilize other crops like maize with nitrogen, or some plants hold moisture from which others benefit); prevent erosion (by protecting the soil surface from the impact of rain); provide natural protection against pests and diseases because crops are scattered among others; spread risk between different crops (not putting all your eggs in one basket); cut down on work (weeds can't grow up on the fully covered plot), and ensure that periods of intensive work don't all come together in an unmanageable bunch. And the farmer also gets a balanced supply of different foods and other products from a small patch of land.[52]

Mixed cropping has now started to be taken seriously by non-peasant experts and crop researchers, along with other hitherto despised peasant techniques, but it has taken a long time and the emphasis still remains on modern technology based on Western science. The World Bank, for example, in a recent major report on Africa, widely acclaimed as more accommodating to its critics than previous reports, admits that:

Attempts to introduce technology into Africa in the past thirty years have been disappointing. Witness the 1960s and 1970s, when 'modern' technologies were planned for cereals, tree crops, oil seeds, cotton and other crops based on higher-yielding varieties, fertilizer, chemical pest and disease control – and in some cases mechanization. This 'off the shelf' technology was frequently a failure.[53]

The Bank also admits in the same report that half of its rural development projects in Africa up to 1987 failed. It is interesting, however, to note *why* it believes modern technology failed. It admits that modern inputs were too expensive for many farmers and that 'sometimes' the failure occurred because the technology was not adapted to local conditions. But the report also emphasizes the inability of farmers to adapt 'slowly to using modern inputs', and argues that pesticides 'were not widely understood'. The Bank recommends a 'new effort to harness agricultural technology to the needs of African farmers'. But this is a call for greater and 'better' transfer of technology, and it still largely ignores the needs and resources of the farmer who should be at the centre of any development strategy.

THINK BIG?

We have seen how understanding food shortage as the root cause of hunger leads to the conclusion that growing more food is the answer. With an eye on the cheap and plentiful food produced by modern Western agriculture, poor countries and aid donors channel resources into building up large-scale farms using modern inputs like chemicals, machines and high-yielding seeds.

These attempts to leap into modern hi-tech farming as a way to solve the problem of hunger have proved misguided. The ecological costs of modern farming – from water supplies contaminated by fertilizers and pesticides to erosion of topsoil by intensive cropping – have caused growing concern in rich countries and encouraged a move back to more organic techniques, and yet the worst environmental excesses of the system are now being transferred to the Third World. In addition, massive state subsidies in rich countries belie the image of great efficiency, running to the equivalent of $21,000 per farmer in the United States and $10,000 in European Community countries. If the expense is increasingly unsustainable in rich countries, how much more so in poor, often indebted, Third World ones?

Pouring resources into increased production on large farms does little to feed the poor. Instead, it may actually stop the hungry feeding themselves, if it takes away the land or wages that give them 'entitlement' to food. This threat is particularly great in Latin America and Asia where the unequal distribution of land is already the biggest single cause of hunger. But it is also a problem in parts of Africa, particularly in countries where white settlers occupied the prime land (such as Zimbabwe or Kenya). Where large farms displace poor farmers they contribute to hunger, no matter how much food they produce, or how efficiently.

The introduction of production-boosting Western technology has also failed to feed the hungry, as many hoped. In part, this is because it has been directed to increasing the production of cash crops and profits on the big farms and plantations. The poor have reaped few of the benefits, while in some cases, where machines have replaced farm jobs, it has increased their likelihood of going hungry. But even where Western technology has been applied with the specific aim of feeding the hungry, it has often been monopolized by rich farmers at the expense of the poor – so increasing, not lessening, hunger.

THE GREEN REVOLUTION

The 'Green Revolution', launched in Asia in the 1960s partly as a way of averting the 'red revolution', promised to use Western science to solve Third World hunger. Special high-yielding varieties (HYVs) of seeds, like the 'miracle rice' IR 8, were grown with a package of fertilizer, irrigation and pesticide to boost food production. Higher yields and extra harvests became possible. They seemed to offer, in the words of one expert, the promise of filling 'millions of rice bowls once only half full'.[54] Green Revolution countries like India and Pakistan *have* dramatically increased their food production since the 1960s, more than keeping pace with population growth. India, once feared as food-short and famine-racked, now has warehouses brimming with food and is a major grain exporter. And yet over half the world's hungry people live in south Asia, centre of the Green Revolution.[55]

The technology has favoured certain crops (wheat and, to a lesser extent, rice) and certain areas already well endowed with flat land, irrigation and reliable weather, such as the north-west plains of India. In India, far fewer rice farmers have taken up the technology in areas prone to waterlogging and flooding, and where they have, the results have been disappointing. Yet these constitute 80 per cent of India's rice-growing areas.[56] In addition, the techniques were supposed to be 'scale-neutral', benefiting big and small farmers alike. But in practice the big landlords were the only ones with enough money and political clout to get hold of the fertilizers, water-pumps, chemicals and machinery needed to realize the seeds' potential.

In the Bangladeshi village of Katni, for example, a tubewell supposed to serve twenty-five to fifty farmers in an irrigation group was installed by the World Bank. But researchers Betsy Hartmann and James K. Boyce, living in the village at the time, soon learned that the tubewell was in fact considered the personal property of Nafis, the big local landlord:

The co-operative irrigation group, of which Nafis was supposedly the manager, was no more than a few signatures he had collected on a scrap of paper. Nafis was the only person in the union to receive a deep tubewell, a distinction he owed mainly to his connections with the ruling Awami League. He told us that the tubewell cost him only 1,500 *taka*, but he was rumoured to have spent several hundred *taka* on bribes to local officials . . . The tubewell will produce much more than Nafis can use, so he says that the peasants who till adjacent plots will also be able to use the water – at a price. But the hourly rate he will charge is so high that few of his neighbours are interested . . . With his extra income, Nafis will be better able to buy out smaller farmers when hard times befall them, driving them into the ever-growing ranks of the landless. In fact, he already has an eye on the plots nearest the tubewell.[57]

Crop-boosting technology uprooted from one place and thrust into another without taking account of the conditions of the local society and economy not only fails to feed the hungry but can make matters worse. The technical package is also often at odds with the local environment and the agricultural techniques that local farmers have built up in harmony with nature over generations. This is increasingly so as the pace of technology quickens.

THE GENE REVOLUTION

The modern age of agriculture based on theories of genetics started in this century, but genetic engineering is only in its second decade. Transnational companies have been quick to exploit this new wave of technology – the 'Gene Revolution'. As in the case of the Green Revolution, the new technology holds the promise of considerable benefits to farmers worldwide. In reality, it serves the interests of those who have carried out the research; transnationals are marketing crop varieties, for example, that have been developed to increase rather than decrease the farmer's need to use chemical herbicides (sold, of course, by the same transnational).

But in addition, the new technology carries with it the potential for environmental catastrophe – the threat of 'genetic erosion'. Previously farmers in different countries across the world grew a mixture of crops, with many different varieties of each species – a diversity of genetic resources that offered protection against the vagaries of disease and weather. As traditional varieties are replaced by single, modern high-yielding varieties, this genetic diversity is reduced. A problem faced by farmers in one part of the world is then multiplied for farmers worldwide if they are using the same new variety.

Furthermore, transnationals are selling packages of seeds, chemicals and know-how to farmers who then become increasingly tied to the company because their traditional knowledge appears redundant. If the seeds can be patented (as commercial pressure groups in the USA and the EC are urging), farmers will be unable to produce their own seed on the farm and will have to return to the company each time. When farmers stop saving seed and start buying it on the market, their families eat the whole of the previous year's crop, and with it the traditional varieties built up over generations. 'Quite literally,' explains scientist Garrison Wilkes, 'the genetic heritage of a millennium can disappear in a single bowl of porridge.'[58]

UN-GREENING FARMING

The ecological problems of Western farming have been imported into many parts of the Third World, where they are frequently magnified. The ecological conditions and farming practices in Third World countries are often different from those of the temperate environments where the technology was originally developed (and where problems enough occur). Add to this the less stringent standards and weaker application of safety and environmental regulations prevalent in the Third World and you have a recipe for disaster – threatening both the human environment and the long-term viability of production itself.

The increasing use of agricultural chemicals – artificial fertilizers and pesticides – is a prominent feature of the move to 'modernize' Third World farming. Although rich countries use the most fertilizers (accounting for three-quarters of world usage) and pesticides (the US alone taking up a third of the world's pesticides), poor countries are now the main growth areas.[59] In the short term their use can dramatically increase crop yields and production. But they also carry considerable costs. As energy costs in the production of chemicals have risen, so have their overall cost to farmers. This is particularly true where farmers have found themselves on a chemical treadmill, and are obliged to apply more and more just to get the same results.

The chemicals – pesticides in particular – also have more direct human costs. Although it is hard to make accurate estimates (most being underestimates, because people do not always report cases), the World Health Organisation estimates that pesticides kill 20,000 people a year.[60] Nearly all these deaths are in the Third World, and many of them are of poor farm workers (often women, who are widely employed as pesticide applicators in the Third World) and farmers. Many thousands more suffer serious damage to their health – including sterility, birth defects, nervous disorders and muscle wasting. Labelling is often poor, sometimes in the wrong language, while widespread illiteracy means the labels are often not understood even when they are in the local language. Farm workers are not always made aware of the risks or are not supplied with protective clothing, regarded as an unnecessary expense by many employers.

The Malaysian environmental group Sahabat Alam Malaysia reports many cases of estate workers applying weedkillers with their bare hands, of pesticide containers thrown away near houses and playgrounds, and the highly poisonous pesticide paraquat carried on estate vehicles together with workers' lunches. The Consumers Association of Penang says:

There is clear evidence that workers are forced by estate managements to work for years as pesticide sprayers, even after they have developed severe health problems as a result. Protective clothing is inadequate or not worn. Managements do not warn their workers of the dangers of the chemicals they are using or educate them on safety precautions.[61]

The impact of pesticides on health not only affects those who directly work with them. Food sold in markets can be contaminated. Researchers in Sri Lanka and in Bombay have found that many vegetables on sale in markets contain pesticide residues way above the official legal limit.[62] In Colombia, it was found that pesticide from local farms was polluting the air of neighbouring cities.

The ecological balance of the environment has been upset by heavy pesticide use. This can lead to pesticides undermining their own effectiveness in the long run, for if they kill off natural predators, certain pests breed without check. In the cotton fields of the Canete Valley in Peru, an increasing range of pesticides had to be used as insects became more and more resistant to them by the mid-1950s. Thirteen new crop-damaging pests appeared, previously unknown or unimportant because natural predators had kept them at bay. Crop yields fell as still more pesticides had to be applied. Only when the government introduced a scheme known as 'integrated pesticide management', where pesticide applications were cut dramatically and beneficial insects were introduced, was the ecological balance restored, and yields then recovered by some 30 per cent.[63]

Governments and aid donors are focusing increasing amounts of scarce resources – particularly in cash-starved debtor countries – on expensive and ecologically damaging chemicals and machinery for big-scale agriculture. Yet poor farmers and landless labourers are starved of the resources to grow food or lose their farm jobs because of labour-saving technology. As the poor become increasingly marginal, with little secure access to the land, they are unable to invest time and resources in building up the long-term sustainability of the land and rural environment. They must think of the pressing needs of today – like food – rather than the longer-term future. This further contributes to the degradation of poor and marginal land. In Africa in particular, this disregard for the peasant farmer is central to the problem of hunger.

FOOD FROM THE GRASS-ROOTS

Food, in human terms, is the most valuable commodity on earth. Yet the poorest people go hungry – not because of shortages of food, but because they are dispossessed of the means to obtain food. A hoarding outside the Zimbabwean Ministry of Agriculture in Harare reads: 'Build on what the farmers know and use what they have.' The example of peasant farmers in Zimbabwe and other countries have shown that they can, with appropriate support and opportunities, provide an effective and ecologically sustainable solution to problems of hunger. The poor themselves are beginning to show that, given the basic means, they can earn or grow food to feed themselves.

4 1992 and All That: Trade and Self-reliance

> You cannot develop in today's world by selling raw materials – no matter on what terms.
>
> Edwin Carrington, ex-Secretary-General of the Africa, Caribbean, Pacific Group
>
> Before the trade we were organic farmers.
>
> Earlene Horne, farmer from St Vincent in the Caribbean

The flow of water into the street gutters turns blood red in the month of April on the Caribbean island of St Lucia. The cause is a surfeit of tomatoes. Ripened under the hot sun during the dry season, the island's annual crop of tomatoes floods the local markets, and those that local traders cannot sell are discarded. Without the facilities to store them, the tomatoes rot within a few days. The gutters, some clogged with tomatoes, are the only way of disposing of the surplus crop. But within two months the street stalls are empty of tomatoes and St Lucia will start once more to import bottles of tomato purée or tomato ketchup from the United States. Cheap local tomatoes are all long gone. For the rest of the year, islanders who can afford it will have to buy ketchup imported from elsewhere.

Like many islands, St Lucia relies on trade. From January to May, during the tropical dry season, the prevailing winds are the 'trade winds'. Exports represent in value half of the island's economy. The history of the island, too, is dominated by trade; colonial powers once competed to control islands in the West Indies to grow sugar and coffee for export to Europe.

While trade comes naturally to St Lucia, the pattern of its trade threatens both the economy and the ecology of the island. Seventy per cent of its exports are made up of one crop – bananas. All the bananas are destined for one market – the United Kingdom. Every banana that leaves the shores of St Lucia is controlled by one firm – the British company Geest.

Seven thousand farmers in St Lucia grow bananas for export. Many thousands more work as labourers. In the two days of the week when harvesting takes place, schools empty as children leave to help on the farms. The whole island depends on the banana trade.

This trade, however, rests on an administrative arrangement which has its origin in Britain's Department of Trade and Industry in London. Bananas from St Lucia and other ex-colonies in the Caribbean, such as Jamaica, Grenada and St Vincent, are granted automatic licences to enter the UK market. Bananas from other suppliers, such as Honduras, Colombia and Costa Rica, are restricted. That arrangement is now being challenged as Britain changes its marketing arrangements in order to enter the European 'single market', set for 1992. In order to compete with the vast and mechanized plantations of Colombia and Costa Rica, St Lucia's farmers would have to cut every corner to reduce costs.

At the moment, bananas are grown on their own on the flat valley floors, and intercropped with tree and root crops on the lower hillsides. With only shallow roots, the banana tree cannot provide soil cover on steep slopes. But if their incomes are pressured by the new competition in European export markets, farmers may be forced to take a short-term view – planting bananas on the hillsides, perhaps cutting down local rainforests to do so, even though in the long term, as the soil is lost, landslides and flooding may occur.

Though St Lucia's trade has provided stable export earnings in the past, it has locked the island into a position where the livelihood of its people rests on decisions taken thousands of miles away in Europe – decisions that are rarely informed by the needs of farmers in poor countries. Trade has made its contribution to St Lucia's development, but it has also undermined the island's own self-reliance.

COMPARATIVE DISADVANTAGE: COMMODITY DEPENDENCE

The colonial era has left many Third World communities and countries, like St Lucia, reliant on exporting primary commodities for economic survival, despite other changes in international trade and industrialization in some parts of the Third World. Africa is the clearest example. Eighty-six per cent of sub-Saharan Africa's export earnings are from primary commodities, virtually the same proportion for some countries as when they won independence in the mid-1960s.[1] Some nations are more vulnerable by being reliant on just one commodity. Uganda, for example, relies on coffee for 95 per cent of its export earnings. Zambia relies on copper for 90 per cent.[2] Taking the poorest countries of the Third World (other than India and China) as a whole, primary commodities account for three-quarters of all their exports.[3] Even relatively industrialized Latin America depends on commodities for 67 per cent of its export earnings.[4]

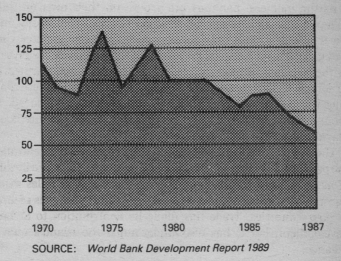

SOURCE: *World Bank Development Report 1989*

Figure 4.1   Non-fuel commodity prices (1970-87)

The reliance on commodities of many poor countries has left them at the mercy of the volatile whims of world commodity markets. The last decade has seen a collapse in commodity prices. By 1986, despite an economic upturn in the rich world, commodity prices (in relation to the price of manufactured goods imported by poor countries) sank to the lowest level recorded this century, with the possible exception of 1932, the deepest trough of the Great Depression.[5] While some commodities – particularly industrial metals and minerals – did rally a little in 1988, they soon took a downward turn again.

SOLD SHORT

Falling world prices do not simply trace a downward line on a financial chart. They threaten whole communities in the Third World. A dramatic fall in world cocoa prices in 1989 left buying agents in the Ivory Coast with unsaleable mountains of cocoa from the previous harvest. As their debts mounted they could not buy the next crop of cocoa from farmers, and cocoa beans piled up in storerooms in the countryside.

One farmer described the impact as the fall in world prices filtered through to the villages:

It is all over for us unless there is a price rise soon. We are finished. Our village and the seven others which make up the co-operative we are part of are collectively owed three million CFA francs [£6,000] and most of us have not been paid for a year. Nobody can afford to buy meat to eat, nor can we afford tools for clearing the ground around the crops. Our children are going without school books and old people in the village cannot afford to buy medicines.[6]

Everybody in the Ivory Coast is praying for a rise in the price of cocoa (as well as coffee – another of the country's major exports which reached a record low). But the prospects are bleak because other countries, like neighbouring Ghana, have been increasing their cocoa production – contributing to a cocoa glut and so to low prices. In both countries the cocoa export drive was part of an IMF package to increase foreign currency earnings to meet foreign debt payments.

THE RISE OF COMMODITY POWER

Since the 1950s economists have debated the theory that the prices of commodities exported by poor countries are in an inevitable long-term decline. The events of the 1970s seemed to repudiate the idea. In 1973 the Arab oil-producing countries, drawn together in protest at the West's support for Israel in the Yom Kippur War, instituted an oil boycott. Prices tripled and the producers realized that a cartel could keep up prices. Throughout the 1970s the Organisation of Petroleum Exporting Countries (OPEC) managed to keep prices rising. The fall of the Shah of Iran in 1979 pushed prices still higher in the face of Western panic about supplies, leaving oil at forty dollars a barrel. At the beginning of the decade it had cost just over one dollar.

OPEC's success gave hope to other Third World countries that at last the producers had started to fight back; the pundits proclaimed the 'era of commodity power'. A few rich trading countries (and latterly giant transnational companies) had for decades controlled the world market to keep commodity prices low, and their profits in processing high. Now it seemed the turn of Third World producers to get together to stabilize and raise prices by controlling supply through strengthened commodity agreements – for example, in tin, coffee and cocoa. These agreements put limits on production through quotas (as in the case of oil), or used buffer stocks to keep prices within an agreed range by buying in stocks to restrict supply as prices fell and selling them when the market picked up again. All producers were meant to benefit, since even if they did not sell as much in volume, they got a higher price.

For a short time it seemed to some that the rich world's fears of the inflationary effect of further raw-material price rises – following the pattern of oil – would lead it to negotiate seriously with the Third World. An added impetus was the warning of environmentalists that the world was rapidly exhausting its resources. Leading business figures, in the shape of the Club of Rome, sponsored the influential *Limits to Growth* report, published in 1972. This gave doomsday computer projections of finite natural resources, including minerals and food being eaten up by ever-increasing economic growth and burgeoning populations.[7] One reaction of the rich countries' governments to such fears was to talk of 'resource wars' – the need to guard access to the 'West's' supplies of vital resources such as oil.[8] Another was for rich countries to make some concessions, in trade talks, to the poor world's demands. The rich countries conceded the principle at the 1976 meeting of the United Nations Conference on Trade and Development (UNCTAD), when it was agreed that eighteen commodities should be regulated by an 'Integrated Programme for Commodities'.

. . . AND ITS FALL

The 1980s brought a rude awakening for those who argued that 'commodity power' was tilting the balance of global economic power towards the Third World. Commodity prices collapsed, and with them any pretence by the rich world to be answering the poor world's call for a 'new international economic order'. By the late 1980s even the oil price itself had dived because of a world glut as OPEC members ignored quotas.

International commodity agreements have also fallen one after the other – both cause and effect of low prices. In 1985 the International Tin Agreement broke down in financial disarray, its final demise being delayed until 1989 only to pay off its creditors. In 1989 the International Coffee Agreement collapsed in a row over quotas, with the United States insisting that its Central American friends should have better quotas and Brazil refusing to take a cut in its traditional 30 per cent share of world exports.[9] A free-for-all market sent prices crashing. By the end of 1989 producers' earnings from coffee were expected to have fallen nearly 40 per cent in a year, from $9.3 billion in 1988–9 to $5.6 billion in 1989–90. Other agreements have been renegotiated, but have lost their teeth as price provisions have been left out. They have simply become forums for the exchange of information; 1977 was the last year in which the sugar agreement contained any economic provisions. The International Rubber Agreement remains the only working commodity agreement successfully to defend prices (other than OPEC, which itself has come under strain).

Prices and their collective defence mechanisms were first undermined from outside by the recession that gripped the rich countries in the early 1980s and hit demand for Third World commodities. The debt crisis – amongst the African debtors, it was partly caused by the commodity crash – has further lowered prices. Policies to promote exports, such as the devaluation of local currency, have been urged on debtors by the IMF. But as individual debtors each try to pay their debts by selling more, the overall effect is simply to add to glutted markets and undermine collective action by producers, pushing down prices yet again. Third World countries find themselves producing more and more for less and less.

For the rich countries, in contrast, the Third World's commodity crisis has been an important boost to industrial recovery. Western politicians made a lot of noise about the success of their 'disciplined' policies in conquering the inflation of the 1970s. But just as important – but rarely noted in rich countries – was the fact that factories and shops were getting Third World commodity inputs, ranging from iron ore to coffee, at knock-down prices.

COMMODITIES AND THE 'IMMATERIAL' ECONOMY

There are long-term forces behind the continuing decline in demand of industrialized countries for Third World commodities. In the 1970s the industrial economies grew by 3.4 per cent a year, while world consumption of non-fuel commodities grew at about the same rate (3.1 per cent).[10] In the 1980s (1980–86) industrial economies grew more slowly, at about 2.3 per cent a year, but the world consumption of commodities grew by even less – only 1.5 per cent. For metals, world consumption was no higher in 1986 than 1979.[11] Forced into energy-saving action by the oil price rises, the rate of energy consumption by industrialized countries has also dropped.

There is undoubtedly room for much greater energy conservation and less wasteful use of resources by industrialized countries which continue to consume the bulk of world resources, quite out of proportion to the numbers of their people. But the trend does undermine earlier predictions of the imminent exhaustion of world resources. It also throws doubt on the bland assurances of Western commentators that increasing prosperity in the rich countries will, through trade, haul up the commodity-producing Third World with it.

The first reason for the declining intensity in the use of resources is that rich countries are shifting their economies away from industry and into services. Information, not coal and steel, is fast becoming the mainspring of the rich countries' economies as they enter the post-industrial age. In the last twenty years the share of industry in the wealth of the rich countries, measured as a percentage of gross domestic product, has fallen from 40 per cent in 1965 to 34 per cent.[12] The south-east of England has become the first region in Britain to become 'de-industrialized', according to a study published in 1990.[13] The region now employs more people in business and financial services than in industry. At the beginning of the 1980s industry supported twice as many jobs as services. The report adds that other regions are following a similar pattern, and nearly all new jobs are expected to be in services.

Even within industry itself the trend has been away from the smoke-stack industries, dependent on raw materials. The consumer society may not be dead, but what people consume is changing. The growth industries are in areas like electronics and computers, which don't use large amounts of raw materials and are constantly being miniaturized further. The first electronic computer had more than 18,000 valves and filled a large room; today a microchip, many times more powerful, is the size of a fingernail.

NEW MATERIALS FOR OLD

Changing technology is reducing the demand for Third World commodities in other ways. New technology has meant swapping traditional, often Third World, raw materials for synthetic ones that are cheaper or more versatile. This process is not new (the introduction of chemical dyes in the nineteenth century ruined Indian indigo growers), but has increased in scale in recent years. Copper from Zambia or Chile is being displaced by plastic pipes in our plumbing and by fibre optics in the telephone cables below our streets. Synthetic fibres in clothes and other textiles ended the dominance of cotton produced in Peru or Sudan.

INDUSTRY: MORE WITH LESS

Previously, new technology was aimed at reducing labour costs, but now it is being directed towards cost-cutting production processes which save on the amounts of materials and commodities used. Computers cut down the amount of waste in production. They make it quicker and easier to calculate ways of cutting sheets of material or metal, and they continuously monitor production in order to avoid waste. Computerized planning of production and fast communication with customers means that factories can shift from the old mass-production methods of producing to stock, to producing to the next immediate order (known as 'just in time' production).

DESIGNER BIOLOGY

Changing technology, particularly the micro-electronics revolution, has brought the biggest cuts in the rate of commodity use of non-renewable metal and mineral resources like iron ore, copper and tin. But the coming wave of technology, especially biotechnology, is likely to bring changes at least as great to farm commodities. Crops grown in the fields of Third World farmers can increasingly be produced in the factories of transnational companies in the rich countries.

The earnings of sugar-exporting poor countries and the jobs of the twelve million sugar workers have already come under threat from the rapid increase in sugar beet production in rich countries – notably the dumping of European Community surpluses on the world market, which has brought world prices tumbling. Increasingly, biotechnology is allowing sweeteners to be manufactured that could replace sugar altogether.

High fructose corn syrup (HFCS) is extracted from corn by new enzyme techniques and modified so that it is interchangeable with sugar for many purposes. HFCS is now widely used in the US, where it accounts for a third of the total sugar and sweetener market, and in Japan.[14] Thirty US soft-drink corporations use HFCS. Coca-Cola now add not only 'life', as the words of its advertising jingle tell us, but also HFCS. Following a cut in the Philippines' US sugar quota in 1985, partly resulting from the rise of HFCS, the sugar-growing island of Negros was devastated and a quarter of a million sugar workers found themselves without jobs. Starvation hit the island and a relief operation had to be mounted. The call from the Philippines' National Federation of Sugar Workers for Pepsi-Cola and Coca-Cola to pay $2.5 million each in compensation fell on deaf ears.[15]

The British sugar giant Tate & Lyle, together with the Anglo-Dutch Unilever, have developed a sweetener called Thaumatin which is 3,000 times as sweet as sugar.[16] At present it is extracted from a plant grown on plantations in West Africa, but this is likely to be a passing phase until the companies have fully developed factory production at home with tissue-culture techniques. Factory-produced substitutes for cocoa – presently largely grown by peasants in countries like Ghana and Bolivia – are being researched by Hershey, Nestlé and Unilever. If successfully produced, an artificial cocoa would wipe out the livelihoods of thousands of peasant producers in West Africa and Latin America.

The big companies who have long profited from the production of commodities like sugar and cocoa are protecting their own future profits by investing now in research on new biotech substitutes. But though many of the new biotech products are developed from genetic material in poor countries, the plantation workers and poor peasants in those countries, who have produced the crop for generations, are likely to be discarded without compensation.

TECHNOLOGICAL CHANGE IN PERSPECTIVE

The implications of technological change on the demand for primary commodities have to be kept in perspective. It is premature to pronounce the end of the 'era of materials'. While the amount of primary commodities used relative to overall economic growth may be declining, this does not always mean there is an absolute decline (although in some cases this is happening). Modern television sets are lighter and less bulky than their predecessors, but many households in rich countries now have more than one set. Some commodity-using industries are also being transferred to the newly industrializing countries (NICs). As they develop and as incomes rise, they will become increasingly important buyers both for minerals – for instance, South Korea's large steel industry will buy iron ore, even if mills in North America and Europe continue to close – and for consumer commodities like coffee and tea. However, the NICs are themselves often adopting, and in some cases actually developing, modern industrial techniques which use fewer raw materials. China, in developing its telecommunications system, is largely using fibre optic technology, bypassing the copper-wire phase of Europe or North America's earlier expansion.

THE EXPORT ROUTE TO DEVELOPMENT

To escape the bleak commodity treadmill, poor countries are urged to switch to exporting manufactured goods as the path to economic prosperity. The World Bank, amongst others, argues that countries should go all out for exports by specializing in particular industries, such as textiles, where they have the international edge in prices ('comparative advantage') because of cheap labour (as compared with the rich countries). They say that countries should bring down their own barriers to trade in order to allow the international free market to force their industries into shape, to become internationally competitive and so be able to win in world export markets. The local currency should be devalued to make exports cheaper abroad. The foreign exchange earned from exports could be used to purchase imports from abroad and to invest in further development. They point to the NICs as the shining example of this approach.

The NICs have been very successful in increasing their exports, mainly to the market of rich countries, and have emerged as major world exporters of manufactured goods, including many hi-tech products such as computers. The four east-Asian 'tigers', Hong Kong, Singapore, South Korea and Taiwan, are the leaders, but Brazil and Mexico have also been marked out as Latin American NICs. Between them, the Asian NICs rang up exports of $220 billion in 1988, not far behind Japan's total of $260 billion.[17] They now produce 8 per cent of all world exports, almost twice the proportion attributable to them at the beginning of the 1980s.[18] As a result, economic growth has been phenomenally rapid. The Asian NICs grew by 10 per cent a year between 1964 and 1973, and nearly 8 per cent between 1973 and 1983, despite the world economic difficulties of that period.[19] This compares with 4.8 per cent and 2.1 per cent respectively for the rich industrialized countries.[20] Some say the development of the NICs represents the 'end of the Third World'[21] and a vindication of the free market, export-led model of development which others should follow.

MYTHS OF THE MIRACLE

There are important lessons to be learnt from the NICs, but these are often obscured by the generalized myths of those who try to fit the NICs into preconceived political boxes. They are held up as models of the success awaiting countries which follow free trade and free market strategies. In fact, their success often involves a high degree of state participation. Contrary to the myth of free market development, the OECD, in a major report on the NICs, commented on the 'resolute government action which has played a major role in influencing economic and industrial development' in at least four of the major NICs (South Korea, Taiwan, Singapore and Brazil).[22]

The NICs have achieved their success by a much broader range of policies than much of the mythology implies. In South Korea, for example, the government has used a series of five-year plans.[23] In the first phase of development, between 1958 and 1964, it built up the country's light industry, using stringent import controls and US aid to pay for imports. In 1964 the government embarked on export-led industrialization, by intervening directly in priority sectors where it gave incentives to exporters, provided generous credit and eased taxes and customs on goods used as industrial inputs in the export sectors. In 1973 the government decided to move the emphasis to developing heavy industry, including steel, chemicals, machinery, construction and shipbuilding – Korea is now the world's second biggest builder of ships. Korea is also a leading exporter of sophisticated consumer electronic products. In the late 1970s the car industry was given great impetus; Korea now produces about a million vehicles a year, half of them for export. In the car industry and other sectors where the government has used foreign investment, it has placed a strong emphasis on maintaining Korean control over production – through, for example, tough rules on foreign investment. It limits the overall level of foreign control allowed in enterprises and insists that a certain proportion of a product should be of local origin. Other key elements of success in Korea's development have been, first, the land reform programme of the 1940s which redistributed land to small farmers, stopped the free market in land and limited farms to an area no larger than three hectares, and second, the government's stress on education.

But in addition to the issue of what development path the NICs have taken, there is a broader question as to whether other poor countries should be urged to follow their example completely. For one thing, there is the question of whether it is a *desirable* model. A number of the NICs are highly authoritarian. Labour laws, for example, have often been very restrictive and unions vigorously repressed. In South Korea a quarter of a million people work in the textile sector – mostly women – but trade unions representing workers from more than one factory are banned. Without an effective national union to establish good working conditions, textile workers will often work twelve hours on one shift.[24] However, there is now growing pressure for improved conditions and representation for workers both in South Korea and Taiwan. Above all, it may not be possible for other countries to follow the NICs' path as a way out of commodity dependence. Changes in trade and technology, coupled with increased protectionism in the rich countries of the North, have altered the specific international configuration that was vital for the NICs' success.

INDUSTRIAL RESTRUCTURING

One of the factors which helped the growth of a number of NICs, such as Mexico and Singapore, was the strategy of transnational companies during the 1960s and 1970s in setting up assembly plants in South-East Asia and Latin America to exploit cheap labour. Local governments often went out of their way to attract foreign companies with tax-free holidays in export-processing zones and promises to enforce 'labour discipline' by banning unions and strikes. In some cases – Singapore is an example – this approach helped the NICs to gain a foothold in markets for high-tech electronic exports, which they have continued to expand. However, more recently transnationals have started to move their assembly back into the rich countries, because technology has cut down the importance of labour costs in the overall product. For instance, the California-based computer company Apple had the components for its first major product, the Apple II, assembled in Malaysia and Singapore. But, its more recent product, the MacIntosh, has been assembled at a highly automated plant in California employing only 200 people (of whom seventy are engineers) and relying on 'just-in-time' delivery of components from nearby suppliers. The plant produces a million units a year, with a product failure rate of less than 5 per cent. Its direct labour costs are less than 3 per cent of total costs.[25]

NEW PATTERNS OF TRADE

The relocation of production back into rich countries has been part of a wider move of transnationals to return to home markets in the 1980s, due to international economic instability, slower economic growth and increasing protectionism. The drive for businesses to become bigger has not, however, halted. Companies did not look to the Third World as they had done before, but instead turned to investment in industrialized countries through international take-over battles, mergers and setting up looser networks of joint ventures and subcontracting to companies in other countries. There has been an explosion of foreign investment by Japanese companies in Europe, and of both Japanese and European businesses in the United States. But the majority of developing countries have shared relatively little in this trend. Foreign investment in the Third World dropped from 29 per cent of world investment in 1975 to 23 per cent in 1985.[26]

Trade is following these patterns of investment. Contrary to classical theory, trade is now growing fastest between countries with similar economic and industrial structures and also between and within companies trying to go global. Final assembly of Ford Escort cars, for example, may take place in Halewood in Britain and Saarlouis in West Germany,[27] but their parts come from fifteen different countries. Governments of rich countries, such as the members of the European Community, have reacted to these pressures by reducing all forms of trade barriers – technical, fiscal, tariff and even environmental – with neighbouring countries. The EC explicitly justifies the 1992 programme of market integration by arguing that European companies are too small and too locally based to meet the challenge of US and Japanese firms. What is needed, it concludes, are larger pan-European companies. The reality is that business is becoming too big for the nation state.

'Globalization' is top of the agenda for industrialists and government economic strategists in the rich countries. But this industrial and trading 'globalization' is scarcely truly global. Most Third World countries who are left out fear that as the blocs bring down barriers between insiders, they will raise them to outsiders. Even hopes of an international 'trickle down' of wealth may be thwarted. As Charles Leadbeater of the *Financial Times* points out:

> The regrouping of national economies into regional blocs (distinct free trading zones that give preferential treatment for its member states) is presented in a spirit of internationalism. But it could become a cloak for born-again protectionism with the formation of trade blocs that might leave debt-burdened Latin America and sub-Saharan Africa out in the cold.[28]

BLOCS AND 1992

Europe's 1992 programme is the most ambitious project in a new trend towards such blocs. Three appear to be emerging among rich countries: a European bloc including the EC in close conjunction with other western and eastern European states; a North American bloc taking in the United States and Canada, under a Free Trade Agreement that may well be strengthened; and Japan, possibly in association with other countries in the west Pacific.

In 1992, for example, the intention is to achieve free trade within the twelve member states of the EC and virtual free trade with other European states, such as Austria and Norway. The EC is pushing through legislation to cover a host of subjects ranging from telecommunications to standards for animal health. Domestic European producers can expect to benefit most from these changes, and other rich countries will be keen to exploit the new economies of scale. Although European producers tend not to compete directly with Third World producers of commodities such as raw coffee beans, they do compete in those products into which poor countries are seeking to diversify, such as processed coffee. Furthermore, 1992 is leading to higher consumer and environmental standards for products, which may raise the start-up costs of diversification for would-be manufacturers from poor countries.[29]

The shift towards trading blocs has, ironically, been coupled with loud assertions on the part of rich countries about the importance of free trade. But in reality, the treatment of exports from poor countries remains discriminatory. The further Third World countries go up the scale of processing, the greater the efforts of rich countries to keep their products out. One example: industrialized countries add an average tariff of 2.6 per cent on cocoa beans, but on processed beans they charge 4.3 per cent, and 11.8 per cent on chocolate. Previous rounds of the GATT trade talks did 'little or nothing' to tackle this problem of escalating tariffs, according to the World Bank.[30] Rich countries know they're on to a good thing, and allowing poor countries to do their own processing would threaten their ability to reap most of the profits.

The greatest trade barriers put up by rich countries tend to be concentrated on the basic industries which Third World countries can most easily set up to process their natural resources. Examples of such industries include the manufacture of textiles and finished clothes, shoes, leather products, furniture, preserving and canning fruits and vegetables, and producing finished vegetable oils from crops like soya and coconut. Eighty per cent of poor countries' manufactured exports to the European Community are in sectors facing protectionist barriers (and 56 per cent in the United States).[31] Poor countries tend to receive harsher treatment despite being more economically vulnerable – or perhaps, more accurately, *because* they are economically vulnerable and politically less powerful, and therefore easier targets than rich countries.

One method which has hit Third World countries particularly hard is so-called 'voluntary export restraints' (VERs). 'Voluntary' is used here in the Mafia sense of the word. Third World countries 'volunteer' to cut their exports in response to 'an offer they can't refuse'. A rich country takes a particular Third World exporting country aside and tells it to agree to cut its imports to a certain level. It warns the exporting country of retribution if it doesn't keep its exports down to this level.

The Omnibus Trade Act passed in 1988 as a way of tackling the US trade deficit crisis strengthened attempts by the United States to retaliate in this and other ways against countries that included some in Asia and Latin America. The Act empowers the United States Trade Representative to retaliate in cases of 'unreasonable trade practices', whether or not these actually violate any legal rights of the US. Of the three countries castigated by the US in 1988 as 'unfair traders', two – Brazil and India – were in the Third World.[32]

DEVELOPMENT WITHOUT TRADE?

The negative picture painted so far calls into question the role of international trade itself. Does trade promote development or hinder it? Critics ranging from Rudolf Bahro of the German Greens to Samir Amin, an African academic, have called on poor countries to 'de-link' their economies from the demands of transnational companies and to seek to withdraw from international trade until they are able to trade on fairer terms.

The argument continues that international trade inevitably damages the environment, partly because of pollution and fuel use resulting from transportation and partly because natural resources such as tropical forests are torn down to make way for export-oriented agriculture. The distance between producer and consumer also gives middlemen, particularly transnational companies, a licence to run down natural resources. The prices charged to the consumer at the end of the day do not include the environmental costs associated with production. International companies can promote intensive farming in one area until the soil is exhausted, and then simply shift to another location, perhaps in another poor country.

However, the link between trade and environmental degradation is far from clear-cut. A report by the University of Amsterdam on the export of cassava from Thailand to feed animals in Europe showed that the trade had both positive and negative environmental effects. On the one hand, cassava is known to deplete soil fertility; on the other, the expansion of production from 100,000 hectares in the mid-1960s to a million hectares today (largely in the hands of small-scale farmers) had not significantly increased deforestation. The greater part of the land used for cultivation was forest land that had already been degraded. Where the cassava was mixed with other crops like peanuts, for example, it reduced the need for fallowing land and hence for other areas to be reclaimed from the forest.[33]

The ecological impact of trade also depends on whether the goods traded are produced in an environmentally sustainable manner. In Chapter 1 we looked at the damaging impact of unsustainable timber extraction. Brazil also offers other examples. A Brazilian court, for instance, suspended the operation of nearly all Brazil's tin mines in early 1990, invoking environmental protection clauses in the Constitution. The Bom Futuro mine, one of the largest in the world, operated by small independent prospectors using unsophisticated methods, was closed so that dams could be built to prevent thousands of tonnes of sludge polluting nearby rivers that supply local drinking water. Courts also ordered Paranapanema, the world's largest tin producer, to close its road to the Pitinga mine, as it threatened the homeland of Indian tribes. The two mines produced about 44,000 tonnes in 1989, making Brazil the world's leading tin producer.[34]

On the other hand, it is not possible to wish away trade. When trade stops, the result is not necessarily ecologically benign. When tin prices collapsed and the Bolivian government closed down its tin mines, 20,000 miners lost their jobs, and, with them, a proud tradition of militancy and collective self-reliance.[35] Thousands of ex-tin miners started to move into the forest to try to escape the destitution that resulted from the tin collapse. They clear the forests either to grow coca, the basis of cocaine, or to search for gold. The poverty that can result from the withdrawal of trade creates its own environmental pressures.

Export earnings from commodities are crucially important for the people, environment and economy of Third World countries. The livelihoods of the mine or plantation workers and peasant smallholders who actually produce the copper, sugar and cocoa may be reliant on international trade. It is true that the working conditions and income of the actual producers of commodities vary widely throughout the world – even if world prices are relatively high and stable. For instance, sugar workers in Mauritius have better pay and conditions than their counterparts in Swaziland.[36] A number of factors explain the differences, including the strength of trades unions and the amounts national governments and foreign companies rake off in revenues and profits. However, all workers would be hit if trade were removed completely.

International trade conjures up ideas of commodities, supertankers and international cartels – of an abstract activity which doesn't impinge on daily lives. But the poor also trade. For vast numbers of women and men in the Third World, trade is a daily activity – often the means of their survival. In most cities in poor countries there is a huge informal economy which may provide a living for up to half the urban population. Whether selling sweets on the roadside or river silt for use in building, bartering, or bringing cattle to the local market in the countryside, trade is an essential way of supporting oneself and one's family.

NATIONAL ECONOMIC IMPACT

Similarly, trade can play a role in wider development of the economy and society. Trade in commodities and manufactured goods is crucial in supplying the foreign exchange that many Third World countries rely on. It is true that foreign exchange in itself does not guarantee sustainable development; it can be wasted by local elites on luxuries, or by corrupt governments on arms or prestige projects that do little to help the poor. But it can also be used positively to purchase tools, medical equipment, books and the like. Equally it may be used for natural resources unavailable locally: otherwise a country with no iron deposits could be condemned to the Stone Age.

Without enough foreign exchange, African countries over the last decade have been suffering acute 'import strangulation' – a condition whereby manufacturing industry is working at a fraction of its full capacity because of a shortage of one or more key parts only available from abroad. Agriculture, too, can be hit by a shortage of fertilizers, and fuel or spare parts for transport.

In fact many poor countries have in the past attempted to break out of dependence on commodities by putting up barriers against international trade within a strategy of 'import substitution'. The aim was for home industry to produce the range of goods required by the home market. However, the record of success has been mixed. Some larger economies, such as China or India, have been partially successful and have as a result been more able to ride out the economic storms of the 1980s. But many countries encountered problems and had abandoned import substitution by the late 1970s. The newly established domestic industries often relied on or even increased the need for imports such as machinery spares and raw materials. The strategy failed to transform the economy: the poor remained poor and the rich were still rich. Some sections of domestic industry produced luxuries for the elite. It was also often inefficient, and with high tariff walls, which led to high prices for consumers inside the country. Agriculture was often neglected. Many countries also found it hard to set up big industries because their own domestic markets were too small. China could do it, but Ghana could not.

BRANCHING OUT

Self-reliance, then, is not withdrawal from trade. Equally it is not self-reliance for poor countries to open up their economies to the volatility and inequalities of the world market. Self-reliance relies on a middle way, one that builds on the human and natural resources available nationally and regionally, and allows for a country to escape the treadmill of commodity dependence. Trade self-reliance means taking control of one's trading destiny. How can this be achieved?

The first step has to be diversification. The ecological as well as the development problems associated with commodity dependence requires this. But while diversification is clearly in the interests of poor countries, it may not be in the interests of some of their wealthier subjects.

Short-term incentives often encourage poor countries to concentrate on a single profitable commodity, for instance, rather than attempt a long-term transformation of trading patterns. Though trade unions in the Dominican Republic, for example, are demanding that land should be turned over to the poor to produce different crops, the land has been sold by the government to US transnationals to supply consumers in the United States.

Diversification programmes cannot simply rely on supplying markets in rich countries. While access to such markets can provide a basis for development, there is no guarantee that the current protectionist barriers to those markets will be lifted. While relying on export earnings generated in this way, in the long term countries must transform their economies internally and regionally to foster appropriate forms of trade – forms that sustain natural resources, are integrated with other sectors of the economy, that help to mobilize resources and investment within the country, and that meet the needs of local people, above all in providing food.

FARMING: FOUNDATION FOR INDUSTRY AND TRADE

One starting-point for alternative economic policies is a place where few conventional economists start – agriculture, and in particular, the kind of peasant-based agriculture described in Chapter 3. A strong, food-centred agricultural base has been a common element of success. Countries ranging from communist China to capitalist South Korea have had some success in meeting basic human needs and building up industry. Ensuring that everyone has enough to eat is in itself a high priority, but there are other important reasons for a primary emphasis on food and peasant agriculture. One is the trading advantage it offers. As Cambridge economist Joan Robinson put it:

> Production of food is the most effective form of import-saving investment. For a country with a deficit on its balance of payments to import food means that it is borrowing in order to eat. The debt remains to be paid after the food has been eaten. This is the rake's progress that has led many Third World countries into the present impasse.[37]

As explained above, many Third World countries – especially in Africa – have pursued a form of industrialization designed to save foreign exchange (import substitution), in the name of self-reliance. Not only has industry in many cases remained heavily reliant on imports, but industrialization has also been carried out at the expense of peasant agriculture and so left countries having to import food on a large scale. A much more practical priority would have been to adopt import substitution in agriculture (although privileged people in the cities would prefer to see a ready supply of consumer products). But the agricultural basis of economic transformation goes further. Land reform and raising peasant incomes will not only tend to direct wealth to the poor majority, it will also provide a mass market for industries producing basic products like clothes, lamps, soap, and foods which involve some processing like cooking oil, sugar and tea. It would also reduce the flow of people migrating from the land to the city, often to appalling human and environmental conditions.

The 'agriculture first' strategy does not, however, ignore industry. In place of predatory forms of industry – whether led by national-based companies or by foreign transnationals – other forms are needed that work with agriculture in a mutually reinforcing way. The emphasis should be on rural-based industrial processing of agricultural output (together with other primary products produced inside the country). In India, small-scale sugar processing has made considerable headway and now accounts for 30 per cent of total production.[38] Products such as refined sugar can be consumed on the domestic market or exported to regional markets, or further afield.

SMALL IS UNDERESTIMATED

'Cottage industries' also have a crucial role to play in the rural economy. Small industries can remain decentralized throughout the countryside since appropriate skills – and small-scale industries – often already exist in villages and small towns: blacksmiths, basket-makers, tailors. Small-scale production makes better use of the resources poor countries *do* have in abundance – labour – with (relative to large-scale industry) less use of the resource they *don't* have – money to invest. By the measures of efficiency of rich countries, these methods might seem 'inefficient'; but many small-scale industries in the Third World often produce far more for the same money than large-scale equivalents. Not only do small-scale industries create more jobs, they also tend to provide them for the poorer people. In Botswana, home brewing of sorghum beer produced about six times the number of jobs for the same output than large-scale production would have done. Furthermore, over half the earnings of home brewing went to the poor majority (the bottom 65 per cent of the population) and only 13 per cent to the richest 5 per cent. In contrast, only 29 per cent of earnings from factory brewing went to the poor majority, with nearly half the income going to the richest 5 per cent.[39] Small-scale industry also provides far more jobs for women – often supplying the only income for households headed by women. Local ownership and control of enterprises is also far more prevalent in the small-scale sector.

Many of the products of the small-scale sector are cheap, and bought by poor consumers. They can, however, sometimes provide inputs for the large-scale sector: in Latin America children collect waste paper and cardboard from city dumps and sell it in bundles to large paper mills for recycling. Small-scale industries also tend to adopt more environmentally-friendly techniques. They often use a higher proportion of locally-grown or collected organic raw or recycled materials. Looking at the goods on sale in an East African market, for example, one sees paraffin lamps skilfully fashioned from old tin cans and soldered on charcoal fires. A familiar sight throughout Africa are the durable sandals made from old tyres which would easily outlast their factory-made equivalents. The flexible inner tube is used to make the straps for the top, while the sole is cut from the hard-wearing outside of the tyre. The value of this kind of activity does not show up in official economic reports and statistics, but its contribution to national economic development is often considerable – above all for the poor. Nevertheless, there is still a role for larger-scale industry. Steel, for instance, can only be produced efficiently in large mills. Economies must walk on the two legs of industry and agriculture, and within industry the two legs of small- and large-scale production – particularly when the intention is to cooperate with neighbouring countries on a regional basis.

PULLING TOGETHER

The trend towards regional trade blocs in the rich countries of the North is adding a new urgency to forging economic and trade alliances in the poor countries of the South. Countries must unite economically to avoid being squeezed out of world trade between the giant blocs, and to provide a strong enough voice to be heard in the rapid changes re-shaping the world economy and trade. But regional cooperation is not a new idea in the Third World – if anything it was an idea current in Africa, for example, before it was considered in Europe. Most Third World countries are, or have been, in some kind of regional economic group. World leaders and international conferences regularly espouse the virtues of regional cooperation, but few of the groupings have real economic teeth, while others have simply collapsed.

There are many obstacles to regional cooperation. Some are internal. Nationalistic and political rivalries can lead to breakdown – as in the case of one of Africa's most successful attempts at regional cooperation, the East Africa Community which collapsed in the late 1970s. Fear of being dominated by one country can also cause problems. Smaller countries in the South Asian Association for Regional Co-operation (SAARC), for instance, fear domination by India. Dependence on outside ties (notably trading links with the rich countries) is one of the major problems Third World regional cooperation has to overcome. But regional groups such as the Economic Community of West African States (ECOWAS) are often grossly underfunded by hard-pressed member governments with mounting debts. One regional grouping that faces all these potential problems is the Southern African Development Co-ordination Conference (SADCC).

SOUTHERN AFRICA AND SADCC

The southern African economies (outside South Africa) display some of the highest levels of external dependence, debt and poverty economies anywhere in Africa. Most, except Zimbabwe which is more heavily industrialized, rely to a great extent on agricultural and mineral exports – Mozambique on fish, nuts and fruit; Malawi on tobacco and tea; Angola on oil; Zambia on copper. A grossly disproportionate amount of production is for markets in the rich countries and for an urban minority. In addition, countries of southern Africa also share dependence upon their powerful neigh-bour South Africa. Less than 5 per cent of southern Africa's trade is between countries in the region.[40] In contrast, about half the trade of European countries is with each other.[41]

SADCC was set up in 1980 with the two aims of lessening members' economic dependence (particularly on South Africa) and of forging links to build genuine regional integration and develop-ment. SADCC countries have learned from the mistakes of past attempts at regional economic cooperation in Africa and elsewhere in the Third World, and so have eschewed grand gestures and over-ambitious plans.

They have instead slowly but surely moved forward practical measures. SADCC has recognized the fears – particularly of the smaller countries – of being overruled by a large economy like Zimbabwe. The principle of national sovereignty is upheld and decisions at all levels are made by consensus, rather than by majority vote. Once projects are decided on, centralized bureau-cracy and costs are kept to a minimum. Each project is coordinated by a different country. Zimbabwe, for example, coordinates SADCC's work on food security, Tanzania the Industry and Trade Sector set up in 1986. The result is greater accountability and fewer squabbles about payments to a central bureaucracy – as have marred the economic community ECOWAS in West Africa.

The first priorities have been building up transport and communications – for instance, establishing a regional electricity grid and rehabilitating the rail link to the Mozambiquan port of Beira, which has been repeatedly cut by South African-backed guerrillas. This has reduced the need for long and expensive journeys for SADCC exports to South African ports like Durban and thus eased SADCC's dependence on South Africa. SADCC is now working towards regionally coordinated industry and trade. Plans currently being formulated will not discourage countries from having their own basic industries, like textiles, nor of some countries continuing to develop already established specialist industries – such as petrochemicals in oil-rich Angola, or steel in Zimbabwe. Nevertheless, certain strategic industries (farm equipment and food processing, for example) are being selected for a regionally coordinated plan. Such plans aim to promote the self-reliant, foreign-exchange-saving production of goods which will help to support the livelihoods of people throughout the region, particularly in agriculture. The aim is not to set up a single massive plant in one country for the whole region, but to establish a series of complementary plants throughout the region. However, while poor countries like those in SADCC can attempt to move towards greater regional self-reliance, their ability to do so successfully may still be greatly influenced by the actions of rich countries.

THE ROLE OF RICH COUNTRIES

Rich countries are less dependent today on trade with poor countries than at any time in the last century. Market surpluses of virtually every major commodity and low prices free rich countries from the threat of radical action by commodity-producing countries. Pressure for trade reform has also to come from within rich countries. In July 1986, for example, a public campaign in Britain organized by the World Development Movement and backed by trade unionists in Bangladesh succeeded in reversing an earlier government decision to impose quotas on imports of shirts from Bangladesh – one of the world's poorest countries, where over 300,000 workers, primarily women, are employed in the garment trade.[42] Bangladesh's textile industry had grown from nothing in 1978 and, in offering women the opportunity to work outside the home (often for the first time), had started something of a social revolution.

Regarding commodities, the prevailing philosophy among the governments of rich countries remains one of minimum interference in the international markets. However, there is still an urgent need for co-ordinated international action on commodities – not least because the commodity markets are not neutral, but based in the North and biased towards the interests of northern speculators, companies and governments. Such action should include the extension and enhancement of mechanisms that are already in place, such as the EC's STABEX and COMPEX systems which compensate poor countries for losses in export earnings, as well as the United Nations Common Fund, which came into force in 1989 and was designed to provide finance for commodity agreements.

In the North it is commercial as much as political pressure that is needed to remove the harsher inequalities of the world trading system, and to assist the move forward to a system of globally sustainable trade. Consumers in the North are presented with an increasing variety of imported products from poor countries – exotic fruit, cut flowers, vegetables – but producers in the poor countries do not have the same luxury of choice. People in the North need to wield their consumer power in order to pressure companies to purchase or produce goods grown or manufactured in an environmentally sustainable way, and to pursue fair employment and marketing practices in poor countries. This means that consumers must put to good effect the 99 per cent of the shopping purse that is spent on ordinary goods, as well as the 1 per cent that is donated to charities. 'Green consumerism' has already made its mark. Now there is a rich potential in a partnership between producers in poor countries and consumers in rich countries. The seeds of change lie in our hands.

5 Money Makes the World Go Round

I don't like Western solutions to the debt crisis – they kill
too many people.

Javier Iguiniz, Peruvian economist

If the Amazon is the lungs of the world then debt is its
pneumonia.

Lula, Brazilian trade unionist and Workers' Party leader

Three days of rioting in the Venezuelan capital Caracas in March
1989 left 250 people dead and many more injured. Streets were
littered with the wreckage of burnt-out cars and shattered glass
from looted shops. In the worst street violence for thirty years,
anger and despair at the crushing weight of economic austerity,
introduced to enable Venezuela to pay its $35-billion foreign debt,
finally spilled on to the streets.

A sudden hike in food prices and bus fares was the spark which
set Caracas alight. These were part of an austerity plan demanded
by Venezuela's creditors as the condition for an injection of new
money to save the debt-ravaged economy from collapse. Deals of
this kind are the 'normal' way of handling debt problems across
the Third World. This time, however, the people who had to bear
the weight of these decisions rebelled.

The roots of the violence lay in years of frustration. The poverty
trap had closed as wages slumped to the level of two decades
earlier, and prices of food and clothing spiralled. At the same time,
Venezuelans were seeing $3 billion a year pour out of the country
in debt payments to Western banks. Millions more were being
spirited away into private accounts in Miami and Switzerland by a
wealthy few.

PATTERN OF VIOLENCE

For Venezuelan leader Carlos Andres Perez, the 'appalling violence
. . . unleashed in the streets of Caracas' was 'shocking and dismay-
ing'.[1] It also dealt Western creditors a sharp reminder that the debt
crisis was far from over. The large number of deaths and the
ferocity of the violence shocked many, but this was not without
warning. Riots as a result of debt-driven austerity programmes
have become commonplace over the last decade. The Dominican
Republic, Jamaica, Sudan, Egypt, Zambia, Jordan, Argentina, Nigeria, Morocco, Tunisia and the Ivory Coast are just some of the
countries hit by the violence.

In itself, the devastating economic impact of years of debt and
austerity on *people* has done little to persuade rich countries to
change their hard-line approach. But worries about the *political*
impact may now be pushing the West towards a change of tack.
The United States in particular is worried that debt is exacerbating
political instability in their Latin American 'backyard'. The World
Bank has advised rich countries to revamp their debt strategy to
avoid the 'erosion of political support for national governments
[in the Third World] . . . and the radicalization of attitudes to
debt servicing'.[2] Even some bankers admit to political jitters.
Speaking a few months before the events in Caracas, Harry L.
Freeman, Executive Vice-President of American Express, told a
British audience:

> To the rational American observer, the Atlantic and Pacific Oceans have
> shielded us from many foreign conflicts and problems for hundreds of
> years. This protection does not exist in the Third World debt crisis. The
> problem is literally next door . . . With approaching elections and the rise
> of opposition parties which advocate debt forgiveness, the threat to de-
> mocratic, market-oriented governments is real.[3]

It is not just sporadic outbursts of violence which worry bankers
and politicians, but also more sustained political trends. In Brazil,
the leader of the Workers' Party, Luis Ignacio da Silva ('Lula'),
standing on a radical anti-debt platform, was only narrowly beaten
in the 1990 presidential election.

Fearing such developments, President Bush announced, soon after taking office at the beginning of 1989, that the United States would 'take a whole new look at the issues' of Third World debt.[4] Significantly, national security advisers were closely involved in the policy review. Events moved too fast and the Venezuelan crisis stampeded Mr Bush's Treasury spokesman, Nicholas Brady, into announcing a new debt initiative. But the prospect of this plan doing anything substantial for the real victims of the debt crisis – the poor, their livelihoods and environment – remains distant (a point to which we return at the end of the chapter).

Headline-catching food riots are the symptoms of an agonizing economic disease afflicting the Third World. Latin Americans have seen their standard of living (or more accurately, their chance of survival) fall by at least 10 per cent since the debt crisis began; Africans by over 20 per cent.[5] The UN Children's Fund (UNICEF) has calculated the human suffering ignored in financial reports: at least half a million children a year die as a result of the debt and recession burdening Third World economies.[6] Despite the horrific human toll, debt only appears on newspapers' financial pages, not front pages. Unlike famine or drought, this crisis cannot easily be captured by TV cameras. Nor, says UNICEF, is it happening because of 'any one visible cause, but because of an unfolding economic drama in which the industrialized countries play a leading role'.[7]

ONE STEP FORWARD, TWO STEPS BACK

In the 1960s and 1970s, there was tangible progress towards meeting basic human needs, even if it was patchy and painfully slow. But now, in many countries, that advance has been stopped in its tracks and even put into reverse. Painstaking progress is being destroyed by a hidden war of economic attrition. Across Africa and Latin America, and in parts of Asia, there are signs not only of endemic poverty, but of decline and decay: life-saving rural clinics now lack even the most basic medicines; silent and dilapidated schools are without teachers; factories lie idle – starved of the foreign currency to buy essential spare parts; thousands in shanty towns go hungry because they have been thrown out of work; forests and soil are plundered to meet interest payments.

It is now clear that an economically disastrous decade of debt for the Third World has made its people poorer, hungrier, sicker, less likely to learn to read and write. In many parts of Africa and Latin America – not just in the disaster areas – malnutrition is again on the increase. People are hungrier, not because there is not enough food to go round, but because debt and austerity have made them poorer and food more expensive. Rising malnutrition is, in turn, pushing up the numbers of children dying in many countries, after decades of improvement. In Brazil, for example, the child mortality rate rose a staggering 12 per cent between 1982 (when the debt crisis broke) and 1984.[8]

As debt payments increase, governments slash already meagre health and education budgets. In the thirty-seven poorest countries, health spending per head has been cut by half and education spending by a quarter in the last few years.[9] As a result, diseases once eradicated – like yaws and yellow fever – have now started to reappear in countries such as Ghana. Families can no longer afford to send their children to school, especially where schools have started to charge fees. Fewer children now start school and many more drop out.

Malawi in southern Africa, for example, spends well over a third of its government budget (38 per cent) in servicing its debt, despite rescheduling. The cost of its debt-servicing has grown by over 7 per cent a year since 1980, while the country has increased spending on education by barely more than half of one per cent.[10] Pupil–teacher ratios in primary schools are now about 63:1; a few years after independence they were 41:1. One headmaster cuts exercise books, of only sixteen sheets each, in half and rations them to pupils – three halves each for the school year. And this is in a relatively well-endowed town school.

The result is that the victims of debt are the poor. And within their ranks, women and children suffer most.[11] Women have to cope and devise survival strategies when the country's debt-stricken economy means that household incomes fall and prices rise. Already, women are overstretched by their dual role. They are producers of both goods and services – as farmers, market traders, industrial workers. On top of this they do most of the unpaid household work, like gathering fuel and water (often from far away), caring for children, nursing the sick and managing the household.

As debt and austerity programmes bite deeper, the economic pressure on women increases. In a desperate attempt to make ends meet, they are forced into working in unstable and badly paid jobs, including 'illicit' activities such as beer brewing, smuggling and prostitution. Yet at the same time they are expected to fill the gap as carers after health and social service cuts. As Maria de Pilar Trujillo Uribe, Director of the Colombian Centre for Labour Studies (CESTRA), told an audience which included senior Western bankers and financial officials:

> It is *our* nations that are suffering and dying through hunger, cold, deprivation, a lack of housing, a lack of education, of health care and of employment. It is on the shoulders of the Latin American woman that the worst effects of the crisis are falling, thanks to external debt. Just as they are borne by the frail shoulders of our children, millions of whom are living, or hardly surviving even, in the streets of our great cities.[12]

COUNTING THE COST

Before looking at how much poor countries owe, it is useful to specify their creditors. It is possible to distinguish between two types of debtor nation (see Figure 5.1). The better-off 'middle income' debtors, largely Latin American countries, but also including the Philippines, have the biggest debt. They owe most of it to Western commercial banks. The world's poorest countries were not considered sufficiently creditworthy for loans from banks and so borrowed from 'official creditors' – rich-country governments and international financial institutions, like the World Bank and International Monetary Fund, controlled by governments. Most of the poorest debtors are in sub-Saharan Africa, but also include Asian countries like Vietnam, Bangladesh and Sri Lanka. (Of course, there are exceptions to prove the geographical rule. The debt of a poor Latin American country like Bolivia has more in common with an average African debtor, while oil-rich Congo's debt is more like Brazil's than a poorer African country like Chad.)

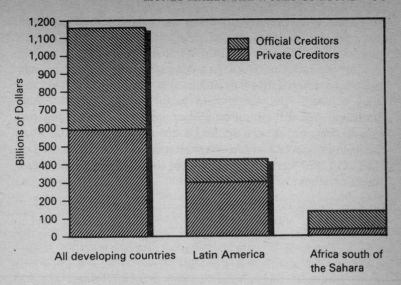

SOURCE: *World Bank Debt Tables 1989/90*

Figure 5.1   Debt totals by type of creditor (1988)[13]

In total, poor countries owe over $1,100 billion – a sum so large that it is almost meaningless. But, in common with other debts, the real problem is not so much the overall size of the debt, but the fact that debtors can't afford to repay. As Figure 5.1 shows, Africa's total debt is small change by the standards of international finance. Brazil alone owes almost as much as Africa put together. But in relation to its ability to repay, Africa – particularly the poorest African nations – has the worst debt problem of all. For the people, economy and environment of debtor countries the catastrophe is that the debt, although unpayable, somehow is being paid. The problem of Third World debt is not so much 'can't pay, won't pay', but 'can't pay, *will* pay'.

A debtor – whether an individual, company or country – gets into trouble when the difference between what they earn and the amount they have to repay on the debt (much of it just interest) becomes too great too quickly. This difference is known as the 'debt service ratio'. In the case of Third World countries, it is the amount of debt they repay each year in comparison with their earnings from trade, since only by exporting can they earn the hard currency, mainly US dollars, in which payments on foreign debt must be made. (Although countries do take out new loans in dollars to keep the other creditors at bay, a move that only drags them deeper into the debt spiral in the long term.)

The fact that the Third World's debt service ratio has more than doubled since the 1970s illustrates just how deep the Third World is in the red. On average, poor countries pay between a quarter and a third of all they earn from trade just to cover their debts.[14] But the figures are even more alarming when one realizes that even these payments are not enough to stop the debt burden growing. Often Third World countries, especially the poorest in Africa, owe a lot more, but just can't pay (see Table 5.1). They fall behind with payments and so reschedule, promising to pay their creditors at some time in the future (though with what isn't clear).

Third World countries thus find themselves on a debt treadmill. While more money flows abroad in debt service, few new loans come in (these dried up after the debt crisis broke in 1982). The combined effect is to bleed debtor economies dry. The debt crisis has changed the overall inflow of finance from rich countries to poor into a perverse and increasing flow *from* poor *to* rich. Third World debtors now transfer over $50 billion a year more to Western banks and governments than they receive in new loans and aid (see Figure 5.2). No other statistics could make a greater mockery of the rich world's idea of itself as a benefactor of the Third World.

PAYING DOWN SOUTH

The price of this transfer of wealth is economic devastation in the Third World. Money cannot be in two places at once. What is paid out in debt – particularly when not replaced by new loans or aid –

Table 5.1 Debt service ratios of selected African countries (scheduled and actual debt payments, as a proportion of export earnings)

Country	Debt service ratio (percentage)	
	Scheduled to pay (1988)	Actually paid (annual average, 1985–7)
Madagascar	95.7	31
Malawi	33.5	31
Senegal	26	17
Sudan	142.5	13.5
Tanzania	85	17
Zambia	59	7
Sub-Saharan Africa	n.a.	18

Source: *World Bank Debt Tables*, 1988–9 edition

cannot be used elsewhere. Debtors, forced to channel their resources into paying off debt, have suffered a decade-long economic slump which has crippled agriculture and industry, thrown thousands out of work, forced down wages and pushed up prices. Money has been sent abroad at the cost of domestic agriculture and industry. In Latin America, levels of investment have been slashed by nearly a third since the beginning of the 1980s.[15] Investment in the economies of the fifteen biggest debtors has dropped by about the same amount as the net wealth they have transferred abroad, according to the World Bank.[16] In the poorest countries of Africa the collapse has been even worse, with investment falling by half during the 1980s.[17]

The investment famine is not merely a symptom of a passing recession; it continues despite the expansion of investment elsewhere in the world since the mid-1980s. Furthermore, the investment squeeze is a vicious circle. Debt starves agriculture and industry of money; less wealth is created; countries have less to pay back debts and meet people's needs; investment is cut back still more – and so it goes on. Debt strangles the prospects of future generations.

The President of Mexico, a country which is regarded as one of the most obedient Latin American debtors, spelt out these dangers in his 1988 inaugural speech, warning that:

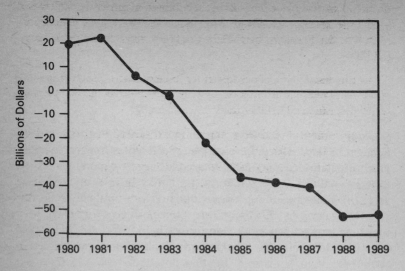

SOURCE: *World Bank Debt Tables 1989/90*

Figure 5.2   Financial flows from poor to rich countries (1980-89)[18]

... external debt impedes economic recovery. The country cannot grow, in a sustained way, if the present net transfer of resources abroad, equivalent to 5 per cent of the domestic product, continues. This situation cannot be accepted and cannot be sustained. I will avoid confrontation. But I categorically state that before the creditors' interests come the interests of the Mexican people. The priority will no longer be to pay debt but to restore growth.[19]

COSTING THE EARTH

Rising poverty and the desperate attempts of Third World countries to earn hard currency carry not only a heavy human and economic cost, but also an environmental one. Many indebted nations rely on their natural resources – whether timber or minerals like copper – to raise foreign exchange from trade. A Philippine grass-roots network, the Freedom from Debt Coalition, says that debt is being paid by:

... tearing down more of our forests for lumber exports, destroying more of our coral reefs for fish exports, and depleting more of our soil through heavy pesticides and fertilizers used for cash crops.[20]

Environmental resources are being exhausted just to pay debt. Senegal in West Africa, for example, effectively earmarks its entire annual catch of export fish (its second largest export) to pay its foreign creditors.[21] Elsewhere, some banks have even dispensed with the time-consuming conventions of international trade. Instead of waiting for debtors to turn their resources into cash, they just take payment in kind. One British bank, Midland, did a deal with Peru to receive fish and raw iron in place of debt payments in cash.

As more and more hard currency is needed to service rising levels of debt, the pressure is to exploit nature as much as possible, as quickly as possible. Little is spent on replanting forests felled for cash. An environmental and economic legacy of decimated natural resources will remain, even if the debt problem itself is resolved.

'Natural resources are being used not for development or to raise living standards, but to meet the financial requirements of industrialized country creditors,' points out the Brundtland Report.[22] The adoption of short-term measures is exacerbated by debt pressures. Taking account of long-term environmental – or even economic – costs becomes an even lower priority than before. Says Brundtland:

Conservation always takes a back seat in times of economic stress. As economic conditions have worsened in developing countries and debt pressures have mounted, planners have tended to ignore environmental planning and conservation in both industrial and rural development projects.[23]

The staff and funding of fledgling pollution control agencies have been the first to be axed in debt-induced budget cuts in countries such as Argentina and Brazil.

Debt hastens environmental destruction in another, less direct, but equally important way. By further impoverishing the poor, debt encourages environmental destruction. As we saw in Chapter 2, the desperation of the poorest is forcing them to over-use fragile environments – like the rainforest and desert fringes – for short-term survival. The burden of debt has been shifted on to the backs of the poor, who in turn have no option but to ease it by exploiting their immediate environment.

On top of this, the original loans were often for projects which were economically and ecologically unsustainable. Mega-projects – which put earning cash first and people and environment last – were the ones that attracted big foreign loans. Ignoring the environment has left countries with massive debts. Mazide Ndiaye, of the Senegalese voluntary organization RADI, tells his country's not untypical story:

Senegal was second only to Nigeria as a world exporter of groundnuts. People persuaded us to build factories to produce oil. We built many factories with the debt. Now we are able to process one million tonnes, but we have destroyed our environment and our production is only four hundred thousand tonnes. So our factories cannot work at full capacity, and we cannot pay the debt because the debt was supposed to make production of one million tonnes a possibility ... We cannot pay, that is the situation.[24]

It is, of course, true that poverty and ecological destruction existed in the Third World before the debt crisis. Even if the debt burden were reduced, these problems would not disappear. Their roots lie in a number of national and international policies introduced before the crisis erupted. Some of these – like the unfair terms of trade and inappropriate agricultural and industrial priorities – are explored in other chapters. Debt is, in this sense, as much a symptom as a cause of ecologically damaging development. Reducing the debt burden does not guarantee an end to poverty, environmental problems or the policies which underlie them. But while major debt relief is not in itself a means to sustainable development, it is a necessary part of any solution.

DEBT WHODUNNIT

Poor people, the environment and sustainable economic progress are all, then, victims of debt. The poor gained little from the lending spree which came before the debt crisis, but they now have to pay the greatest price. They are innocent victims, but where are the villains? Tracking them down, by understanding how the crisis came about, is of more than historical interest as different solutions are offered on the basis of different accounts of events.

The former British Chancellor of the Exchequer, Nigel Lawson, typifies the views of Western governments. His explanation of how the debt arose is that it was just like any other case of foolish borrowing and rash lending – only on a bigger scale:

> The debt problem did not arise from any single global development: it arose because individual countries sought to borrow from individual creditors – primarily from the commercial banks, but also to some extent from governments and the international financial institutions – and the creditors, by and large, lent the money willingly.[25]

It is not surprising, then, that he dismisses talk of 'grand designs and global solutions' as 'not only mistaken, but counterproductive'.

The rich countries reject Third World calls to negotiate a way out of the debt crisis on the same grounds. The official line in Western capitals is that debts were run up in private deals between banks and sovereign governments; Western governments have no business supplying a solution. And in case we should think they are singling out the Third World for this treatment, they would assure us, in Mr Lawson's words, that 'there can be no question of taxpayers bailing [the banks] out'.

Having no truck with 'global solutions', the rich countries have adopted the so-called 'case-by-case' approach as their guiding principle. Each debtor must agree rescheduling deals with their creditors as and when payment problems occur. In addition, they argue, since countries chose to borrow as a way of avoiding their economic problems, they must now accept the consequences. Debtors have to swallow the bitter medicine of austerity administered by the IMF to 'get their economies into shape' by adopting 'sensible' (i.e. Western free market) policies.

But the attitude of the Western governments is not as prudent and even-handed as it seems. This is partly because – as we shall see later – Western governments *have* heavily intervened since the crisis began. Their taxpayers *are* bailing out the commercial banks on a massive scale. But fundamentally, the taken-as-given bedrock of most Western debt solutions is a version of events rewritten to suit the political and financial priorities of the rich countries, hidden beneath layers of mystifying jargon. The solutions look only at 'individual creditors' and 'individual debtors'. They turn the spotlight away from Western finance and trade policies which were central to the whole disastrous chain of events.

WHERE DID IT ALL BEGIN?

There are two questions to answer in untangling the roots of the crisis. How did Third World countries accumulate a trillion-dollar debt? And how did this debt lead to a crisis?

The conception of the crisis is often traced to the oil price rises of the early 1970s. They supplied rich countries with both the wherewithal and a reason for the massive lending spree. Arab oil wealth was deposited in Western bank vaults. These 'petrodollars' provided much of the cash lent to Third World borrowers. Western leaders feared the impact of rising oil prices. If the oil producers could not spend all the money, someone else should, they argued. 'Recycling' oil money to the Third World meant that it could keep buying Western exports, despite bigger oil bills. Rich-country governments hoped this would keep factories in Europe and America open and stave off a further descent into recession. But equally important in bringing on the debt disaster was the *way* in which money was lent. For this we have briefly to go further back.

BANKING ON THE WORLD

Since 1945, Western governments and international government institutions like the World Bank had been the principal lenders to the Third World. During the 1970s private commercial banks began to eclipse these official lenders. Armed with oil money, the banks moved in on the market in a big way. At the height of the lending in 1982, banks were lending $63 billion a year to the Third World, nearly twice the amount lent by official government sources.[26]

The banks were propelled into this new prominence by the changes which swept the global financial system in the 1970s. With the rise of the West German and Japanese economies, the United States' top position was threatened. The dollar-centred, post-war global financial consensus (the Bretton Woods system) was faltering. In the early 1970s managed international exchange rates based around the dollar were dropped in favour of floating exchange rates. Suddenly a lot of money could be made by buying and selling currencies as they fluctuated in value. A new expansion of international banking took off outside the financially restrictive United States. The 'Eurocurrency' markets were born and grew rapidly from a market worth $300 billion in 1973 to over $2,000 billion in 1983.[27]

Arab fears that a hostile US government might freeze their assets if they put them in US banks ensured that the oil wealth found its way into the headstrong Euro-market. The search for new ways of making money out of the oil windfall took banks to the distant shores of rising Third World hopefuls, mainly in more industrialized Latin America, but also in oil-rich countries in Africa, like Nigeria and the Ivory Coast.

Big banks bought money on the burgeoning Eurocurrency market and resold it as loans to the Third World. In the increasingly footloose and competitive environment of international finance, bankers began to see overseas lending as a key to the future. Soon, even the smallest banks got in on the act through syndicated loans organized by a large lead bank, sometimes involving hundreds of other banks. As the Third World lending gathered pace, more and more banks began to lend more and more money to more and more countries.

Loan scouts toured the world in their search for 'under-borrowed' countries, trying to make deals to use up the 'loan quotas' their banks told them to fill. One bank economist recalls:

The international side looked glamorous ... Bankers like travel and exotic locations. It was certainly more exciting than Cleveland or Pittsburgh, and an easier way to make money than nursing along a $100,000 loan to some scrap-metal smelter.[28]

The old rules of prudent banking were cast aside in the rush to lend. Banks over-extended themselves to a greater extent than ever before. By 1982 the nine biggest US banks had lent nearly three times their total capital to the Third World.[29] Bankers were convinced that because loans were to governments (or were guaranteed by them), they were secure. 'Countries do not fail to exist,' reassured the chairman of the biggest US bank, Citicorp, in 1983.[30] Banks believed Third World countries, unlike companies, could not go bankrupt.

The business was also very profitable for banks. Third World countries were still marked as relatively high-risk and therefore loans carried a higher rate of interest. For banks putting deals together, there was a commission averaging about 1 per cent of the loan; big money when the loans were so large. On a hundred-million-dollar loan a bank could pick up a million-dollar fee.

Thanks to the protection of their governments, many Western banks continue to do very well out of their outstanding Third World loans. Since the debt crisis broke in 1982, Britain's four main banks (Lloyd's, Midland, National Westminster and Barclays) have amassed a total profit of £15 billion, sustained by an estimated net transfer (payments minus new lending) of some £8.5 billion from the major debtors between 1983 and 1987 alone.[31] Clearly the 'crisis' has not been all bad for the banks.

OFFICIAL NOD OF APPROVAL

Western governments were more than happy to let banks do the job of recycling for them. It fitted in with the growth of governments' free-market thinking. Planned lending through international bodies like the IMF was rejected as out of step with the new way of doing things. But now that lending has gone sour, banks want government to shelter them from losses. Clearly the banks were motivated by profit, not patriotic duty. Nevertheless, they were encouraged by Western governments. More importantly, governments were responsible through their failure to control the lending or to seek another, more secure way out of recession.

SPENDING A TRILLION

Western banks had their reasons to lend, as their governments had to encourage them. But why did their clients borrow and what was the money used for? Stories of extravagant Third World leaders and corrupt politicians spending their way through borrowed millions make good newspaper headlines, but they do little more than comfort rich countries trying to blame someone else for the problem. In reality a substantial proportion of what was borrowed cannot be written off to simple corruption and waste. Furthermore, in what was undoubtedly a profligate and decadent lending tango, dictators and the wealthy were partnered by the very banks and governments that are now so quick to moralize.

Many Third World governments did see easy borrowing as a way of bolstering their own positions. They imported consumer luxuries with it to pamper the rich elite that kept them in power. Loans were used to buy foreign arms, particularly in Latin America, which was largely under military rule at the time. Money was blown on prestige events pandering to the vanity of politicians. Liberia, for example, borrowed heavily just to host a meeting of the Organisation of African Unity. Money was sent abroad by corrupt politicians like Zaire's President Mobutu or the Marcos family in the Philippines.

Millions more, in countries like Venezuela, were spirited out of the country as 'capital flight' into safe-haven Western banks through the dealings of rich individuals. (Revealingly, most banks, though quick to criticize the evils of capital flight, refuse to cooperate in identifying and returning money to the debtor nations from which it was illegally taken.) Money was borrowed for ill-conceived and environmentally damaging projects which failed to be economically viable – or even earn enough to cover the original loan.

Other loans, however, were used to fund profitable economic expansion according to the orthodox rule-book: roads, factories, mines, irrigation schemes. Third World governments were well versed in the accepted theory that capital and technology were the missing links needed to propel them into 'advanced' Western-style development. Back in the 1970s, borrowing was so cheap that it seemed almost financially imprudent not to do so. Interest rates were low and in real terms (because of world inflation) even negative. To oil exporters, like Nigeria or Mexico, borrowing seemed a way of drawing an advance on the oil riches still lying below their soil. Nobody thought oil prices would actually fall (as they later did). Countries without oil borrowed to offset the costs of their increased fuel bills, to keep factories and economies going. Raw-material exporting countries like copper-reliant Zambia borrowed to offset low commodity prices. They believed prices would pick up again when rich countries pulled out of industrial recession. Instead, prices continued to fall.

Assuming low interest rates, countries calculated that their economies would grow enough to enable them to pay back their debts, and leave sufficient money for them to reinvest (the same reckoning Western governments made in supporting debt recycling – since it meant Third World countries would carry on buying their exports). And indeed, during the 1970s, investment and economic growth rates did rise. The economies of the group of countries now officially listed by the World Bank as 'highly indebted' were growing at more than 6 per cent a year in the big borrowing period in the decade and a half before 1980. But in the 1980s they struggled to grow by more than 1 per cent a year on average; some economies even shrank.[32]

INTEREST, OIL AND EARNINGS: THE DEBT DISASTER

The impression we get from listening to bankers and Western governments is that if only we had had more profitable investment and less corruption and bad economic policies, things would have been all right. This is only part of the picture. Poor countries were hit by a series of external shocks of such ferocity that even if all the money borrowed had been invested with utter honesty and financial acumen, a debt crisis would still have resulted.

The first of these shocks was a meteoric rise in the cost of borrowing, says Tim Congdon, one-time Chief Economist with Shearson Lehman Hutton: 'The debt problems of the 1980s have been caused by very high real interest rates.'[33] As the international cost of borrowing turned from rock-bottom to sky-high, countries' payments on debt went through the roof. Raising interest rates was the policy adopted by the US administration under President Reagan in 1981. Rates went still higher as US tax cuts conspired with massive government spending – notably on a major rearmament programme – to send the US heavily into deficit. High interest rates were a way of sucking in money from the rest of the world to fuel the deficit. Interest rates in other Western countries rose to keep up. With every 1 per cent rise in the interest rate an estimated $2 billion was added to poor countries' annual interest bill.[34]

Another oil-price hike in 1979 was a second blow to debtors, the majority of whom had no oil of their own. The hike came just as they were learning to live with oil prices set after the original 'oil crisis' in 1973.

Third, not only was the Third World paying out more for oil, but the value of their non-oil exports was falling. Countries reliant on exporting commodities like copper or tea were being paid less and less for them by rich countries. 'The heart of the debt crisis,' says Zambian President Kenneth Kaunda, 'is the prices paid to us for what we produce.'[35] The poorest debtors – many of them in Africa – were the most dependent on commodity exports and were hardest hit by the decline. More industrialized Latin America found its manufactured exports to rich countries faced rising trade barriers, as Western countries pinned the blame for industrial decline on 'cheap imports from the Third World'.

The torrent of external financial pressures on debtors built up. In 1982, Mexico gave way and declared that it couldn't pay its debts. 'It was like an atom bomb being dropped on the world financial system,' said one banker.[36] Bankers panicked and tried to recover their loans. The massive lending spree came to a halt, depriving debtors of their financial lifeline. Western governments and banks launched a rescue package. They came up with enough cash and rescheduling to keep Mexico afloat, and so stop the much-feared slide towards mass default. With the IMF setting out an austerity programme, which was the condition of the new package for Mexico, the blueprint for the Western debt 'solution' had been established. Despite the responsibility of creditors as well as debtors for building the debt bomb, it is a solution which ensures that the fallout hits only the debtors.

AN OFFER YOU CAN'T REFUSE

The IMF was originally set up in 1945 to stop the financial sneezes of one country giving the whole world trade system a cold, as had happened in the worldwide slump in the 1930s. Its brief was to help with temporary balance-of-payments problems between the big economies; it was not set up to deal with the problems of Third World economies. But as rich countries had a majority vote, they used it to manage the debt crisis.

The IMF became the creditors' police force – keeping debtors on the straight and narrow. It obliged debtors to adopt policies for full and quick repayment, while managing the concessions needed to avert outright default. By using the IMF, rich-country governments could also keep out of the limelight and avoid being seen to be 'bailing out the banks'.

In reality, governments stepped in with money and political muscle to save the banks – and have continued to do so since. As one official of a West European central bank remarked around that time: 'We cannot say what they already know, that the big banks will not be allowed to go under.'[37] Bankers are also clear on the debt-collecting purpose of IMF programmes, which takes priority over other economic problems. Sir Jeremy Morse, Chairman of Lloyd's, the British bank with the biggest Third World loans, says the purpose of the IMF should be to ensure economic policy in the Third World is addressed to 'containing inflation and earning a sufficiently large trade surplus to enable them to service their debt'.[38]

IMF deals do not involve legally binding treaties. Yet the power of the IMF, and now the World Bank, to enforce programmes is as strong as if they did. To get IMF help, debtors must promise to change their policies in a so-called 'letter of intent', approved by the IMF Executive Board. The country receives some money on approval, getting the rest in quarterly instalments if the country's IMF team says it is sticking to the set targets. The Fund's position is made even more powerful because a country usually needs an IMF seal of approval to be eligible for funds from the World Bank, commercial banks and governments.

The IMF says policies are carried out by national governments who come to them for advice. But for most debtors the IMF offer is Hobson's choice – like it or lump it. Countries which have opted not to follow an IMF path have become financial pariahs. For instance, food price rises – resulting in riots – and massive currency devaluations ordered by the IMF led Zambia to break off its IMF programme in 1987. Not only did the IMF halt its own payments, but Britain alone cancelled £30 million of aid already pledged to the country.[39] In June 1990, riots again hit Zambia after an attempt to reintroduce an IMF programme.

THE IMF MEDICINE

'Adjustment' is the name usually given to the policy packages which countries have to undertake. Adjustment is 'inescapable', according to IMF chief Michel Camdessus.[40] 'Economic adjustment is a process of adapting an economy to live within its means,' says a member of staff of the IMF, Peter Heller.[41] But beneath the Fund's apparent realism lie two sacred assumptions.

First, it is taken for granted that paying debt comes before everything else. Once you accept that your means are determined by what is left *only* after debt is paid, then some kind of belt-tightening is unavoidable. Second, the IMF assumes that financial difficulties are largely the result of debtors' own bad policies. ('Adjustment' by rich countries – for example, to lower interest rates or trade barriers – is *not* part of the deal the IMF strikes with debtors.)

However, as we have already seen, the policies of Third World countries were only one cause of the debt crisis. It is therefore not only unfair to expect them to accept all the costs of adjustment, but it is also unlikely to be effective. Successful treatment relies on correct diagnosis of the illness. The classic IMF treatment consists of short, sharp shock-tactics of financial belt-tightening to skim off foreign exchange for debt payment. The strategy relies on cutting imports (to save foreign currency), increasing exports (to earn more of it), and cutting government spending.

First, countries are told they consume too much (and so import too much). Cutting overall 'demand' in the economy is the remedy, they are told. Crash austerity programmes (involving credit squeezes and wage freezes to cut local spending power) did curb imports, helping Latin America go into a trade surplus with the rest of the world. In that sense they 'worked'. The major debtors slashed their imports by 14 per cent in 1982, followed by a further dramatic cut of 20 per cent in 1983.[42] Their trade balance moved from a deficit of $6.5 billion in 1981 to a surplus of nearly $28 billion in 1987.[43] But the price of the short-term benefit of generating more foreign currency to meet spiralling debt payments was recession and terrible human hardship.

The second strand of the IMF approach is in boosting exports. The central tool here is devaluation of the country's currency (often in sudden drastic moves) to make a country's exports cost less abroad. Local industry and agriculture are encouraged to switch from selling locally to producing for export. Often such a switch is difficult for smaller producers who have little experience of selling abroad. In addition, the advice seems to take little account of a world trading environment of slack demand for the Third World's goods and the growing trade barriers put up by rich countries.

The other side of devaluation is, of course, that it makes imports more expensive. One might imagine this to be a blow struck for self-reliance: cutting out wasteful imported luxuries. Unfortunately, these are not the main type of imports hit. Introduced so suddenly, on top of the fact that foreign currency is being eaten up by debt payments, devaluation leads to chronic shortages of vital imports like medicines and spare parts to keep factories open. In countries who need to import food, it leads to shortages and higher food prices. In Africa, fragile industrial output has plummeted as the cost of spares, fuels, raw materials and goods for processing and assembly has shot up. On top of this, more expensive imports push up prices and fuel inflation – further eroding the living standards of the poor.

The third plank in the IMF solution is to force governments to cut their own deficits. Government spending and investment is pared down to the bone – putting a further brake on the economy. Third World governments are told to reduce deficits, even though debt itself eats away at their budgets. In some cases governments are even obliged to nationalize the debts of private companies in arrears to Western creditors – a notable exception to their general enthusiasm for 'market solutions'. The social impact is devastating, with spending on health and education, wages of government workers and food subsidies all prominent on the list of cuts.

BAKER BREAKS IN

The first chapter in the debt saga was about crisis management. The central concern was to prevent an international banking collapse. After a few years the IMF began to admit that pure austerity, while squeezing funds for debt service in the short term, was so destroying debtor economies that there would be nothing left with which to pay debt in the longer term. In 1985, US Treasury Secretary James Baker announced a new debt initiative which was supposed to herald a new beginning in solving the debt crisis. In reality the Baker Plan marked only a minor modification of the original theme.

Under the plan, international financial institutions and, significantly, the commercial banks promised to lend more money to the seventeen big debtors (mostly Latin American) to enable them to follow a so-called 'adjustment with growth' strategy. It was supposed to allow debtors to boost their economies and so earn enough to pay off their debts. Rich countries supported the plan because they preferred more lending to anything that even smacked of writing off old debt. Banks grudgingly assented because they knew that countries needed new money if they were to keep paying back their old debts. But the 'solution' amounted to tackling debt with more debt.

THE WORLD BANK AND MARKET MAGIC

Under 'adjustment with growth', debtors have done plenty of very painful adjusting, but only their debts, not their economies, have grown. Old-style IMF programmes, measured in months, have been supplemented by ones of a couple of years. The IMF and its sister organization the World Bank (traditionally an aid institution rather than policy manager) have moved closer together. Increasingly the World Bank has used its money in the IMF manner, to cajole countries into ever more wide-ranging policy changes through its Structural Adjustment Programmes (SAPs). Few areas of policy have been left for the countries themselves to decide.

Structural adjustment entails countries adopting the whole gambit of free-market and aggressively outward-orientated policies which are presented as the path to economic salvation. They must throw open their borders to trade and expose their fragile industries to competition from foreign goods – despite the barriers blocking the export of their own goods to rich countries. Widespread privatization is often instituted. Between 1985 and 1987, some eighty public enterprises were privatized under adjustment programmes in nineteen African countries, while a further seventy-eight were liquidated completely.[44]

Some Third World state enterprises have undoubtedly been inefficient and have been manipulated by small interest groups to prey on the poor. A greater role for free markets in such situations can help to improve the livelihoods of the poor, as well as overall national productivity and efficiency. In Chapter 3 we saw such a case, with a number of agricultural marketing boards. But the scale of the assault mounted through adjustment programmes on state enterprises has been based more on the sweeping ideological assumption that 'state is bad: private is good' than on economic or political reality. The assumption of World Bank and IMF mandarins is that *more* private sector control of the economy always means economic control is in the 'hands of the people', and that it is the golden key to the door of efficient and fair development, is a grand – and dangerous – delusion. (As is the notion that *more* state control is generally an expression of the popular will, ensuring rational economic planning and just sharing of wealth.)

One reason for this is that policies are drawn up from abstracted models of the experience of markets in rich industrial economies. The dogmatic adherence to privatization, for example, ignores many of the economic and political realities of the way markets do – or more often don't – work in Third World countries. The inappropriateness of some of the panaceas is beginning to be admitted by some of their former supporters – particularly as campaigners have highlighted the social, economic and environmental costs of adjustment.

Chris Patten, addressing the World Development Movement's AGM in June 1989, shortly before being moved from his position as Britain's Minister for Overseas Development, confided that, looking back, he had been 'too gung-ho' in setting out the argument for structural adjustment. 'I should have said more about the problems in implementing adjustment programmes and the problems in designing good adjustment programmes,' he said. On privatization, he said that 'it doesn't seem very valuable if all that privatization means is the transfer of assets from being run by a minister through his ministry to being run by a minister's family'.

PAIN – BUT WHAT GAIN?

After all this radical restructuring and self-sacrifice, have things got better for the countries swallowing the 'new improved' IMF/World Bank medicine? Following a major internal survey of the economic success of adjustment, the World Bank itself could only claim that 'by and large' countries who did accept their programmes did 'moderately better than countries that did not'.[45] Many independent analysts argue that even this self-assessment is highly optimistic.

Another World Bank progress report[46] on adjustment in Africa was even more complacent than the first, purporting to prove that reforms were producing recovery, but was criticized by experts for its spurious statistics and dubious argument. It also provoked heated debate within the Bank, where a substantial body of opinion questioned the 'evidence' used. Another department of the Bank produced a more rigorous and measured report[47] which failed to come up with the same conclusions. Indeed, if there was any improvement in adjusting countries (an assumption which is still wide open to debate), it probably had more to do with the fact that accepting a programme was the passport to getting more foreign aid, rather than because the policies themselves had achieved anything.

ADJUSTMENT WITH A HUMAN FACE

Growing outrage at the human and environmental effects of adjustment programmes has been voiced by popular organizations in the Third World, together with international organizations and non-governmental groups in rich countries. In a landmark report, UNICEF not only documented the way that adjustment programmes have hit the poorest and most vulnerable people hardest, but went on to chart an alternative 'adjustment with a human face'.[48] While the report underlines that rich countries must cut the overall debt burden, it also sets out policies to protect the poor that are practicable at the national level for countries with severe financial constraints. Nor is 'adjustment with a human face' simply putting forward a costly welfare programme for the poor, as some critics contend, as three of its key points make clear:

1. *Protecting education and health*

During adjustment, the poor suffer because health and education spending are often the first to be cut. But spending can be restructured for the benefit of the poor without necessarily costing the government more. Resources can be redirected to priority areas – for example, from military to health budgets. Even within the same sector, money can be re-allocated to make better use of it. In Pakistan, the cost of immunizing most of the country's children (and so saving

100,000 lives) was met by the government's decision to postpone building an expensive urban hospital.[49]

2. Safeguarding nutrition and food security

Cutting food subsidies – to reduce government 'interference' in the free market – has to be reassessed in countries where the urban poor are dependent on such supplies. Other lower-priority subsidies can be cut instead – such as those on national airlines or types of food rarely consumed by the poor. The IMF and World Bank are keen to say that adjustment helps the rural poor, particularly through higher farm-gate prices for small farmers, but often the effects are mixed.[50]

3. Supporting jobs and wages

The emphasis must be shifted away from short-term austerity cuts in jobs and wages towards measures that generate economic growth by building up the incomes of the poor through productive employment. In the short term, public works schemes can boost local economies. In Sierra Leone, for example, a school-building programme increased school enrolment by 30 per cent; the construction of wells has freed women's time, noticeably reduced water-borne diseases, and is expected to increase palm-oil production. Support for small-scale industry – through access to credit, for instance – can often be more economically efficient than the present support for the large-scale.[51]

Mounting pressure on the governments of rich countries and on the IMF and World Bank has led to some concessions. In Britain, members of the World Development Movement mounted a historic lobbying campaign which resulted in 400 MPs signing a cross-party letter to the President of the World Bank demanding that World Bank policies should be assessed for their impact on the poor. Instead, they said, policies should be targeted to meet the needs of the poor – as measured by 'human indicators', such as rates of child mortality. The letter, which was subsequently signed by members of all major parties in Germany and the United States, won World Bank agreement that adjustment programmes should follow new guidelines. From denying the social impact of adjustment, the Bank now concedes that 'support for programs designed to ameliorate the social costs of adjustment should be intensified'.[52]

One well-publicized example of this is the Programme to Mitigate the Social Costs of Adjustment (PAMSCAD), introduced in 1987 under Ghana's structural adjustment programme. A group of international agencies, including the World Bank (although initially under duress, according to some reports),[53] supported an $85 million scheme to strengthen employment programmes, nutrition, primary education and community initiatives over two years.[54] Similar elements have been included in adjustment programmes in countries like Morocco, and a 'Social Dimensions of Adjustment' project has been initiated by the World Bank, the UN Development Programme and others. Under the scheme two dozen African countries are receiving the advice of experts on ways to 'improve the design of adjustment operations and to monitor the social effects of adjustment'. Although such moves are concrete signs that the Bank has been forced to rethink, they have to be kept in perspective. PAMSCAD, for example, only amounts to 6 to 8 per cent of the estimated total cost of Ghana's adjustment programme.[55]

It is not only the small size of such programmes that leaves them wanting. The Bank seems to believe that social programmes can be bolted on to old-style adjustment to 'compensate' the poor for the 'short-term' harm it causes. But this does not lead them to question the basic policy formula of orthodox adjustment, which makes such 'compensation' necessary in the first place. A thin sugar coating may have been added to the pill, but the pill itself is still made from the same bitter ingredients.

The Bank defends these fundamentals of adjustment on the grounds that the 'failure to adjust is likely to hurt the poor'.[56] The implication is that its critics shirk tough financial decisions in favour of a 'do nothing' position which, in practice, would lead to economic chaos. But criticizing the IMF/World Bank formulation of adjustment is not the same as saying the economic policies of poor countries have been perfect, or that there should be no change. The question is not, in this sense, whether there should be adjustment, but what form it should take, over what time-scale and, crucially, with what priority of aims.

The response of the IMF has been even weaker. Although IMF chief Michel Camdessus admits that adjustment programmes hit the poorest, the IMF opts out of changing its policies with the generalized assurance that in the 'long term' the poor will be better-off. It has the attitude that it only deals with the large-scale financial issues and that 'social' issues are not its department; they are up to the World Bank to deal with. Of course this is a fiction, since it is precisely those measures introduced in the name of large-scale financial goals which have such devastating effects. Furthermore, neither the IMF nor the World Bank – despite the latter's much-heralded 'greening' – has given serious thought to the environmental implications of adjustment programmes. The World Bank and the IMF, and the rich-country governments that control them, remain entrenched in a 'there is no alternative' view of orthodox adjustment which leads them to resist suggestions for a different approach.

AFRICAN ALTERNATIVES

One such suggestion was put forward in 1989 in a major African initiative set out in a report by the UN Economic Commission for Africa (ECA).[57] Statistically analysing the poor record of IMF programmes in Africa in even producing growth (let alone relieving poverty), it sets out to make adjustment address the deep-rooted problems of Africa's cycle of 'excruciating poverty and abysmally low levels of production', which in turn underlie much of the continent's environmental crisis. It is these deep-rooted problems which the IMF and the World Bank – with their emphasis on controlling short-term financial balances – have failed to tackle. The ECA report proposes a thorough rethink, it argues for 'adjustment with transformation' which is human-focused, and contains practical measures to strengthen the domestic economy.

But the report does not dodge the difficult issues. It says that proposing a different approach to adjustment does not mean that 'balance of payments disequilibrium, fiscal imbalance, inflationary pressures and acute shortages of goods are to be wished away or passed off unaddressed. On the contrary, Africa has to adjust.'[58] It criticizes the lack of effective democracy in many African countries, and the fact that in government spending 'social priorities have increasingly taken second place to defence spending'. The report accepts some IMF adjustment proposals, such as an increase in farm prices and greater financial efficiency in public enterprises – including 'selective privatization' where the state has 'over-extended itself'. But despite the ECA's self-critical pragmatism, rich-country governments have made little attempt to meet it half-way or engage in constructive dialogue with African governments over its detailed analysis or proposals. Britain's overseas aid minister criticized the ECA report in Parliament as soon as it came out, saying that it meant a return to 'dirigiste policies from which increasing numbers of African countries have been moving away'.[59]

BANKS BOTTLE OUT

During the phase of 'adjustment with growth' and the Baker Plan, the Third World accepted more stringent adjustment. But the commercial banks (and, to some extent, government aid donors in Africa) reneged on their side of the bargain by refusing to lend debtors more. In fact, banks have lent less, while debt payments continue to roll in. With this wealth transfer from the debtors, banks have set about securing their own financial position.

The commercial banks have put aside money in reserves (known as 'provisions') against the possibility of default on outstanding Third World loans. In 1989 the US banks increased their provisions further. J. P. Morgan, for example, used two billion dollars' worth of its profits to finally cover 100 per cent of its Third World loans.[60] In 1990 British banks followed, as Barclays, Lloyd's and National Westminster all made large provisions (see Table 5.2), putting them in a position where they *could* afford to write off 70 per cent of their Third World loans.

Despite extravagant press claims that large provisions mark the

Table 5.2   Provisions against Third World debt by British banks (1989)

	(£ million)
Barclays	983
Lloyd's	1763
Midland	846
National Westminster	990
Standard Chartered	427

SOURCE: *Financial Times*, 21 March 1990

'beginning of the end of the Third World debt crisis'[61] or that debt is 'fast becoming just a bad memory',[62] banks have not actually written off anything. Provisions are primarily an internal accounting method. The debtor nations are no better off, as banks still expect them to pay the full face value of the debt. Provisioning is not prompted for any 'moral or political reason', as Anatole Kaletsky noted in the *Financial Times* when J. P. Morgan made its dramatic move, but on account of 'cold business judgement'.[63] Because they represent a cushion against potential losses, provisions improve the look of a bank's books, reassure its investors and so boost its share value.

Furthermore, in Europe and Canada banks get generous tax relief on their provisions. European banks have received an estimated seven billion dollars' worth; Britain's 'big four' banks alone had received £1.65 billion by the end of 1989, larger than Britain's annual aid programme.[64] Stephany Griffith-Jones, a leading expert on debt at Sussex University, says that tax relief can actually discourage banks from going further and writing off debt. In a 1990 submission to the British government on behalf of the 'In Whose Interest?' campaign of Friends of the Earth, Third World First and the World Development Movement, she suggests that governments should give an incentive to banks by saying that tax relief would effectively be clawed back after a certain period – say, three years – if the banks had not written off the debt they had made provisions on.[65] The scheme would not cost taxpayers any more than under present arrangements, and public money would be going to facilitate genuine debt relief rather than just to help the banks.

Tax relief is not the only help banks have had in wriggling out of the bind of Third World debt. They have relied on the covering fire of continued IMF and World Bank lending to save debtors from total collapse and default under the strain of transferring so much wealth to banks. Contrary to their public statements, governments are indeed 'bailing out the banks' – and in a way that does nothing to help the debtors.

WINNERS AND LOSERS IN THE DEBT GAME

Has the debt strategy worked? From the rich countries' and bankers' point of view it has achieved a fair degree of success – given how near they came to disaster in 1982. The World Bank says that although 'some achievements have been made, an end to the debt crisis remains elusive'.[66] On the plus side, 'the threat to the international banking system has abated' and debtors are 'restructuring and reforming their economies' along lines approved of by the IMF and World Bank. Unfortunately, the Bank has to admit that 'most of the indebted countries are still no better off than in 1982 – when the debt crisis first erupted'. Gains and losses in the debt game have been distributed according to the rich world's rules: tails we win, heads you lose.

In recent years two further debt initiatives have been launched with a great fanfare by the rich countries, as addressing the need for actual debt relief: the Toronto initiative on official African debt and the Brady Plan for commercial debtors. They are politically significant in that they show that banks and governments of the rich countries have been forced at long last to concede the principle of debt relief (rather than just lending more money or postponing repayments). They demonstrate that concessions can be won and that greater pressure could yield more. But in both cases the financial significance is much more limited in relation to the size of the debt problem; they concede too little too late.

OUT OF AFRICA

The main 'solution' offered to African debtors has been for them to undertake adjustment while rescheduling their payments through the so-called 'Paris Club' of rich-country creditors. But agreements to put off payments do little good when the real problem is that countries cannot pay at all – it simply becomes a process of unending deferral. Between September 1982 and June 1989, some 188 reschedulings were agreed between rich-country creditors and fifty-three poor countries through the Paris Club.[67]

Following a parallel logic of 'borrow your way out of debt' as advocated by the Baker Plan for commercial debtors, some new sources of loans were made available to Africa's official debtors. The IMF's three-billion-dollar Structural Adjustment Facility (SAF) was set up in March 1986 to lend on relatively soft terms to the poorest debtors who were implementing adjustment programmes. The size of the fund was tripled eighteen months later. But rich countries were increasingly pushed to concede the need for some kind of debt relief.

As Africa's debt crisis deepened, the move was a simple recognition of reality – countries just could not pay and were not doing so. It was also prompted by the concern of Western voters following the African famines of the mid-1980s, and by the message from their industrialists of a collapse in exports to cash-strapped African countries (particularly in France and Britain, with the enduring importance of their colonial-based trade links with the continent).

Following initiatives from the then British Chancellor of the Exchequer, Nigel Lawson, and from President Mitterrand of France, a 'menu' of debt relief was at last agreed by the seven major industrialized countries at their 1988 summit in Toronto. Under the scheme, creditors could choose from the following:[68]

(a) *cancel a third of debt service*, but reschedule the rest at market interest rates over fourteen years;

(b) *reschedule all payments*, over a longer period of twenty-five years;

(c) *reduce interest payments* by either half or 3.5 percentage points – whichever is greater, but to be paid back over fourteen years.

The deal signified an important breakthrough in conceding the principle of officially sanctioned debt relief. However, given the amount of political effort that went into achieving the Toronto deal, financially the outcome is 'desultory', says Percy Mistry, a former senior World Bank staff member and Senior Fellow in International Finance at Oxford University.[69] The World Bank estimates that taking up the options will perhaps save Africa 5 per cent of its overall debt service obligations.[70]

One major problem with the plan is that option (b) is effectively a get-out clause, largely included to please the United States, and is not really debt relief at all. All in all, Toronto was only a starting-point towards effective and realistic debt relief for Africa. But the rich countries have seen it as an opportunity to rest complacently on their pitifully scant laurels. If the rich world was looking for a single effective contribution towards solving Africa's human and ecological crisis, it need hardly look further than a really effective plan of debt relief for Africa. It would cost the rich countries relatively little (perhaps from funds redirected as part of any savings made on arms spending following the thaw in the Cold War), but could make a huge difference to Africa.

BRADY AND THE BANKS

In Latin America, the failure of the Baker plan to alleviate the debt crisis has threatened political stability. The Venezuelan riots precipitated a plan which marked some change of principle in Western handling of the crisis. While it does not insist on the absolute principle of full debt repayment, this does not mean that Washington is uttering that taboo word 'forgiveness' (of debts).

If 'adjustment with growth' was the catch-phrase of the defunct Baker Plan, then 'debt reduction' is that of the 1989 Brady Plan. The plan amounts to an official pat-on-the-back for something commercial banks have already started doing in recent years. It is ideologically sound for the free marketeers, since it is a technique first certified as acceptable by 'The Market'.

Banks wanting to get rid of their Third World loans started selling them as far back as 1984. The banks selling do not mind getting less than the face value of the debt – say, 70 per cent – because they swap it for a more secure, though smaller, payment. It helps ease doubts of shareholders and customers over Third World loans. On the other hand, banks and speculators buying the debts accept the risk associated with them, because they can carry on getting back as much of the face value of the debt as they can. Any debt payments they get back above the discount level – in our imaginary case, above 70 per cent – is profit.

The 'secondary market' in inter-bank trading of Third World debt is now a booming business, with a turnover of about $50 billion a year.[71] But, in itself, the fact that debts are being traded by banks at an average of only 35 per cent of their face value (as was the case for the major debtors in 1989) does little to help the debtors, who are still required to honour the debt at full value. As with provisions, they could only point to the secondary market as a debating issue by arguing, 'If the free market says our country's debt is only worth half its face value, why should we still have to pay back at the full face value?'

Debt reduction is a way of capturing some of the secondary market discounts for the debtors' benefit. A variety of techniques have emerged in which debtors gain the discount on a particular debt by agreeing to exchange it for something else of value to the creditor, like an investment in a profitable local company, or a more secure bond. Four main types of debt conversion scheme have emerged:

1. *Debt-for-equity swaps*

A foreign company buys, say, Brazilian debt at the going secondary market rate, perhaps half its face value. It then trades in the debt with the Brazilian government at its full value, but is paid in the local currency – in this case Brazilian cruzados. It then uses the money to invest in a Brazilian company. Although the government pays the full value of debt, it agrees to the deal because it does not have to use any of its scarce foreign exchange, and the money stays in the country. From the foreign company's point of view, it gets an investment in Brazil at about half-price.

However, debtor governments are often wary of swap deals because they increase foreign control of their industry, and with it the likelihood that profits will be repatriated abroad. Swaps also carry economic side-effects, like inflation, because governments print extra local currency to finance them. Also, public debt can only be reduced in this way if governments are prepared to swap public assets in return for debt (i.e. privatize them). Nevertheless, debt-for-equity swaps are the leading method of debt conversion – with about nine billion dollars' worth of debt being swapped in 1988.[72]

2. Debt for bonds

Banks agree to swap their existing loans for more secure bonds at, say, 50 per cent of the face value of uncertain debt. One of the most notable attempts at this was Mexico's 'Aztec' bonds, but they found disappointingly few buyers among Western banks.

3. Debt buybacks

A debtor is allowed to buy its own debts directly on the secondary market, and so cancel the difference between the going price and the debt's face value. Chile (using a windfall from a rise in copper prices) and Bolivia have done this. In a way, this is the most attractive route for debtors. But in practice, to make it work they need plenty of hard currency, which as debtors, almost by definition, they simply do not have.

4. Debt-for-nature and debt-for-development swaps

Using the same mechanism as the debt–equity swap, non-governmental organizations (NGOs) in rich countries buy a portion of a country's foreign debt at the discounted secondary market rate. They then cancel it in return for the government providing local funds for, say, preserving forests or carrying out a vaccination campaign. One US environmental group, for example, bought a slice of Bolivian debt with a face value of $650,000 for the cash price of $100,000.[73] In return for the cancellation of the debt, the

Bolivian government set up a fund to finance the running costs of the Beni Biosphere Reserve in north-east Bolivia and, in a non-money aspect of the deal, the government increased its protection of the reserve under Bolivian law. Other debt-for-nature swaps have followed, including schemes in Costa Rica, Ecuador and the Philippines, but the total value of all such swaps only amounts to less than 100 million dollars' worth of commercial debt.

Debt-for-nature swaps have been hailed as an innovative debt solution which avoids the social and ecological damage of conventional debt solutions. But there are serious drawbacks. Some of the swap-funded projects have come in for criticism; in the Bolivian scheme, for example, a forest reserve was set up before taking account of the opinions and needs of local people. More fundamentally, by concentrating time, energy and money on what are (relative to the debt as a whole) tiny schemes, NGOs risk winning a few minor immediate battles while undermining their ability to secure the major long-term solution that is clearly needed to solve the debt problem.

By playing the debt game according to the banks' rules, even for well-meaning ends, NGOs legitimize the way that most debt is collected at the expense of the poor and the environment. The ability of NGOs to challenge the injustice of the debt mechanism is compromised. Banks can buy, for a relatively small price, social and environmental kudos from involvement in a swap and so improve their image in the eyes of a public increasingly aware of the real costs of repayments to the banks.

The Brady plan embraces debt reduction as the next big step towards solving the debt crisis. It aims to speed up debt reduction by changing banking laws which slow down debt swaps; by using the IMF and World Bank as guarantors between banks and debtors in debt-reduction deals; and by getting the same institutions, along with rich-country governments – notably Japan – to come up with money to back the schemes. But the Brady plan poses problems of both quality and quantity. First, debt reduction deals themselves carry a range of drawbacks for debtors, of the type outlined above. But second, and more importantly, the plan is too little, too late, in too few countries. The all-party parliamentary Treasury and Civil Service Committee concluded, 'The Brady initiative will be partial in its effect; and that in the case of those countries which have adopted a Brady package, its impact will be modest.'[74] A year after the Brady plan was launched, deals had been arranged in only three countries (Mexico, the Philippines and Costa Rica), all favoured because of their importance to US foreign policy. Overall it will do little to halt, let alone reverse, the flow of money from poor to rich – the number one priority for action.

Some of the figures quoted for debt reduction sound impressive – billions of dollars a year. But these are for cuts in the overall debt stock. And as discussed at the beginning of the chapter, the real problem is debt service. Many countries are so snowed under with debt that they are rarely servicing all the debt at any one time. *Unless debt reduction is on a really big scale it will only marginally improve the plight of debtors.* A conservative UN estimate says that the net wealth transfer to the banks needs to be cut by $10 billion a year at least if the minimal target of 2 per cent growth a year is to be reached and even a faint hope of tackling poverty achieved.[75] According to UN and World Bank studies, to achieve this the stock of bank debt must be written off to the tune of at least thirty to forty cents in the dollar, way short of what banks are prepared to accept. Mr Brady and other Western leaders refuse to consider bringing pressure on the banks to accept the scale of write-offs needed – something the banks have persistently ducked since the start of the crisis.

Until governments and banks are forced to do so – by debtor actions and the pressure of people in rich countries as shareholders, bank customers and voters – then the prospect remains bleak. Without these write-offs, the hope of tackling poverty and defending the environment from Amazonia to Zambia remains thwarted.

6 Aid in Perspective

There is no such thing as a free lunch.

Anon., often attributed to the economist Milton Friedman

A large new coal-fired power station rises above Lake Rihand in the northern Indian state of Uttar Pradesh. It has been built to produce a thousand megawatts of electricity, as part of a vast new 'energy park' of fifteen power stations. Constructed to fuel India's economic growth, and in particular its expanding heavy industries, the whole scheme will eventually produce 20,000 megawatts, probably the largest concentration of power generation in the world.[1] The project is probably not the kind of thing that would come to mind for many people if one talks of 'overseas aid'. But the Rihand Super Thermal Power Station is one of Britain's biggest-ever aid projects, and it reflects the content of much of the British aid programme to India, the country which receives the biggest share of British aid.

Built by the British company Northern Engineering Industries (NEI), the Rihand Power Station received £120 million of British aid money between 1982 and 1989.[2] Aid has also gone to equip the large coal mines nearby with British machinery. Thirty million pounds' worth of mining equipment is being supplied to develop the Amlohri Coal Mine to enable it to feed the Rihand Power Station with the estimated 20,000 to 30,000 tonnes of coal it will use every day.[3]

The benefits *to* the poor of such schemes for the poor are remote. Locally, over 250 families, mostly tribal people who are impoverished farmers, have been displaced by the power station.

Researcher-reporters Steve Percy and Mike Hall report that many of them have not received the promised compensation because they have no land titles. Even among those that do, some are still waiting to be paid.[4] Jobs promised to local families have also not materialized. Environmental problems are growing: forest has been cleared, coal dust and ash heaps increasingly dot the landscape, and slurry from ash is already seeping into the lake, according to one report.[5] Recently, the National Audit Office, the official but independent watchdog for British government bodies, produced a report on the last ten years of British aid to India. It reported that at the Amlohri Coal Mine requirements for reafforestation and land reclamation had been 'flouted' and that there had been 'unrest between villagers and mine staff'. It reported 'serious environmental problems', including 'considerable devastation of the landscape; spontaneous surface fires; the lack of a watering system for the mines and the associated dust problem'.[6]

Over the last decade, 42 per cent of Britain's aid to India has been spent on the power and mining sectors with the aim of promoting economic growth, in comparison with just 17 per cent on projects officially classified as 'poverty alleviation' (such as housing, agriculture and education; but how much benefit from these projects actually reaches poor people is strongly debated).[7] (See Figure 6.1.) The types of projects outlined above are clearly, then, in the mainstream of British aid to India; but even in other very poor countries, such as Sudan and Bangladesh, big power projects have swallowed up large chunks of British aid. However, simply cataloguing a further series of disastrous projects is not enough. We must look behind them at the underlying determinants of aid in its different forms to understand why such projects go on attracting funds.

GETTING AID IN PERSPECTIVE

For or against, the importance of aid is often exaggerated. This is both because the rich world has an inflated image of its own largesse and because, for those frustrated by the slow progress in

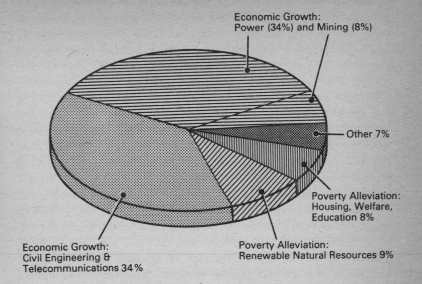

SOURCE: National Audit Office, *Bilateral Aid to India*, 1990, p.10 (as amended)

Figure 6.1   UK bilateral aid to India, by sector (1980–88)

the fight against world poverty and environmental problems, aid provides the most obvious handle on which to hang their hopes and criticisms. Controversy tends to focus on aid; and even then, mainly on high-profile aid such as disaster relief which only makes up a small proportion of aid spending. It is undoubtedly important to keep turning a critical searchlight on aid and work towards improving its effectiveness. But before looking at these issues it is equally important to see aid in perspective, recognizing that many of the other links between the rich world and the fate of people and environments in the Third World, explored elsewhere in this book, have greater overall significance than aid.

The fate of a poor country's economy is more likely to be affected by a downturn in the price for its main export crop or a rise in international interest rates than by fluctuations in aid spending. All world aid together equals only 1.4 per cent of the economies of the Third World (as measured by total GNP); even in Africa it makes up only 7.5 per cent.[8] For the givers, too, aid has to be put in perspective. The total of world aid is still only half what Britain spends on its social services.[9] A few Third World countries are heavily aid-dependent, such as Bangladesh or Somalia. But other aid-dependent economies can, in some respects, be seen as exceptions: for instance, some of the small Pacific or Caribbean island states, or colonial territories like French New Caledonia, the Netherlands Antilles, or British St Helena.

However, the significance of aid is greater than its straight cash value. Aid reflects what the giving countries hold greatest store by in their relationship with the Third World. Donors have therefore used aid for many purposes other than the one commonly assumed to be the most central – helping poor people in poor countries. Aid is used in promoting commercial deals, buying strategic allies, promoting free-market policies in the Third World and, perhaps increasingly, the adoption of environmental policies. But before going on to look in more detail at what kind of aid is given, we must take an overview of how much is given and by whom.

WORLD AID – WHO GIVES WHAT?

Overall, the level of world aid remained roughly constant during the 1980s, hovering around $50 billion a year, in real terms. A slow increase in giving from the rich countries cancelled out the decline of Arab aid, which fell with oil prices just as it had risen with them in the 1970s.[10] But despite its stagnation, aid's *relative* importance as a source of outside finance for the Third World increased considerably. When the tide of private bank lending to the Third World rapidly receded in the 1980s, after the debt crisis, it increased the relative importance of the stream of aid money as a source of financial buoyancy. Aid now accounts for half of all the new outside finance coming to poor countries, when in 1980 it made up less than a third of the total.[11]

Most (84 per cent) of the world's aid comes from the eighteen Western industrialized countries who are represented on the Development Assistance Committee (DAC) of the Organisation for Economic Co-operation and Development (OECD).[12] The Soviet Union, along with eastern Europe, accounts for about 9 per cent ($4.7 billion) of the global total, with a programme largely focused on the Third World members of the Council of Mutual Economic Assistance (CMEA) – Cuba, Mongolia and Vietnam – as well as Cambodia and Laos. However, it should be noted that these are 1988 figures (the most recent comprehensive ones available at the time of writing) and so are prior to the changes in eastern Europe and the Soviet Union, which are likely to change established patterns considerably. Not only is eastern Europe set to become a much larger recipient of Western aid, and so perhaps draw aid away from the Third World. Its own, and particularly the Soviet Union's, aid programme may be constrained by the financial demands of internal restructuring.

The European Community (EC), which has been co-ordinating aid to eastern Europe, has its own aid programme. This programme, which started with an exclusive focus on ex-colonies in Africa, the Caribbean and Pacific, has helped make poorer countries in Europe such as Portugal and Greece both donors and recipients of international aid. EC aid has tended to reflect the EC's own experience, with a strong emphasis on agricultural development and on supporting regional cooperation in the Third World. More recently, however, hard-line states within the EC, such as the UK, have encouraged the EC to act as a partner, and almost always a junior partner, to the World Bank and IMF.

Arab donors make up 5 per cent (2.7 billion dollars' worth) of world aid – a faint shadow of their 1975 heyday when they gave a third of all aid.[13] Interestingly, some Third World countries like China, India and Venezuela are themselves aid donors, but altogether account for less than 1 per cent of total world aid. Clearly, then, while the rich countries are not the only aid donors they are the main players in the aid game.

In cash terms, the league of rich-country donors is topped by the so-called 'Group of Seven' richest industrialized countries. However, to compare performance more accurately – internationally and over time – aid-giving is expressed as a proportion of the donor's economy: as a percentage of its gross national product (GNP). Not only does this measure adjust for the donor economies' uneven size, but also helps to smooth out the distortions of exchange rate fluctuations.

GOING UP

The GNP measure reveals a very different pattern from the straight cash graph. For some years the most generous aid donors by this yardstick have been the Netherlands and the 'Nordic' group of donors – Norway, Sweden and Denmark. The Nordics have also won official international praise for giving more of their aid as grants, not loans, and for their attempts to make sure it gets to the poor. Finland is also

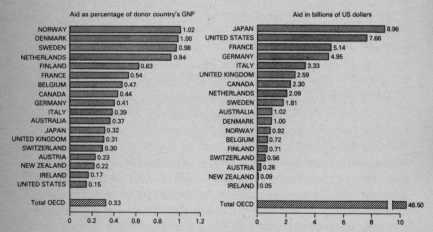

NOTE: Figures for France do not include aid to overseas territories

SOURCE: Development Assistance Committee, OECD (June 1990)

Figure 6.2   Aid from Western industrialized countries, as a percentage of donor's Gross National Product and in billions of dollars.

moving towards the Scandinavian pattern, following the government's 1980 decision to achieve, by the end of the decade, the 0.7 per cent of GNP aid target set by the United Nations. Italy too is set to increase its aid programme, having grown from one of the smallest of Western donors (taking aid as a proportion of its GNP) to become one of the largest. The French are also likely to continue expanding their aid programme, as they have done over the last decade.

COMING DOWN

On the other side are countries whose aid programmes have shrunk significantly relative to their economic strength over the last decade, notably Belgium, Britain and New Zealand. Despite still being the second biggest aid donor in cash terms, the United States is the least generous in relation to its economic strength. Pressure to reduce the budget deficit has taken its toll on US aid spending – and is likely to keep it at roughly its present level for the near future. German aid, which had expanded in the early 1980s, has been cut back again in more recent years and is predicted to stay stable in relation to GNP. In addition, many now fear that large-scale spending on German reunification and on eastern Europe will divert German aid away from the Third World.

BRITAIN'S DECLINE

Britain has dramatically cut the size of its aid budget since the Conservative government came to power in 1979. Despite a promise from the Prime Minister during the 1983 election that, 'when economic circumstances permit, we will move towards the UN target of 0.7 per cent of GNP', the UK has in fact slipped back further and further.[14] In 1979 Britain gave more of its GNP (0.52) in aid than any of the other seven richest industrialized countries. By 1987 it had slumped to sixth place (above only the United States) at 0.28 per cent of GNP, the UK's worst figure on record.[15] Following criticism of Britain's record by the OECD and the all-party parliamentary Foreign Affairs Committee, and after an intense national lobbying campaign by the World Development Movement, in 1988 the government announced plans to increase the aid budget in real terms. But these increases have been eaten away by higher-than-forecast inflation. The long downward trend in the size of Britain's aid budget as a proportion of the country's wealth may have been stemmed, but the OECD estimates that the planned increase is unlikely to raise aid as a share of GNP above its present low level of 0.31 per cent.[16]

JAPAN: THE RISING GIANT

Japan is already a leading, if little-recognized, player in the aid game. In 1989 it overtook the United States to become the world's biggest donor in cash terms. The drive to give and lend more to the Third World is one expression of Japan's desire to take a political place in world affairs which better matches its vast economic might. The Japanese doubled their aid budget in the five years from 1976 to 1980, then again between 1981 and 1985; in 1988 they announced their intention to double it once more, by spending more than $50 billion up to 1992.[17] It is significant that they continue to expand aid apace while domestic spending is reined in. To complete the picture of Japan's move to centre stage in Third World economic coopera-tion, it has earmarked large funds from its trade surplus for debt relief in Africa and Latin America. However, there must now be the caveat that Japanese attentions are being diverted away from the Third World towards eastern Europe.

It is common in Europe and America to hear Japanese aid decried as simply a vehicle for extending their commercial empire in the Third World (particularly in Asia), or as a crass attempt at chequebook diplomacy. Attention is focused on the damaging human and environmental impact of Japanese aid. Much of this is hypocritical Western humbug. Japanese motives are undoubtedly heavily rooted in economic and political self-interest, but so are those of nearly all aid donors. The scorn poured on Japanese aid reflects as much the self-delusion of other countries that their aid programmes stem from an altruistic desire to help the poor as it counts for objective criticism of the contemporary Japanese aid programme itself.

Japan has certainly encountered problems in achieving a high quality of aid because of the rapid rate of increase in its quantity, but so have countries like Italy which have rapidly expanded their programmes. As Yoshiji Nogami, acting Director of the Japan

Institute of International Affairs, points out: 'One basic problem is that there is too much emphasis on increasing volume and no agreement on how to spend it.'[18] Japan still dispenses a greater proportion of its aid as loans, rather than grants, than other donors. But contrary to widespread belief, it now ties less of its aid to buying its own goods than do other countries, such as Britain or the United States.

For geographical and historical reasons, Japan's main focus for aid is South-East Asia. But recently it has increased its aid to Africa – which now accounts for 10 per cent of the government-to-government total[19] and is now the biggest contributor to the World Bank's Special Facility for Sub-Saharan Africa.[20] Japan is increasing the amount of aid it gives through voluntary agencies and to smaller-scale projects, though, as in other donor countries, the Trade Ministry and private companies continue to push for funding of big infrastructure projects with benefits for Japanese business.[21]

AID: WHAT COMES FIRST?

The debate over Japanese aid highlights the fact that aid must be measured not only by its quantity, but by its quality. To do this means looking again at what aid is meant to achieve, to provide criteria against which its success or failure can be measured. Aid is most commonly understood to be money, together with expertise and goods such as food or machinery, that is given by the governments of rich countries to help poor people in poor countries. Government aid is viewed as something like a state equivalent of the funds sent overseas to the Third World by charities, or perhaps as an international extension of domestic state welfare provision. Governments reinforce this impression in their public statements. 'We concentrate British aid on poor countries, on poor people and on their basic needs,' asserts the government Overseas Development Administration's glossy 1989 *Anniversary Review*, produced for its silver jubilee.[22]

It is hardly surprising, then, that the public becomes indignant when stories emerge of aid 'not getting through' to the poor, or of being spent on huge dams or roads which destroy the forest homelands of poor people. UNICEF notes the gap between this disillusionment with official aid and the rapid expansion of public support for the voluntary Third World agencies whose 'primary purpose is to alleviate poverty – by helping poor people to improve their own lives'. UNICEF argues that:

> The truth is that there is little idealistic support for significantly increased aid and a renewed commitment to the international development effort because there is a widespread perception that such efforts are not primarily designed to meet the needs or enhance the capacities of the poorest or to make rapid progress towards the eradication of poverty.[23]

Cynicism often arises from the way aid is diverted 'in handling' from helping the poor. The main culprits are held to be the corrupt governments of receiving countries and the activities of blundering, short-sighted officials of Western aid ministries which attract shocking stories of tractors wastefully rusting away in foreign fields, and of environmentally misplaced dams which take no account of local ecology and are left useless and silted up after a few years.

Bad implementation of aid must take its share of the blame. More attention should be given to improved social, environmental and financial monitoring and procedures.[24] But no amount of this will help poor people or their environment if policy-makers who control aid place other commercial, ideological and political factors higher in their list of priorities. This is frequently the case. Britain's aid programme demonstrates these mixed motives.

The British government says its aid programme is designed 'to promote sustainable economic and social progress and alleviate poverty in developing countries'.[25] It rejects criticisms such as that voiced by the all-party parliamentary Foreign Affairs Committee:

> In practice, the purpose of bilateral aid programmes in the UK, as in most other countries, has rarely been viewed as the purely selfless promotion of other countries' and peoples' welfare. It has always been understood that such programmes should be carried out with British commercial and industrial interests and political interests in mind.[26]

The government, however, rejects such distinctions, asserting that 'separate "developmental", "commercial" and "political" objectives' do not exist.

> There is one objective, which is the promotion of development. This is entirely compatible with also serving our political, industrial and commercial interests.[27]

Governments, then, have to concede that aid is given with mixed motives, but maintain that these motives can be married together without interfering with each other. But in reality there are fundamental clashes which mean that poor people only rarely benefit, and sometimes suffer, from aid. This is not what the taxpayers of rich countries want, nor the poor majorities in poor countries.

DRUMMING UP BUSINESS

Aid is commonly thought of as handing over money to Third World governments for development. In fact, aid largely consists of funding from Western governments for services, machines, technical experts and consultants to be supplied by companies in rich countries, frequently their own. Most aid money is actually spent in the rich world. The former Chairman of British construction giant Balfour Beatty, Don Holland, backs calls for a bigger aid programme because, he says:

I believe that a larger bilateral aid programme would assist us [Britain] in securing more British goods overseas and therefore help our balance of payments situation.[28]

He lists other advantages of aid projects for Britain: creating jobs, encouraging small businesses (through sub-contracting on major projects), and giving 'further long-term benefits to the UK through follow-on orders and spares'. He recognizes that aid focusing on 'the rural sector, rehabilitation of rundown plants, maintenance of projects, smaller projects which are more manageable, greater use of internal resources and manpower, emphasis on cost recovery' might play 'a very important part in the scheme of things in these territories'. But he cautions against it, lest it should 'reduce the possibilities of UK trade' and lest British companies miss out on the kind of large aid projects which are such a good 'introduction to further business' in the Third World.

AID STRINGS

One obvious way in which aid is designed to help businesses in the donor's country is the practice of 'tying' aid. Under tied aid, any goods and services used in the project must be bought from the country giving the aid – whether or not a cheaper or more suitable equivalent can be bought from another country or from within the Third World country itself. The UK is a particularly bad offender in this respect as virtually all British bilateral aid is tied to buying British goods. In addition, Britain imposes a 'local costs' ceiling on many countries that limits the proportion of aid that can be spent on locally bought materials. (By comparison, over three-quarters of Swedish and Norwegian aid is not tied.)

The business aid bonanza applies not only to country-to-country (bilateral) aid, where it is specifically tied to buying goods and services from the donor country; it also applies to the multilateral lending agencies. Britain's aid minister, Lynda Chalker, boasts how Britain gets orders worth £1.75 for every £1 it put into the multilateral agencies.[29] Britain receives over £650 million worth of business a year from the multilateral agencies.[30] Similarly, European Community aid is tied to reciprocal buying from EC member countries.

Although the World Bank puts its aid contracts out to international tender, donors still reap a lot of the business generated. Raghavan Srinivasan, chief of the World Bank's Procurement Policy Unit, told a conference of British businesspeople that 'the procurement cake presented by the World Bank is a very large one'.[31] He is not exaggerating. In 1988, of the total $20 billion the Bank lent to the Third World, it 'disbursed $15 billion to contractors, suppliers and consultants functioning under the Bank's projects,' he says.[32] His audience were particularly pleased to hear that 5 per cent of all the World Bank's lending ends up as orders for British companies. In Africa, the boon was greater, with one in every five World Bank dollars coming to the UK in 1987.

AIDING TRADING

One of the most controversial commercial uses of aid is as a sweetener to win contracts for the donor country's companies against international competition. Aid is reduced to little more than an official bribe to pep up government trade financing and so

make deals cheaper and more attractive to Third World governments. It also avoids international trade rules against straight
subsidies. In Britain the Aid-Trade Provision (ATP) has used
about £650 million of aid money to win two and a half billion
pounds' worth of business for British companies since it was set up
in 1978.[33] However, the ATP in its present form may now be
on the way out, not because of the argument that it diverts aid
away from helping the poor, but because under the European
Community's 1992 programme such nationally based subsidy programmes will become obsolete.

But Britain is not alone in using aid to win business. Indeed,
countries frequently justify using aid to win Third World contracts by pointing to the use of aid by other countries to subsidize
the bids of their own companies. This plea of ensuring a 'level
field of competition' has led to a spiralling abuse of aid which
the OECD struggles, unsuccessfully, to bring under control. Aid
is reduced to funding a price-cutting war between donors, making
it ever more remote from its supposed purpose of helping the
poor.

Asia is now the focus for the aid-financed scramble for business,
as new projects have been hit by debt in Latin America and Africa,
and by declining oil revenues in the Middle East. In Indonesia,
Western countries are trying to outbid each other with what the
Financial Times called the 'rampant use of aid as an export
subsidy'.[34] In a recent case, Washington accused Japan of using
some of its massive two-billion-dollar aid programme in Indonesia
to support the Japanese company NEC in a bid to win a 300-
million-dollar contract to supply Indonesia with digital switching
gear for its public telephone exchanges (with the prospect of two
billion dollars' worth of repeat orders in the future). But the US
has indicated that it is prepared to use a special 'war chest' of
government soft loans to counter competitors in important markets
like Indonesia – in this case, to support a counter-bid by the US
telecommunications company AT&T.[35] President Bush himself
intervened in February 1990 to support AT&T's bid, with the
backing of the Netherlands and Spain, where much of the work
would be done if AT&T won the contract.

Britain is also keen not to miss out in such markets. It signed arrangements with Indonesia for soft loans and mixed credits of £140 million in 1986 and £100 million in 1988.[36] The loans have been arranged with an eye on the opportunities for British companies in the power sector. The state electricity utility PLN set out a four-and-a-half-billion-dollar expansion scheme for the 1989–94 five-year plan – 83 per cent of which is to be funded by foreign aid.[37] Britain hopes to use its soft loans to secure some of the vast numbers of orders flowing from the plan against competition from Japan and elsewhere.

BUSINESS BEFORE PEOPLE

While the scramble continues, the poor and their environment are left on the sidelines or are overrun in the mêlée. Governments defend the aid-trade link by saying it is a case of mutual benefit – the country concerned gets what it wants and the donor gets business and jobs. But criticism of this kind of aid is not just prompted by a negative reaction at seeing a donor's businesses doing well; the problem is that the type of aid which benefits business in the donor country is unlikely to benefit the poor by meeting their basic needs or supporting an environmentally sustainable, secure livelihood.

Commercial objectives in aid tend, right from the start, to favour large-scale, hi-tech, capital-intensive industrial and infrastructure projects because these mean big exports and lots of technical advice from Western companies. It works against low-cost rural solutions focused on the poor because they generate less export business and fewer jobs back home. This bias is further encouraged by the fact that officials find it easier to administer, say, one big ten-million-pound road project than ten rural development projects costing one million pounds each.

The result is that an environmentally damaging coal-fired power station or large hydro-electric dam has priority over help to increase the poor's production of and access to fuels they normally use, like wood and charcoal. Hi-tech agricultural projects, using chemical pesticides and fertilizers, are favoured over those that provide basic inputs, like credit, to enable the poor to grow more food. Research is concentrated on estate-grown cash crops instead of on the staple food crops of the poor. A steel plant is set up, rather than support for small-scale industries that could provide jobs for many poor people – in particular, women – at much lower investment cost. Professor Paul Mosley, Director of the University of Manchester's Institute for Development Policy and Management, sums it up:

What the poor want to buy . . . is generally small, simple and locally made; what the aid agencies offer them is very often big, complex and imported.[38]

In aid-trade deals there are particular problems. The vetting of proposed aid-trade projects is often hurried and half-done. In Britain, for example, ATP projects are only supposed to be accepted if they are 'developmentally sound'. But in practice the need to move rapidly to sew up commercial deals before competitors are able to do so means that corners are cut in the environmental and social assessment of projects. Approval has to be gained on very limited information because the funding proposal first comes from the company (via the Department of Trade and Industry), rather than being devised between the recipient government and the Overseas Development Administration (ODA), as happens with other projects. Even so, business still complains of time-wasting scruples that get in the way of winning contracts, scruples concerning details such as whether the project is going to harm the environment or leave the poor worse off.

In its report on Britain's aid to India, the National Audit Office found that the ODA

. . . were often subjected to considerable pressure to complete their appraisals quickly where Aid and Trade Provision finance was involved . . . [and were] not always able to provide as full an assurance on the developmental value of projects as would be required for those funded from country programmes.[39]

In the case of the Rihand Power Station, the ODA had to give urgent approval in principle, because of the commercial pressures, without even knowing where the plant was to be built or its detailed specification. Although, as the NAO points out, 'there was no prior assessment of its priority or soundness', the project was given the initial go-ahead simply on the basis of the 'known shortage of generating capacity in the Indian power system'.

Despite their free-market rhetoric, donor governments such as Britain are prepared to use aid to subsidize private companies, often to the economic detriment of the country receiving the aid. Both trade-supporting and tied aid can work against self-reliance in the recipient country by favouring the donor country's suppliers over local ones. But if anything, the bias should be the other way round. Opportunities to create local jobs and build up experience are lost. Britain made a vast pledge of £131 million, including £33 million from the ATP, to help British engineering giant GEC undercut Indian state-owned Bharat Heavy Electrical Ltd in a bid for a power station contract.[40] Yet the Indian company had already built another plant hailed as one of the most efficient in Asia and had won productivity awards. But British taxpayers' money was used to deprive it of a contract it could have fulfilled.

TOWARDS PEOPLE-FIRST AID

It is not only commercial and political self-interest which distances government aid from the poorest and leads to a low priority for environmental protection. Present patterns of aid are also justified by the donors on the grounds that they help increase the national economic growth of the country concerned, and that, at some point, this will improve the lot of the poor. This view of aid reflects a prominent approach to development in general. But it does not consider how often poor people fail to benefit from the growth, or are even harmed by it, nor does it accept the true scale of environmental costs.[41]

Aid should aim to benefit the poor directly by helping them to increase their income and productivity, by providing them with better basic services, improving their living conditions and helping them to protect their environment. To many, all these points seem to be what aid is obviously about, but in fact, as we have seen, they rarely are. If these were made the central aims of aid, replacing those of commercial and political self-interest, they would bring a very different set of methods to those that exist at present. Certainly such a redirection is not easy – needing a radical reorientation in existing practices and running up against the vested interests of the rich and powerful, both in donor countries and in the Third World. But it is the kind of change that many Third World people, as well as the taxpayers in rich countries, are waiting for, and it could be made a reality.

THE FALL AND RISE OF POVERTY-FOCUSED AID

Calls to focus aid on the poorest people are not new. In the mid-1970s, partly because of the much-publicised famines in the Sahel and Bangladesh, there was an upsurge of criticism at the failure of aid to alleviate poverty and a move to focus aid on the poorest. The World Bank, under the presidency of Robert McNamara, sought to put far more emphasis on agriculture and 'integrated rural development' aimed more directly at raising standards of living in the countryside, where most of the poorest lived. Other donors moved in a similar direction. In Britain, the Labour government set out its intended policy of more help for the poorest people in the poorest countries. Agencies such as the International Labour Organisation (ILO) set out a 'basic needs' approach to development. In 1977, the International Fund for Agricultural Development (IFAD) was established with a mandate to reduce malnutrition and alleviate rural poverty specifically by supporting small farmers, the landless and others of the rural poor. Although some attempts to redirect aid to the poorest failed, others, such as those of IFAD, did make significant, though underfunded, steps. But the general movement was brought to a halt by the pressures of the debt crisis and because aid officials were only too quick to pronounce that poverty-focus aid had 'failed'.

Aid policy-makers quietly forgot the concerns of 'poverty-focus' as they turned to an overriding obsession with adjustment programmes. We explored the terrible social and environmental costs of this in the previous chapter. More and more aid was used to back packages of free-market policy reforms, while the more traditional aid for individual projects was put on the back-burner. In some countries, such as Britain and the United States, there was an explicit move to upgrade the commercial use of aid, further distancing it from the poor.

But more recently there are signs that the tide is turning. There is now a movement against the dehumanized aid of the 1980s and growing pressure for aid to become refocused on the needs of the poor, together with the environmental problems that affect them. In part, it has again taken the shock of famine, this time in Ethiopia and Sudan, to force policy-makers to question whether aid is doing anything to meet the needs of the poor. But it has also partly been a result of growing public and international pressure.

Environmental groups have been successful in forcing a major restructuring of the World Bank to take account of environmental issues. Two members of the Bank's Environment Department concede that the heated criticism of the environmental damage caused by some of the Bank's projects – such as the Polonoroeste project in Brazil – 'spurred' the Bank, in 1987, to 'sharply adjust its policy so as to favour environmental management'.[42] The Bank says it has increased its personnel allocated to the environment by more than a hundred staff years, that it expects to spend $1.3 billion on environmental projects in the three years from 1989 and has 'fully integrated environmental issues into the Bank's approach to development'.[43] In Britain, former aid minister Chris Patten said:

> We not only have to direct our aid programme in part at measures which will conserve and restore the environment . . . we must also see that environmental factors enter as by right into the complex calculations which lie behind aid in whatever form.[44]

As we saw in the previous chapter, the World Bank and other official agencies have also come under increasing pressure over the effect on the poor of their adjustment and aid policies, and have been urged to take more account of making sure aid reaches the poorest people. A growing number of voices are pressing for change. Third World non-governmental organizations are setting out demands for a new agenda, abandoning the dehumanizing despair generated by the standard austerity programmes. More recently, the thirty-two governments who are donors to the International Development Association (IDA), the part of the World Bank that lends to the poorest countries, accepted proposals to link the amount of aid a country receives with its efforts to stamp out poverty. They also agreed to make 'poverty reduction' a central part of the discussions between the World Bank and the recipient country, not just the standard issue of what macro-economic policies the country is pursuing. This followed an intensive international lobbying campaign by the World Development Movement.

The speeches of the aid policy-makers are now ringing with messages similar to those used by World Bank President Barber Conable, that the 'fight against poverty is at the core of our mission' and that 'we have to ensure . . . that change does not destroy the resources on which human progress is based'.[45] The official watch-dog of the rich countries' aid, the OECD's Development Assistance Committee, is calling for aid and development in the 1990s which has 'a more determined equity and anti-poverty orientation', 'a new emphasis on investing in people' and a 'stronger concern with environmentally sustainable development'.[46]

The words, and in some cases the broad policy positions, of the official aid agencies have moved in the right direction; a change that needs to be welcomed and encouraged by their critics. But too often in the past there have been the right phrases without the substance of practical change. The challenge is to hold the agencies to their promises. While the rhetoric is moving in the right direction, concrete action is now needed. Principles for ensuring that the grand new promises for aid begin to be translated into practice are set out below. It is crucial that these principles underlie not only the projects that are funded by aid, but also the all-important policy packages of aid-funded adjustment programmes.

NEW PRIORITIES

The first test of whether the intentions are serious is whether the bulk of aid is no longer assigned to large-scale infrastructure projects like power plants, roads and bridges, and high-level city services such as telephone systems. Aid should be switched instead to the rural and natural resources sector – agriculture, forestry and fishing (together with cottage industries and basic urban services such as sewerage) and to social provision (including health and education). This is essential, for three reasons.

(1) These sectors remain grossly under-represented in aid budgets and have suffered in the commercialization of aid over the last decade. In 1979, education, for example, received 17 per cent of all aid from Western industrialized countries, but by 1987 only 10.5 per cent. Health, nutrition and family planning together got 7.5 per cent and 5 per cent for the respective years.[47] And yet there are highly effective, low-cost ways of improving health, such as the provision of clean water and childhood immunization programmes. The treatment of diarrhoea – one of the major killers in the Third World – can be improved by promoting the use of a simple but effective rehydration treatment using a solution of salt, sugar and water.

(2) The poorest people tend to live in the countryside and are often dependent on the land, forests and waters for their livelihood. If aid is to sustain the livelihoods of the poor and help them to play an active part in their own and their countries' development, it must be directed to the areas where most of them live and work. This will also help to stem the migration of the rural poor and jobless into the city slums. Any serious strategy to tackle poverty and its associated environmental degradation must be centred on providing a secure food supply. If aid is to play a part, it must support the efforts of the rural poor to grow food. The shift of aid to rural and natural resources is, of course, a question of redressing past imbalance. Aid could also usefully go to the cities, if it benefits the urban poor, whose ranks are swelling in much of the Third World.

(3) The present emphasis is on the kind of projects that have been shown to have a devastating environmental impact, like transport and energy infrastructure. Instead, aid should be used to tackle the major environmental problems that afflict the countryside – like the dwindling forests and spreading deserts – in a way that nurtures the natural-resource base on which many poor people rely for their livelihood.

NEW WAYS OF DOING THINGS

Apart from being channelled to new sectors of the economy, aid should be managed in a different way. It is only a first step, for example, to argue for more overall spending on forestry. Good forestry projects are not simply a matter of getting the most trees planted. It must be asked: What kind of forestry project? Does it address the poor's priorities, not only for trees for firewood, but for diverse needs, ranging from fodder from branches in the dry season to fruits for sale for a little extra cash income? More forestry spending will have little direct benefit for the poor if it is confined to large-scale 'farm forestry' of one species, such as eucalyptus, which ends up benefiting the richer people in an area. Instead the emphasis should be on 'community forestry', where the priorities are set by the whole local community and the benefits accrue to all.

A key component of this new way of doing things is that the poor people, and women in particular, who are supposed to benefit from a project should be involved in it right from the early planning stages, through to implementing and evaluating it. By enabling people to participate, the project can draw on the great store of knowledge the rural poor often have about their local environment. This would be a major change, for much existing aid is based on the idea that the outsider who has come to implement the project is the 'expert', and has come to impart knowledge and 'development' to the local people.

Through participation, the project can build on the many innovative ideas which spring up from local people once they really know that they will be listened to and given support. It also helps to build up self-reliance and community strength – so helping the group become more aware of its rights and strengths, and so more assertive in defending them. This also helps to ensure that the grains of a project are sustained after aid is withdrawn.

Another key priority is to place women at the centre of the development process. The role of women in development projects is frequently overlooked and their contribution is ignored. It is mainly women, particularly in Africa, who are the farmers, but only a few projects are directly aimed at helping them grow more food. Women often find it hard to get seeds and credit. Although many development agencies now pay lip-service to the central role of women in economic development, change in the practice of development programmes is slow. As Kenyan Dr Miriam K. Were, head of health and nutrition for UNICEF in Ethiopia, says:

Women ... have been dispossessed because they don't have power, because the speed of development has moved so fast they have not had the possibility of influencing its direction, and the structures of decision-making have not helped them get into this process.[48]

PRODUCTION, NOT HAND-OUTS

The official agencies also need to take on board the fact that poverty-focused aid is not simply, or even predominantly, a question of more welfare. It is concerned with improving the poor's access to economically productive assets like land, or sewing-machines, or fishing-boats, and helping them improve their productive potential with these assets, by, for example, widening their access to credit or training. Aid will only play a useful role if it offers the poor the assets, services and skills that they actually want and can use. But much present aid, as we have seen, offers things that are remote from them, such as power stations, which are chosen because they serve the interests of the donor's exporters and government planners. Poverty-focused aid can be economically highly successful. For example, IFAD, which concentrates its funds in action of this kind, found that of the $2.6 billion it has invested in self-help participatory development around the world, over 90 per cent of it has been repaid.[49]

LONG ROAD

We should not pretend that getting effective aid to the poorest people is easy. 'People's participation' frequently trips off the tongue of development agencies nowadays; as Mohiuddin Alamgir, Director of the Policy Review Division of IFAD, remarks:

It is easy to say that participatory development embracing the poor is fundamental to effective poverty alleviation, but the rhetoric of grassroots mobilization is too often not matched by action.[50]

There are problems of benefits being usurped by richer people, or of local groups becoming controlled by a powerful faction. 'The poor' are not a homogenous group. Poverty-focused projects have failed because of 'the opposition of the rich, or diluted into impotence by their enthusiastic support', says Paul Mosley.[51] But these kinds of problems can be overcome with persistence and ingenuity. For example, in Pakistan the locally based Aga Khan Foundation, which receives both voluntary funding and grants from the British ODA, has tackled the problem in a way that has proved effective:

The villagers are required to form a village organization (VO), of which all families, rich or poor, are members. The VO must meet at least once a month, must not be run by a committee, and there must be public reading of accounts [to ensure that it is not monopolized by only those who can read]. In this way [the project] has managed to ensure that the VOs are not hijacked by an elite group, and that the benefits of the VOs' activities flow to all members of the community. The VOs are the key. From the outset, they make the decisions as to what their priorities are.[52]

FOLLOW-UP AND MONITORING

Evaluation and monitoring seem like a bureaucratic irrelevance in institutions and aid agencies, which are often already highly bureaucratic, but they are essential if 'people first' projects are to succeed. (This also applies to NGOs, who in the past tended to skimp on this.) Evaluation and monitoring allow them to learn from their mistakes and to capitalize on and replicate successes. For example, the highly successful IFAD-funded Grameen Bank scheme, which extends credit to poor landless people in Bangladesh to enable them to establish small-scale ways of generating an income, is now being modified and spread into other countries. Increased staffing for environmental and social assessment of projects at their outset, and for subsequent evaluation, may be needed in some agencies. As Professor Mosley points out:

. . . of the thousands of evaluation reports which have so far issued from aid agencies the number which measure how far the poor have benefited from the project can be counted on the fingers of one hand.[53]

Pressure is mounting on the official agencies to redirect aid to help the poor and to tackle environmental problems from the viewpoint of poor people. Increasingly, the response of the aid officials is that it isn't really possible for the official agencies to reach the poor. But in their defence they say they are increasing their support for the NGOs. Britain has rapidly increased the amount of aid it channels through NGOs, through its Joint Funding Scheme, to £20 million for 1990, a 25 per cent increase on the previous year. The Minister for Overseas Development, Lynda Chalker, says that this shows that the ODA is 'putting our money where our mouth is'.[54] The support for NGOs is based on her belief that 'by working in direct partnership with local communities [NGOs] can provide the direct inputs necessary to poverty alleviation, which are often difficult to achieve at a government-to-government level'.

Greater government funding for NGO aid projects is likely to increase the chances of aid reaching the poor, of projects being carried out in a way that enables the poor genuinely to participate in them, and of helping to tackle ecological problems effectively. But there is a danger that greater NGO funding will become the fig-leaf of public credibility, behind which official agencies will try to hide the fact that most aid is carried on in the same old way. Funding for the voluntary organizations can only ever be part of the solution for improving aid.

For one thing, there has to be a limit on the amount of money the NGOs get from government, if they are to preserve their identity and independence. For another, as they themselves freely admit, they are too small to make a really substantial impact on world poverty beyond a number of local projects. Greater funding for the NGOs should not become a substitute for the government aid agencies making real efforts to ensure that the bulk of their aid – instead of a small percentage – reaches the poorest. Although the task is not easy for governments (or for anyone, for that matter), it is by no means impossible. The primary obstacles are not technical, but lie in the fact that most aid is subject to other priorities, such as the commercial interest in the aid 'giver's' exporters and the promotion of dogmatic adjustment programmes which often harm rather than help the poor. New talk of 'people-centred aid' will bring little tangible change towards promoting sustainable livelihoods for poor people unless it is made to challenge these entrenched interests. Nor will it unless it is also allowed to challenge the many other policy areas – from trade to debt – which, ultimately, are more decisive than aid itself.

7 War of the Worlds

> They are going to fight our movement with violence and intimidation.
>
> > Chico Mendes, leader of Amazonian rubber-tappers,
> > shortly before his murder

> When two elephants fight, it's always the grass that gets hurt.
>
> > African proverb

In Brazil, just before Christmas 1988, the winter season's torrential rain was falling around the home of rubber-tappers' leader Chico Mendes near Xapuri, in the western Amazon. It had temporarily dampened the forest fires, deliberately lit, that Chico Mendes had tried to stop. But its battering roar on the tin roof of his house also covered the sound of the *pistoleiros* (hired gunmen), in the pay of local landlords, as they hid outside. When he stepped out of his back door to walk across to the wash-house, they shot him in the chest. He staggered inside and died soon afterwards in front of his wife and children. Mendes had long feared he would be murdered.

His murderers thought that by striking during the Christmas holidays his killing would go unnoticed. They were amazed by the worldwide shock and anger created by the elimination of someone they saw as just another troublesome union leader. Several of Chico's predecessors had met a similar end without the outside world taking notice, but this time the world's eyes were on the Amazon.

Chico's murder brought into bloody relief a war being waged by Brazil's large landowners. Hundreds of poor people are murdered every year as they try to defend the forests and land which are home and livelihood to them. His death is just one example of the violence meted out to poor communities throughout the Third World for standing up for a just share of nature's resources. Chico

Mendes knew that he risked death for his stand. Just weeks before his death he described the dangers for himself and other activists:

We are all on the death list of the UDR's [União Democratica Rural-ista, the landowners' organization] assassination squads. Here in Xapuri, these squads are led by Darli and Alvarino Alves da Silva, owners of the Parana and other ranches round here. They lead a gang of about thirty gunmen – I say thirty because we've counted them as they patrol around the town . . . Now they're both in hiding and have said they'll only give themselves up when I'm dead . . . We are sure this will be the landowners' main tactic from now on.[1]

The local police took no action immediately after the murder. But the unprecedented international public outcry that followed prompted the Brazilian authorities to arrest Darli Alves da Silva for organizing the killing, and one of his sons, Darci, for carrying it out. Although the UDR denies involvement in the murder, two UDR lawyers defended the accused.[2]

KILLING THE DREAM

Chico Mendes was killed for campaigning, in his words, to 'stop the deforestation which is threatening the Amazon and all human life on this planet'.[3] By organizing community protests like *empates* (non-violent stand-offs with the chainsaw gangs sent by landlords to clear the forest), he helped to save thousands of acres of forest. But these protests were not a blanket opposition to change or to all economic development. The aim was not to turn the Amazon into 'some kind of sanctuary that nobody could touch,' said Mendes. He was struggling to protect the forest as a way of defending the livelihoods of local poor people – rubber-tappers, Indians and fisher-folk – dependent on harvesting the rubber, nuts, fibres, oils and fish in a way that left the forest intact for future generations. 'My dream is to see this entire forest conserved,' he said, 'because we know it can guarantee the future of all the people who live in it. Not only that, I believe that in a few years the Amazon can become an economically viable region not only for us, but for the nation as a whole, for all of humanity, and the whole planet.'[4]

To the big landowners, however, this was an unacceptable dream. It stood in the way of profits and 'progress'. They wanted to raze the forest to make way for cattle pasture and commercial farms, so Chico Mendes, and the movement to which he belonged, had to be stopped. The cattle barons enforced their own 'dream', using money and murder. As Mendes explained:

> The landowners use all the economic power at their disposal. They bribe the authorities; it's common knowledge that they've bought off the [government's] Brazilian Forestry Development Institute [IBDF] staff in the Amazon region. They also use the law . . . They accuse rubber-tappers of trespassing when we try and stop the deforestation. They turn to the courts for support and protection, claiming the land is private property. But the rubber-tappers have been here for centuries![5]

When landowners resort to killing to get their way, the courts always side with the rich, he said, recounting one example from many:

> The police even refused to carry out an inquiry into who shot the rubber-tappers who were camped outside the IBDF offices on 27 May 1988. The gunmen were recognized and are well known round here and witnesses have made statements to the police, but they haven't done a thing.[6]

Powerful landowners getting away with murder is nothing new in Brazil. They have not hesitated to use force when the landless dare to demand enough land to grow food or local people try to resist their attempts to make a quick buck at the expense of the forest and soil. For many years the landowners relied on the military, who ruled Brazil until 1985, to turn a blind eye to their execution of 'justice'.

DECLARING WAR ON THE FOREST

The overthrow of the centre-left civilian government of João Goulart in the US-backed coup of April 1964 ushered in twenty-one years of repressive military rule. Staunch allies of the landowners, the military abandoned Goulart's plans for land reform and suppressed the peasant leagues who had been campaigning for it. The generals'

'Operation Amazonia', a vast plan to occupy and 'develop' Brazil's forest interior, encouraged entrepreneurs – through subsidies, cheap land and new roads – to set up large ranches on forest land. Land speculation on the back of these state incentives was rife, unleashing an environmental holocaust in Amazonia.

The policy's original aims were partly economic – to provide cheap beef for the industrial cities and for export, as well as to spearhead future development of the region. But the military regime also embraced the Amazon plan as providing a sense of national purpose and as an expression of national security doctrines. 'Amazonian occupation will proceed as though we are waging a strategically conducted war,' proclaimed Brazilian dictator General Castello Branco.[7] The ranchers were to pacify and occupy the Amazon, both to secure Brazil's frontiers against its neighbours and to pre-empt communist subversion from within.

The military's style of development won warm approval from Washington. Brazil's military coup was recalled as 'the single most decisive victory of freedom in the mid-twentieth century' by Lincoln Gordon, US Ambassador to Brazil at the time of the coup.[8] The United States supported Brazil's military government as a stalwart of its 'Alliance for Progress' in Latin America in the 1960s. The programme was mounted to support governments friendly to US economic interests and to counter 'communist subversion' in the region with a mixture of economic and military aid. Brazil received one of the region's largest and most sustained programmes of US military assistance for equipment, arms and training, designed to strengthen the police and army's techniques of counter-insurgency and to maintain 'internal order'.

The end of military rule has not, however, put a stop to the landowners getting their way by force, as shown by the rising numbers of killings, including that of Chico Mendes. The UDR has used big money and powerful lobbying to thwart the possibility of real land reform, one of the great promises of the return to civilian government.

The forest people's fight for their livelihoods parallels other conflicts where the majority are kept from a fair share of the country's natural wealth by a small minority who protect their interests by armed force. The poor are not only subject to violence as they try to defend the environment on which their livelihoods rely, but they and their environment are the first to suffer the effects of conflict. The ensuing environmental stress and resource conflict further exacerbate political and social tensions, as exemplified in Central America.

CONFLICT IN THE ISTHMUS

Central America is scarred by this vicious circle of poverty, ecological destruction and armed conflict. In this 'slender waist of tears' more than 150,000 people have been killed in political violence and civil war since 1978.[9] Violence has destroyed farms, crops and factories and starved the economy of resources that have been squandered on the military.

The cycle has been fuelled further from outside. Economic development, poor communities and their environment have all been sacrificed in the name of stamping out 'Soviet–Cuban subversion', as the United States describes any challenge to its traditional control of events in the region. To retain control, the US has allocated over five billion dollars in military and economic aid to the regimes in the region over the last decade.[10] Peace remains a distant prospect while the roots of the conflict go unaddressed.

LANDED CONFLICT

Many Central American farms are too small to feed a family (as many as 88 per cent in Guatemala, and 92 per cent in El Salvador, according to one report).[11] Alongside vast under-used farms, tiny peasant plots on poor, steep land barely stave off hunger, even when farmed for all their worth. Combined with rapid deforestation by large landowners for cattle ranching,[12] over-cultivation of these tiny plots is producing land degradation of crisis proportions in Central America. The fundamental causes of the present conflict are at once environmental and political, stemming from unequal access to, and distribution of, natural resources – particularly land.

El Salvador suffers the worst soil erosion and most skewed land distribution in the region. Nearly all its original deciduous forests have gone, all the major watersheds are degraded and over half the country's land mass is facing serious erosion.[13] Soil cover in parts of the Cordillera Norte, the northern mountains, 'is now almost entirely eroded, with deep gullies and exposed rocks in many places making productive use of the land impossible without extensive rehabilitation'.[14] As the soil washes away, so does the food supply. It is wasting away, not because peasant farmers are ignorant of the right methods, but because they are deprived of enough land to survive on. Only one in ten people has access to clean drinking water and half the children die before their fifth birthday. As one Salvadorean environmentalist says, 'We're not going to resolve the ecological crisis if we don't resolve the social crisis.'[15]

El Salvador's peasant majority are crowded on to the poorest, most ecologically vulnerable land because 2 per cent of the people – known as the 'Fourteen Families' – control 60 per cent of the land,[16] particularly the flattest and most fertile land for growing cotton, sugar and coffee, and for raising livestock. Thousands of poor migrant workers journey across the country to find work in the hot cotton fields of El Salvador's Pacific coast. Added to the ordeal of long hours and poor pay is the threat of pesticide poisoning from the crop-duster planes that fly overhead as they work and from the water sources and soil which are dangerously contaminated.

As a leader of the National Association of Farm Workers (ANTA) explained:

The owners think of their own interests and not the interests of the workers. So even if a different kind of pesticide application would be safer, the owner won't adopt it if there are cheaper ways for them to spray . . . In El Salvador there isn't any protective law for workers with regard to pesticides and other workplace conditions.[17]

Trade unions organizing protests against these conditions face repression. In 1987 ANTA's Secretary General, Jesus Hernandez Martinez, was kidnapped by the army and tortured. His body was only found weeks later.

To add insult to the poor's injury, big chunks of fertile land on the large farms are under-used. In El Salvador up to 46 per cent of the land on large farms is used for pasture (instead of crops), and an additional one third is totally unused.[18] As in other parts of Central America, the system leads to a human, economic and ecological madness in which the ecologically best land is used less intensively than the poorest soils. The poor are forced on to marginal land which is unsuitable for agriculture. Today some ·campesinos (peasant farmers) are tilling land so steep that they must tie themselves to a stake so that they do not fall down the hillside as they work. The ANTA leader spells out their dilemma:

What does a poor campesino do? He starts working what little land he does have year after year without letting it lie fallow to recuperate. Soon it doesn't produce and becomes barren: the soil is gone. This isn't the fault of the farmer, but the fault of those who own the land but refuse to make it available to those who need it.[19]

Poverty, protest and ultimately armed uprising have developed in response. Moves for reform have been continuously frustrated, brutally cut short by the government and the army. The result is that, like other countries in the region, El Salvador runs 'red with the blood of hundreds of thousands killed and tortured in order to stave off social change'.[20]

THE ECOLOGY OF WAR

By conservative estimates, between 1979 and 1987 68,000 Salvadoreans met violent deaths, two thirds of them civilians murdered by death squads and the security forces.[21] The murders are not just random killings. As Congressman Miller of the US Congressional Task Force, sent to El Salvador after the killing of six Jesuit priests in November 1989, stated:

The fact of the matter is, this is part of the policy of the military to go out and kill people who they disagree with or they believe are a threat to them . . . They are a very efficient killing machine and thanks to us they are very well financed.[22]

In the countryside the army has directed the war against the civilian population and their environment in guerrilla-held areas. According to the classic maxim of guerrilla war, the fighters depend on local people's support as fish do on the sea. US military advisers counselled the Salvadorean army to borrow a tactical leaf out of their Vietnam book: they must drain this sea. Ground sweeps by US-directed elite Salvadorean army units have been supplemented by intense aerial bombardment. The Salvadorean air force has dropped more than 3,000 tons of US-made bombs in the countryside – leaving it scarred with craters and setting off great forest fires.[23] US planes from the Palmerola base in Honduras provide reconnaissance which enables more accurate locating of human targets. Napalm, white phosphorus and fragmentation bombs (anti-personnel weapons) have been reported to have been used to inflict maximum destruction on people, crops, livestock and forest – deemed to be the 'sea' of potential support. People, their land and crops have all become legitimate targets.

In 1988 community leaders from the region of Morazan, where 4,800 acres of pine forests were destroyed by bombing and fires, placed an advertisement in the national newspaper El Mundo appealing for an end to the ecological devastation wrought by the military:

We are very worried by the grave damage from the devastating forest fires caused by aerial bombing and indiscriminate mortar fire, as well as by soldiers carrying out patrols and operations. The armed forces commonly burn the forest during the dry season, accelerating the destruction of the resources of the zone, including natural forests, logging areas, coffee crops and food crops. Because they have deforested large areas in our zone, the scorched earth and bombing campaigns have notably affected rainfall patterns. The length of the rainy season has shortened, and the levels of streams and rivers have dropped. This situation is becoming more critical, and we are worried now because it is affecting us directly. Our crops have diminished and this worsens our already agonizing economic situation.[24]

In El Salvador, the violence has clear ecological roots. This is the most densely populated mainland country in the Western hemisphere and faces a serious shortage of resources. It is not merely a question of 'over-population', but is due to extremely unequal landholding and the expansion of commercial agriculture.

The conflicts are not amongst the peasants themselves, but between the poor and the larger landholders. The destruction is exacerbated by the scorched-earth policy of the military. Environmental problems are a result of conflict and serve to intensify those conflicts. Violence cannot break this vicious circle, but merely deepens the ecological crisis and fuels the poverty behind the conflict.

It is scarcely surprising, then, that over a million Salvadoreans (a fifth of the nation's total population) have fled from the fighting – about 600,000 within the country and another half million as refugees in neighbouring countries.[25] The military 'solution' can never work without tackling the underlying roots of the problem. Central American history has shown that further 'development' rooted in economic inequality will only worsen the already existing environmental crisis. As a recent USAID report on Guatemala said, 'it is the poor who are most affected by environmental problems and environmental problems are often the result of poverty ... the only way to break this spiral is to infuse a change into the system'.[26] Meaningful agrarian reform is the best hope of bringing sustainable development, of providing real security rather than repression and death squads.

UNCLE SAM DRAWS THE LINE

The United States has put El Salvador at the centre of its military policy for Central America. The social revolution spawned by the mounting pressures of land hunger, environmental degradation and poverty has been written off as part of Soviet designs within the region and used to justify propping up the Salvadorean regime. The US pumped more than three billion dollars' worth of military and 'economic' aid into El Salvador during the 1980s.[27] (A report prepared for Congress showed that 69 per cent of 'economic' aid had in fact been used directly or indirectly for the war.)[28] Former Secretary of State Alexander Haig argued for 'drawing the line' against 'communist aggression' in El Salvador on the basis that:

What we are watching is a four-phased operation of which phase one has already been completed – the seizure of Nicaragua. Next is El Salvador, to be followed by Honduras and Guatemala . . . a hit-list, if you will, for the ultimate take-over of Central America.[29]

To sustain the idea of imported revolution, the Sandinista government of Nicaragua was constantly accused of being the conduit for weapons going to the rebels in El Salvador. In Britain, Prime Minister Margaret Thatcher also repeated the charge that Nicaragua was supporting 'attempts to destabilize democratic governments elsewhere in Central America'.[30] But according to David MacMichael, a former CIA analyst on the issue, 'the evidence for this arms flow is almost totally lacking'.[31] (In fact much more evidence exists that the rebels get US-made weapons from corrupt members of the Salvadorean army and similar sources within Honduras, as well as Costa Rica and Mexico.) When he tried to report this fact to his superiors, he found them 'fixated' with the 'Moscow–Havana–Managua pipeline', so that 'often when a piece of finished intelligence went out, the evidence would be so thin, so unconvincing, that you would have to say that the conclusions are more or less dictated by what the policy-makers want to hear'.[32]

EAST–WEST GOES SOUTH

Central America has formed the centrepiece of US military concern in the Third World, but was also part of a wider strategy in which the Third World was seen through East–West tinted spectacles. Reviving the old Cold War theory of 'containment militarism', US strategists said the Soviets were extending their domination through fomenting Third World revolutions which would spread and eventually surround and dominate the United States. President Reagan said:

Let us not delude ourselves. The Soviet Union underlies all the unrest that is going on. If they weren't engaged in this game of dominoes, there wouldn't be any hot spots in the world.[33]

US hawks pressed for a more concerted strategy to 'roll back' this threat. In part, this included a renewed commitment by the

United States to direct military intervention: the 1983 invasion of Grenada, the bombing of Libya in 1986, the ill-fated action in Lebanon in 1983–4 (withdrawn after the death of 230 US marines in a bomb attack), the naval deployment directed against Iran during the Gulf War and the invasion of Panama in 1989. In all these instances, except Grenada, the US received a varying degree of diplomatic or military support from allies in Europe (notably Britain and France) and elsewhere (especially Israel).

A more important part of the strategy was indirect military action in the Third World through active support for 'anti-Communist' forces wherever they could be found. A host of pro-Western governments received renewed support, regardless of their human rights record, particularly those fighting internal wars against guerrillas – from El Salvador to Morocco, from the Philippines to Zaire. At least as important was the strategy of supporting, or instigating where deemed necessary, anti-government guerrillas – notably in support for Jonas Savimbi's Unita forces in Angola, the Contras in Nicaragua, the Mojahedin in Afghanistan (the biggest of the support programmes, running at between a half and one billion dollars a year) and, incredibly, the guerrilla coalition in Cambodia dominated by the infamous Pol Pot's genocidal Khmer Rouge.

A further element was the stress on long-drawn-out and supposedly 'low-level' wars, known as 'low intensity conflicts'. As a White House document explained in 1988:

Our own military forces have demonstrated capabilities to engage in low intensity conflict, and these capabilities have improved substantially over recent years. But the most appropriate application of US military power is usually indirect through security assistance – training, advisory help, logistics support, and the supply of essential military support equipment. Recipients of such assistance bear the primary responsibility for promoting their own security interests with the US aid provided. Our program of assistance to El Salvador illustrates a successful indirect application of US military power.[34]

BRITAIN PITCHES IN

US allies often give support for such action. There was outrage in Britain in 1989 when it became known that Britain, along with China, France, Thailand, Singapore, Malaysia and the United States, was giving direct military assistance to the Khmer Rouge-dominated guerrillas fighting to overthrow the Cambodian government. *Jane's Defence Weekly* revealed that since 1985 British army officers, veterans of the Falklands conflict, had been training guerrillas in basic battle skills and 'hit-and-run' sabotage tactics at secret bases in Thailand.[35] In 1987 the Foreign Secretary admitted to Parliament, following previous denials, that there had been clandestine sales of British Blowpipe anti-aircraft missiles to the Afghan guerrillas. The then Foreign Office Minister (and present aid minister), Lynda Chalker, justified the sale, saying: 'We have to strengthen the ability to resist aggression in the hope of protecting Western interests.'[36]

WAR AND FAMINE

Despite the thaw in East–West relations and some moves towards the resolution of regional conflicts in the Third World where there is superpower involvement, many of these conflicts have continued or even intensified. Despite its troubles at home, the Soviet Union is still involved in some Third World trouble-spots. In Ethiopia, for example, it continues to support (albeit on less favourable terms) the military regime of Colonel Haile-Mariam Mengistu as it ruthlessly prosecutes its internal war against Eritrean, Tigrayan and Oromo claims to national and cultural self-determination. These wars have crippled the agriculture and economy of Ethiopia. The government has been propped up by an estimated six billion dollars of Soviet aid, much of it military, and arms imports accounted for about 60 per cent of total imports from 1980 to 1986.[37] The fighting has greatly hampered relief efforts and forced thousands into exile as refugees in neighbouring countries, notably Sudan. It has also blocked development which would have tackled the drought and prevented it from turning into famine.

Elsewhere the West is taking what opportunities it can to push its advantage in the face of whatever concessions the Soviet Union makes. Western support for the Khmer Rouge-dominated guerrilla coalition continues, despite Vietnamese withdrawal from Cambodia. The United States renewed vigorous support in 1989 for the Unita guerrillas in Angola,[38] and also resisted full dismantling of the Contras – despite moves by Central American governments to do so – until after the election defeat of the Sandinistas in 1990. In Afghanistan, hailed as a model for the superpower resolution of regional conflicts, Western support for the Mojahedin continues, despite Soviet withdrawal.

NEW THINKING?

While these examples show that it is premature to proclaim the end of the Cold War in the Third World, there are also hopeful signs of movement away from the era of the 'Third World wars' which have killed many millions of people and have been inflamed by the interference of East and West for forty years. The reforms of Mikhail Gorbachev in the Soviet Union, far-reaching changes in eastern Europe, and moves towards nuclear and conventional disarmament have radically shaken the assumptions of international policy-makers. Although much of the discussion has focused on the dramatic political and military implications for Europe, the developments have also brought hope of a less conflictual approach to the Third World by both East and West.

GORBACHEV, GLASNOST AND THE THIRD WORLD

Gorbachev fostered 'new thinking' in Soviet approaches to international policy, including dealings with the Third World. Glasnost has also led to stronger internal criticism of past foreign policy – notably over the Soviet invasion of Afghanistan. Soviet foreign policy planners increasingly uncouple Third World conflict from the superpower relationship – focusing on factors such as ethnic conflict and religion, rather than 'western imperialism' as in the past. The willingness of the Soviet Union to accept compromise in the Third World, particularly in a number of long-running regional conflicts with superpower entanglement, has been heavily influenced by the practical necessity of concentrating its attention nearer to home on the challenges of restructuring its own affairs and coping with the changes in eastern Europe.

FROM EAST–WEST TO NORTH–SOUTH?

The Soviet Union has therefore brought some pressure to bear on its Third World allies to resolve a number of internal and international conflicts. Soviet diplomats pressed for rapid withdrawal of Cuban troops from Angola and the closure of ANC bases there to speed up a UN agreement to end South Africa's occupation of Namibia, which in turn led to its independence in 1990. The Soviets also encouraged the Vietnamese to withdraw from Cambodia in 1989, which they had occupied after driving out Pol Pot's Khmer Rouge. The Soviets themselves withdrew from Afghanistan in 1989 following the signing of the Geneva Accords in April 1988. In the Horn of Africa the hostility between Western-backed Somalia and Soviet-backed Ethiopia, which had rumbled on since the 1977–8 Ogaden war, was greatly reduced and Cuban forces stationed on the border were pulled out.

Elsewhere there have been hopeful signs that superpower rapprochement could help resolve some of the most deeply entrenched and long-running conflicts. The United States has increased its pressure on Israel to negotiate with the Palestinians following the PLO's recognition of Israel, a conciliatory move encouraged by the Soviets. In the uneasy tension that has continued between North and South Korea since the Korean war of 1954, the Chinese and Soviets have been pressing the North to continue negotiation.

In the Western defence establishment there are mixed reactions to such moves. Some insist that it is still too early to proclaim the Soviet threat over – in the Third World as much as anywhere else. A Pentagon policy document for the 1990s, leaked to the press in February 1990, stated that 'fundamental Soviet objectives in the Third World do not appear to have changed'.[39] Others do concede that the theme of the Soviet threat to the Third World is becoming politically and publicly less credible, and are urging military withdrawal from Third World conflict. However, in some quarters there is a growing belief that the greatest threats to national security now come from the Third World itself. As the 'Soviet threat' recedes, it is possible that a fresh *raison d'être* for military power and military action in the Third World will be forged around a new official agenda of security threats visited on the North by the South – drugs, fundamentalism, terrorism and what are dubbed 'rogue states'.

The fact that East and West are increasingly taking a joint approach to Third World conflict creates enormous potential for resolving those long-standing conflicts wedded to superpower rivalry, but it also carries new dangers, for there are growing Third World worries that it may take the form of joint control – a kind of condominium. Some fear that the destructive confrontation of capitalist West and communist East may be being broken down only to be replaced by a confrontation between rich North – combining the old Cold War foes – and poor South.

Things are unlikely to be so clear-cut. The remaining tensions between East and West should not be underestimated, nor the determination of the superpowers' Third World allies – whether governments or guerrillas – to resist having their own agenda simply dictated to them from outside. Nevertheless, calls for East–West cooperation are now emerging.

Former British government minister Norman Tebbit recently warned of new threats to 'national security and prosperity':

> As the shadow of superpower war is lifting, the darkness of international crime, drugs, civil unrest, civil war and terrorism will spread widely through the world. *There is common cause to be made with our Cold War allies and adversaries alike to deal with these dangers* and it is in our interest to do so.[40]

He called for a 'British initiative to develop new understanding to deal with the new dangers', and described how 'shared concerns at the possibility of the drug cartel buying virtual control of one of the Caribbean mini-states, should make Anglo–French–US military action possible in that region'.

CANAL MOVES

The shift away from the 'Soviet threat' as the main rationale for intervention was highlighted dramatically on 19 December 1989 when President Bush ordered 24,000 US troops into Panama to arrest President Manuel Noriega on drugs charges and to send 'a clear signal that the United States is serious in its determination that those charged with promoting the distribution of drugs cannot escape the scrutiny of justice'.[41] The move was vigorously endorsed by the British Prime Minister. The massive military operation which left as many as 7,000 Panamanians dead, 13,000 homeless and caused two billion dollars' worth of damage was, however, not only about apprehending, in President Bush's words, a 'drug-dealing dictator'.[42]

Although it is hard to doubt his extensive drug links, there is much evidence that up until a few years before the invasion the United States turned a blind eye to Noriega's involvement in the drug trade, in return for his help in arming and training the US-backed Contras in their attempts to overthrow the Sandinista government in Nicaragua.[43] Noriega had been on the CIA pay-roll since the 1960s when, as an army major, he was paid $50 a month plus a bottle of whiskey for the information he provided. By the mid-1980s he was earning thousands of dollars, both from the CIA and the US Drug Enforcement Agency. Drugs were patently not the real reason why the United States finally acted, nor was it Noriega's disregard for democracy, bearing in mind the long history of US support for Latin American dictatorships deemed to be defending Western interests, such as the bloody Somoza dynasty in Nicaragua.

The key difference was that he had turned so decisively against his former masters. In the words of the Mexican writer Carlos Fuentes, Noriega's crime was to be the 'tin soldier who started talking back'.[44] His populist, nationalist stance worried the United States. President Bush became frustrated as Noriega outwitted his attempts to remove him, and grew sensitive to charges of lacking decisiveness in foreign policy, particularly after a botched attempted coup to overthrow Noriega in October 1989. The invasion was launched just weeks before the first stage of the US handback of the

Canal to Panama, to be completed by the year 2000 under the Canal Treaty of 1977. The prospect of having a troublesome go-it-alone leader in the lead-up to the transition was clearly not one the United States relished.

THE DRUGS WAR

However high on the list of reasons for the US invasion of Panama was the excuse of Noriega's drug-running, countries throughout Latin America condemned the invasion. They criticized the US approach of attempting a military 'solution' to prevent the supply of cocaine from Latin America. Reports that the United States was planning to mount a naval blockade against Colombia to prevent drug shipments sparked outrage in Latin America. In addition, the United States – together with countries like Britain – appeared to prefer giving assistance for more military-style programmes, such as aerial spraying of fields to eradicate the coca crop.

In reality, attacking crops is not the answer to the drugs crisis. What fuels the trade is the demand in rich countries. Furthermore, any solution which fails to give alternatives to growing coca to the rural poor in Latin America will fail to halt drugs production in years to come. It is too easy to pass the blame for the drugs problem in rich countries on to producers in poor countries, while ignoring the fact that drugs are one of the few crops that provide an economic return for farmers whose main concern is survival. One of the principal alternative crops for Colombia would be coffee, but, ironically, predatory action by consumer countries such as the United States has undermined the International Coffee Agreement that had stabilized and supported world prices. The Agreement collapsed in 1989 and coffee prices fell to a fourteen-year low.

The important new feature of the drugs war is that it represents Great Power military involvement in the Third World outside the prism of East–West relations. It is significant that although the Soviet Union condemned the US invasion of Panama, it was not allowed to endanger the improving relations with the United States. Many observers asked whether military action in Panama, not justified in terms of the 'Soviet threat', was a one-off or whether it marked a renewed readiness to take direct military action in the Third World – against a new set of threats to 'national security'.

GUNNING FOR BLACK GOLD

Western military involvement in the Gulf demonstrates the same web of pious and confusing double-talk that surrounds military action over the drugs issue in Panama or the alleged Soviet threat in Central America. Behind this double-talk there is a growing potential for conflict stemming from competition for resources. Revolutionary Iran embodied the long-perceived Third World threat to the West's oil and strategic raw materials. President Reagan himself claimed:

> Iran's geography gives it a critical position from which adversaries could interfere with oil flows from the Arab states that border the Persian Gulf. Apart from that geography, Iran's oil deposits are important to the long-term health of the world economy.[45]

RESOURCE CONFLICTS

We have already seen, taking the cases of Brazil and Central America, the way in which environmental destruction and poverty can underlie conflict and even civil war. The rich and powerful enforce their monopoly over environmental resources at the expense of those who rely on them for their survival. Unsustainable forms of development create conflict which often causes further environmental destruction. This may be true even if the rhetoric focuses on other factors, such as 'the Soviet threat' or 'US imperialism'. As the sources of tension between states become less linked to East–West rivalry, environmentally based sources of conflict may take greater prominence. As the Brundtland Report says:

> Nations have often fought to assert or resist control over raw materials, energy supplies, land, river basins, sea passages, and other key environmental resources. Such conflicts are likely to increase as these resources become scarcer and competition for them increases.[46]

As environmental capital is further depleted by the demands of Western consumer society, we face the growing threat of resource wars in which rich countries will enforce their 'right' to the resources of the Third World at the low prices they are used to paying. Poor countries may be cast as having an illegitimate stranglehold over vital commodities, which rich countries will take by force.

In the 1970s, doomsday predictions of the imminent exhaustion of key natural resources added an extra note of alarm to 'national security' concerns. Instead of taking the path of conservation of resources and reduction of wasteful economic growth, the hawks' answer was to prepare to fight to safeguard access. Belligerency over supplies of oil and other resources mounted in Western business and military circles throughout the 1970s and became influential in the interventionist thinking of the 1980s. In 1981, former US Secretary of State Alexander Haig sounded a warning:

The escalating setbacks to our interests abroad, increasing lawlessness and terrorism, and the so-called wars of national liberation are putting in jeopardy our ability to influence world events . . . and to assure access to raw materials.[47]

He said that 'disruption from abroad threatens a more vulnerable West as we draw energy and raw material from regions in which the throes of rapid change and conflict prevail'.[48] He warned that the 'era of the "resource war"' had arrived.

Despite the easing of immediate concern over resources (commodity prices have fallen dramatically and economically vulnerable Third World economies have been forced to sell their raw materials at any price) securing their supply remains an important part of Western military strategy. A 1988 White House report setting out the reasons for the use of 'low intensity conflict' in the Third World claims, for example, that:

In mineral-rich southern Africa, insurgencies, economic instability and apartheid, as well as ethnic tribal conflicts, pose potential threats to the extraction of essential raw materials and their export to industries in the West and Japan. The conflicts endemic in the region are exacerbated by the activity of the Soviet Union and its surrogates.[49]

IRAN—IRAQ: TAKING SIDES

Sabre-rattling over Gulf oil dates back to the Arab oil embargo of 1973, which had raised the spectre that Western industry, consumers and oil companies could be brought to their knees by a disruption in oil supplies. The Gulf War of the 1980s, the most destructive conflict of recent years, killed a million and a half people. Many of them were soldiers, but thousands of civilians also died in missile attacks during the 'war of the cities'.[50]

The war has been portrayed as a private Middle Eastern quarrel, but Western countries and the Soviet Union played an important direct and indirect role. In part, this took the form of their arms dealers making cynical profits from the war by selling, legally and illegally, equipment to both sides.[51] Britain was one of fifty-three countries, many of them signatories of United Nations resolutions calling for peace in the Gulf, to sell military equipment to Iran and Iraq during the war, according to the Stockholm International Peace Research Institute (SIPRI).[52]

Outsiders also took a more direct military role during the Gulf conflict. More than eighty Western warships (forty-five from the United States and nearly forty from western Europe) were deployed in the Gulf.[53] Officially the force was not there to take sides but was to act as an impartial 'police force' maintaining freedom of navigation for commercial shipping. However, Iran became the main object of Western naval action as it was widely blamed by Western governments as the main perpetrator of attacks on neutral shipping. Domestic political and public support for the anti-Iranian military action by the United States and Europe was also strengthened by the Iranian regime's reputation, undoubtedly well-earned, for brutality.

In fact, Iraq not only initiated the whole Gulf conflict by its invasion of Iran in 1980, but also started the attacks on oil tankers and commercial ships. Iraq was the main perpetrator of these attacks. Of the 173 attacks on such ships between March 1984 and March 1987, 70 per cent were carried out by the Iraqis.[54] This was part of a deliberate Iraqi policy. The aim was partly to disrupt Iran's oil exports and undermine its ability to finance the war effort, but there were other motives, as the *Sunday Times* reported at the time:

Most observers agree that Baghdad also aims to provoke the Iranians into retaliating against third parties, thus drawing outside forces into the conflict.[55]

Despite claims to 'neutrality', *Western warships only ever 're-taliated' against Iranian targets.* The contradiction between the reality of Iraqi policy and the anti-Iranian orientation of Western military action, despite its guise of impartiality, is illustrated by the incident in 1987 when the frigate USS *Stark* was hit by an Iraqi Exocet missile, killing thirty-seven crew members. President Reagan readily accepted Iraqi apologies. In a classic piece of double-think he went on to paint the 'barbaric country' of Iran as the real villain of the piece and, in a prelude to the decision to re-flag Kuwaiti tankers under Western colours, lashed out at Iran for interfering with Gulf shipping. In April the following year the United States did not show the same inclination to excuse Iran from mistakes as they had done over the *Stark*; when damage was inflicted on a US ship by a mine alleged to have been lain by Iran, US and Iraqi forces mounted a joint revenge attack on Iranian ships and oil platforms.

The myth of impartiality was revealed as the Western naval force sided against Iran with Iraq and its allies. Furthermore, any moral backing for the Western deployment based on the repugnance of the Iranian regime wore thin in the face of the human rights record of the country which the naval force was bailing out. A report by the human rights group Middle East Watch says that Iraq, under the rule of Saddam Hussein,

... is a well-organized police state and its government is one of the most brutal and repressive in power today ... With the exception of freedom of worship, the Iraqi government denies its citizens all fundamental human rights and freedoms, and ruthlessly suppresses even the smallest gestures of dissent.[56]

A GROWING EUROPEAN ROLE?

A second significant feature of the Gulf War was that it demonstrated a much higher profile than in recent years for European countries in military action in the Third World. Seven months after the ceasefire in the Gulf, the military magazine *Jane's Defence Weekly* argued that;

On a strategic level, the Gulf crisis appeared to reinforce the case for Western nations to maintain forces for out of [NATO] area (OOA) operations. These could become increasingly important as East–West tensions in Europe decrease.[57]

Western Europe maintained a coordinated fleet of up to forty ships in the Gulf war zone (from France, Britain, Italy, Belgium and the Netherlands), roughly the same number as the United States. In fact, as one senior British naval official was keen to point out, 'We were there before the Americans,' referring to the Royal Navy's Armilla Patrol which went into the Gulf in 1981.[58] Similarly, the French were forthright on the need for European involvement, reportedly resisting one US move to scale down the size of the Gulf operation in 1988. Europe's collective muscle-flexing surprised many people. Cesare Merlini, director of the Italian Institute for International Affairs, noted at the time, 'You would have been dismissed as a dreamer six months ago if you had predicted Europe would be in the Gulf in such force.'[59]

The move was viewed as very significant in the United States. One Pentagon official said, 'A generation gap is emerging with an emerging generation of European officials challenging the cautious approach that has prevailed'.[60] Whether this indicates a general trend towards a renewed European military role in the Third World as European unity progresses is premature to say. But many find the Gulf precedent worrying.

More widely, the role of Europe, as well as Japan, in Third World conflict in the decade has been broadly twofold. First, to give tacit or active diplomatic support for renewed US adventurism in the Third World. Britain, with its 'special relationship' with the United States, has generally been one of the leading supporters of American policy in the Third World. In addition, Britain's former colonial role gives it an important relationship with the Third World within the NATO alliance. Britain has spoken up for US Third World military involvement in areas such as Central America. It has also concretely facilitated US military action. The US planes which bombed

Libya took off from air bases in the UK. France, the other big former colonial power of recent history, is not a member of NATO, though it has cooperated with the United States while staging interventions in former colonies, such as Chad, in recent years. Second, some European countries have their own forces for direct intervention, including Italy and France's 'Force d'Action Rapide' (FAR). Britain, too, has developed its own capability.

THE JOINT FORCE HEADQUARTERS

During the 1980s, Britain set up its own 'go anywhere anytime' Third World intervention force. The aim, in the words of its former commander Lieutenant-General Sir Geoffrey Howlett, was to:

... make it quite clear that Britain has both the capability and the resolve to deploy beyond the NATO area either in response to a request for assistance by an endangered friend or if we see our interests threatened.[61]

These forces can be deployed at 'very, very short notice', according to Lieutenant-General Howlett, over long distances, for anything up to six months in land-, sea- and air-based operations.

The units involved have been given tours of duty in Belize (formerly British Honduras, in Central America) specifically to afford them 'the opportunity to acquire jungle training, get used to hot climates and operate outside a NATO environment' as a preparation for possible out-of-area deployment, says Lieutenant-General Howlett. The Joint Force Headquarters (JFHQ) have also carried out UK-based and overseas exercises. In July 1984 they simulated an exercise in which a friendly African government asked for Britain's help to put down an internal revolution by sending in British airborne troops.[62]

In November 1986, while the Iran–Iraq war still raged, 5,000 JFHQ troops carried out the major 'Swift Sword' joint exercise with Iraq's ally Oman, just twenty or so miles across the sea from Iran. It was altogether a 'bloody good exercise', according to Major Rick Ginn of 5 Airborne Brigade, in which 'we learned we could deploy long distances with our kit and perform very well'.[63] He added: 'The opportunity to train in that sort of terrain for the brigade is perhaps unique, an area, or one like it, we could be fighting in at the nod of a head.' The operation was part of the long-standing role of the British army in Oman and other Gulf states. In fact until 1987 the head of the Omani armed forces was a British general on loan. British forces played a major role in putting down the Dhofari rebellion against the autocratic rule of the Sultan of Oman in the 1970s and an SAS regiment has played an ongoing role in security force training.[64]

The prospect of Oman as an actual battleground is not that far-fetched, given the way Western powers have raised it – and other conservative Gulf states – in the military stakes. Real-life external enemies which the Sultan of Oman and his Western allies might confront could include not only Iran to the north, but South Yemen to the west (depending on its international realignment following the unification of North and South Yemen in 1990). If a serious threat to his rule were to emerge, Britain and the United States might intervene to protect him as a key regional ally; regional and international conflict could escalate.

PEACE DIVIDEND

There has been something of a peaceful pay-off from better East–West relations for Third World conflicts long aggravated by super-power involvement. But this pay-off must be capitalized on in order to redirect efforts away from conflict and militarization towards the vast challenges of poverty and environmental destruction. With the superpower grip loosened, international forums such as the United Nations can start to take a more effective role in turning peace proposals into reality. Global changes do offer possibilities of positive gains. Fewer wars are being fought in the world at this moment than at any time in the last half-century. Demilitarization could bring a valuable peace dividend, a fact already realized by the Soviet Union. It now recognizes that spending the equivalent of nearly 20 per cent of national output on the military has handicapped the country's ability to feed and provide for its citizens.[65] The United States is also likely to curb its spending boom, with talks of arms cuts of 50 per cent over the next ten years. The scale of the human and environmental challenge facing the world makes it imperative that military spending be diverted to positive uses.

WASTED RESOURCES

Annual military spending is still greater than the combined income of half of humanity. Production of arms is a waste of human and physical resources, a form of consumption, not productive investment. Even the diversion of quite a small fraction of military spending could achieve significant benefits. For example, the World Health Organisation waged a twenty-year war against smallpox and eventually eradicated the disease. The cost of this remarkable battle was the same as the world spends on its arms in just one hour of every day of every year. Military spending in the poor world appears particularly perverse. Since the early 1960s, military spending in poor countries has increased fivefold[66] – nearly twice as much as the growth in income. According to UNICEF, governments of poor countries on average now devote half their annual expenditure to the unproductive maintenance of the military and to servicing debt – more than \$400 a year for each family in the Third World.[67] This is a scandalous waste of resources, scientific skills and scarce foreign currency (defence spending is import-intensive), and merely adds to the conflict it is supposed to quell (as in the cases of El Salvador and Ethiopia, outlined above).

In 1988, military spending in poor countries totalled \$145 billion, enough to end absolute poverty within the next ten years.[68] However, just because there is a prospect at last of less money being spent on the military, at least in rich countries, it does not of itself mean that people will be clothed and fed. In order to ensure that 'a peace dividend' is spent in productive and progressive ways – indeed that there is a peace dividend at all – we need a new attitude to development, a realization of global interdependence and a new vision of security that can only come from 'sustainable development'.

TOWARDS REAL SECURITY

Conflicts over resources foster violence at many different levels, as we have seen, from landlords fighting peasants for land to great powers fighting for oil. As we destroy what is left of our globe, these conflicts are likely to intensify. Resource war may become more commonplace, while global warming could have a destabilizing effect if, as some predict, large portions of highly populated and agriculturally vital land are drowned. Military 'solutions' may be implemented by the strong at the expense of the weak. But the crisis points in today's world require non-military solutions. A preventative approach to conflict, built on real human and environmental security, is needed.

The status quo of the last forty years is crumbling, but security remains a major unresolved issue. The task now is to work towards a new vision of human security, the kind of security Chico Mendes was fighting for, based on sustainable livelihoods, on living in harmony with people and nature.

8 Putting People First

If you are thinking a year ahead, sow seed.
If you are thinking ten years ahead, plant a tree.
If you are thinking one hundred years ahead,
make people aware.

Anonymous Chinese poet, 500 B.C.

Poverty and the destruction of poor people's environments in the Third World have a long history. But both have intensified sharply in the last decade as poor countries have been sent spinning into a downward economic spiral of debt, collapsing trade and food insecurity. The central solution proposed by the policy-makers of the rich world is to stimulate faster economic growth – both in the world economy as a whole (since this, it is argued, would boost poor economies through increased trade) and in Third World countries in particular.

The 'more growth' solution to Third World poverty is not a new one, but it has recently been revived in a particularly uncompromising version of 'development' aimed at increasing production for profit – particularly for export. As we saw in Chapter 5, the debt crisis has given rich countries the power to promulgate this new development gospel in poor countries, through adjustment programmes.

This approach is adopted partly because it serves powerful interests in both rich and poor countries (as we saw in Chapter 2, there is often a 'logic' behind environmental destruction – it is not all a 'mistake'). It is justified as 'the only practical way' of producing the wealth needed to solve the problems of poverty and ecological degradation. This approach focuses on production itself, the first priority being to expand the size of the national economic cake. Only then will a country be able to afford to tackle its problems.

This line of argument has a commonsense appeal because if the problem is one of people not having enough (whether not enough food for the hungry or income for the poor), then the answer must be to increase wealth and produce more. According to the 'more growth' solution, the best way of achieving this is by allowing the free play of market forces, so that people will pursue profit more eagerly, thus generating wealth to enrich the whole society.

With the primary aim of maximizing economic growth taken for granted, most of the debate amongst the development experts centres on abstract technical analysis – much of it derived from the experience of industrialized countries – of how to increase the 'efficiency' of production for profit. Economic growth therefore becomes virtually synonymous with 'development' or even 'progress' in the Third World. Increasing the gross national product (GNP) per head thus becomes the key measure of success.

However, the emphasis on boosting production ignores the problems of who gets the fruits of that production (as we have seen, for example, simply growing more food is not the answer to hunger), and how it is achieved (is it at the expense of poor groups of people and the environment?). Before looking at these two problems in detail, one must consider the way in which the grow-out-of-poverty solution is failing even within its own terms. Whilst the rich countries have been able to recover from the economic difficulties of the early 1980s, many Third World economies, particularly in Africa and Latin America, remain stagnant. They are strangled by a world economy loaded against them, and by vast debt payments which suck resources out of the Third World and away from investment in farms and factories to create growth.

Even without large debt payments, many argue that Third World countries are still unlikely to achieve high rates of growth with the policies proposed by the free market purists. Governments have to intervene, for example, by investing in new industries and protecting them against the full blast of competition from established rivals in rich countries, and to foster economic growth in the long term. But more deep-rooted criticisms centre not only on whether the traditional remedy of economic growth is possible with present national and international policies, but also on whether it is really desirable at all.

WHO GAINS FROM GROWTH?

The second main criticism of the 'more growth' solution, therefore, centres on the assumption that if only economic growth were to pick up, the poor would necessarily share in increased wealth. An important lesson of the 1960s and 1970s, when many Third World economies did grow rapidly, was that faster growth was often associated with little, if any, improvement in the position of the poor. In Brazil, for instance, the poor shared little in the country's 'economic miracle'. As Keith Griffin, an academic studying development, points out, there is considerable evidence from a number of Third World countries to show that

... poverty among certain groups, above all in rural areas, has failed to decline significantly even where growth in per capita production has occurred. In such countries hunger has persisted despite greater average prosperity.[1]

The main measure of economic growth – GNP per person – only takes account of the average value of goods for sale. It fails to ask the questions: 'What kind of production?' (luxury consumer goods and arms, or staple food and farm tools), and 'Production for whom?' (a rich elite or the mass of poor people gaining some of the basics of life like food, a reasonable income and essential goods).

In fact, GNP per head is a particularly misleading indicator of the welfare of the poor in the Third World because it focuses narrowly on production of goods traded in the market – reflecting the belief that only things denominated in dollars and cents are of value and that buying and selling in the market authenticates 'real production'. GNP therefore ignores work within the household, much of it carried out by women (from collecting wood to growing food for the family to eat), and much of the work in the informal industrial sector which is of particular importance to poor people, especially women.

COSTING THE EARTH

Third, the 'more growth' argument fails to take into account environmental costs. Environmental destruction in the Third World is often justified as a necessary sacrifice for the urgent goal of increasing national growth. Rainforests are cleared for the revenue they bring as timber, to unlock the mineral assets of iron ore or gold that lie below them, and to make way for cash-earning ranches. Industries pour out poisonous pollutants because the costs of cleaning them up are said to be too expensive for poor countries and would slow the growth rate.

The exclusive focus on GNP per head means that environmental costs are taken as incidental, as uncounted 'externalities'. For example, conventional economics measures the income from timber as the monetary value of the timber extracted, minus the costs of felling, transporting and processing it. The costs of replanting the forest do not often enter the calculation, because short-term profit is the criterion of success.

Thus economic gain from an economic activity entered in the cash-ledgers of national economic growth may be dwarfed by a much larger loss of ecological capital – forests, soils, rivers – incurred without being counted into the deficit side of national wealth. The environment is often assumed to have an infinite capacity to absorb pollution, and therefore goes uncosted in the balance-books of economic growth. The environment's capacity to regenerate itself despite the damage wrought by economic activity is taken as a free gift of nature. Increasingly, though, development experts are accepting the need to place an economic value on the environment. The Pearce Report to the UK government, *A Blueprint for a Green Economy*, notes that:

One of the central themes of environmental economics . . . is the need to place proper values on the services provided by natural environments. The central problem is that many of these services are provided 'free'. They have a zero price simply because no market place exists in which their true values can be revealed through the acts of buying and selling. Examples might be a fine view, the water purification and storm protection functions of coastal wetlands, or the biological diversity within a tropical rainforest.[2]

The stress on economic growth as the goal for development also fails to take account of the future impact of present actions. It places the emphasis on profitable living now without considering the price – environmentally (and therefore probably economically) – to be paid later. For many environmentalists the greatest weakness of the 'more growth' solution is its failure to anticipate the future threat to the environment.

NO GROWTH NO ANSWER

The problems of 'more growth' as a solution for the Third World has led some to attack economic growth itself as the cause of poverty and environmental destruction. Far from being the solution, economic growth itself was said to be the problem. The 'no growth' argument gained great popularity during the 1970s, particularly with the publication of the *Limits to Growth* report by the Club of Rome in 1972. It was argued that there was a trade-off – either economic growth or the environment. The world had to aim for a steady economic equilibrium to head off a 'sudden and uncontrolled' environmental nightmare of pollution, resource depletion, overpopulation and food scarcity as the planet reached its finite ecological limits.

This argument angered many in the Third World who believed that the rich countries, having attained their high living standards, were now calling a global halt – for development levels to be frozen where they were – in the name of ecology. The debate has moved on substantially since then. But the issue remains a live one, as shown by the accusations of Brazilian leaders that environmentalists are 'anti-progress'. Similarly, much popular debate about the environment and the Third World is still couched in simple anti-growth terms, even though many leading Greens no longer subscribe to a simple 'no growth' stance.[3]

The problem with the arguments of the 'no-growthers' is that by inverting the arguments of the 'more-growthers' they fall into the same trap of concentrating on the overall *quantity* of economic development instead of its human and environmental *quality*. There is no reason to believe that the poor will reap the benefits of no growth any more than they will of more growth. The experience of recent years bears this out, for many countries in Africa and Latin America have experienced no or even negative growth while environmental destruction and poverty have continued to increase.

Poor communities must be allowed to improve their economic productivity (and so create some growth) to meet their basic needs and aspirations – and it is in the interests of the environment that they are allowed to do so. The real question is *how* – locally, nationally and internationally – they can do this.

Neither more growth nor no growth are in themselves solutions to poverty and environmental destruction. The urgent need is to build new patterns of economic development which serve the priorities of people, particularly poor people, and their living environments, rather than subordinating them to indiscriminate economic growth. This brings us into a debate of less resounding simplicity, but it is undoubtedly what is needed. There are therefore growing calls for 'sustainable development'. But as with many ideals, like democracy and freedom, the concept can mean many things to many people. To some it means an environmental and social tweaking of existing development policies, while for others it means a radical re-think from first principles.

PEOPLE AS PROBLEM

For some, the first priority of 'sustainable development' is to cut population growth. They argue that much of the pressure to increase economic growth (and so pressure on the environment) comes from the growth in population, and that population is growing fastest in the Third World.

But concentrating on the simple balance between the overall number of people and the level of resources is misleading. It underplays the rate at which different people and different countries use resources (the rich world far more than the poor world). The economic and political realities that mediate between the individual and the resources they act upon. Too often it fails to take account of *why* poor people have large families. Though if asked, the poor can explain what to many in the rich world seems inexplicable, if not inexcusable. Ramchandra Ghanekar, a poor and elderly Indian who comes from a coastal village called Chiplun in Maharashtra State – but went to work in Bombay as a labourer – explains. He describes how, for poor people, children provide a very rational survival strategy and insurance:

I have just two children living. Others have died in childhood. Most people like to have more children as the death rate of children in villages is very high. Moreover it is good to have more hands to work on the land and thereafter in the cities. I was lucky that we have a village school where my children finished their middle school. My elder son studied up to the tenth standard in the school and then tried to get a clerical job in Bombay. He did not want to be a domestic servant like me.[4]

To solve the problems caused by population pressure, which are severe in some countries, a secure and decent livelihood must be the starting point for any substantive progress.

PEOPLE FIRST: PIECING IT TOGETHER

Both the 'more growth' developers and economists and the 'no growth' and population control school of environmentalists failed to take people, particularly poor people, as their starting-point. The 'more-growthers' took production as their starting-point and economic expansion as their aim. The key point of reference for the 'no-growthers' was the physical environment, with conservation of natural resources and ecological diversity as the chief goals.[5] Although both include important elements in the jigsaw, they fail to take account of the central piece – poor people themselves and their right to a decent, secure livelihood.

Robert Chambers, who has spent many years in academic study and working in the Third World, argues that both approaches fail because they start with 'physical problems rather than people, and often with the concerns and values of the rich rather than those of the poor'. He insists, instead, on making poor people the starting-point – of putting the last first:

When the priorities of the poor are the starting-point, the elements in the analysis arrange themselves in a different pattern, and nothing is ever quite the same again. The first priority is not the environment or production but livelihoods, stressing both short-term satisfaction of basic needs and long-term security.[6]

The case for putting poor people first is not only the strong moral imperative to do so, powerful though this is. It is also, he argues, the way to achieve the objectives of protecting the environment and increasing production. Putting people first does not have to be a slogan divorced from the world of economic and environmental realities, but a way of re-entering it. The aim is to establish a kind of virtuous circle of grassroots initiatives, instead of the vicious circle of poverty, inappropriate development and environmental destruction.

If poor people are allowed a decent and secure livelihood through having their own land or a job, they no longer have to live from hand to mouth and can plan for the long term. They are far more likely, therefore, to invest time and energy in, say, conserving soil. Communities are likely to be stronger and more able to prevent incursions into their environment. With the land offering more secure livelihoods for the rural poor and the government providing better education for women, people are much more likely to have smaller families and not to be pushed by poverty out of the countryside into the overcrowded cities.

The economic returns would also be considerable. Putting people first would make more efficient use of human skills and labour for local and national economic development. Measures to increase poor people's access to literacy and health would no longer be seen as burdens on the nation's wealth, but as a way of building it up. Healthier and better-educated people are not only an end in themselves but, as examples of successful economies show, a crucial means to increasing economic productivity.

There are three principal pillars of people-first development:

1. Building livelihoods to meet essential needs

At base, development should be about expanding what people are capable of doing and being. This contradicts the conventional definition of development as producing more things to expand economic growth. The criteria of success should be focused not on things, but on people's essential needs: having enough to eat; escaping from avoidable illness themselves and protecting their children from early death; having access to clean water and energy for cooking and keeping warm; finding adequate shelter, and gaining access to basic education for themselves and their children. One priority, then, is for national and international development strategies to concentrate efforts on how better to deliver these essentials to the poor through, say, literacy and vaccination campaigns. And more than this, training local people in primary health care techniques so that improvements are long-lasting, once national campaigns have passed by.

But beyond this is the priority poor people place on a decent and secure livelihood for themselves and their communities. As Mahatma Gandhi once said: 'I must refuse to insult the naked by giving them clothes they do not need, instead of giving them work which they sorely need.'[7] A livelihood will increase people's ability to find the basic essentials of life (by, for example, allowing them to grow enough food or earn enough to buy it). On top of this, an adequate livelihood brings people greater self-respect and dignity to replace the powerlessness of poverty and economic insecurity, and gives them greater freedom to control their destiny.

2. Defending the poor's environment

Throughout, we have stressed how poor people often suffer most when environments are degraded and natural resources are over-exploited. The environment directly underpins the long-term viability and security of many poor people's livelihoods and culture. Only if soils are cared for will they keep producing crops or withstand the shocks of natural disasters like drought. The environment is also the medium through which many of their essential human needs are met or not met. Health, for example, is often dependent on whether the river or well gives clean drinking water and whether there is decent sanitation. Equally, future development of the national economy depends on careful use of natural resources in the long term and recognition of the many 'free services' which the environment performs. These begin to break down where the environment is pushed beyond certain bounds.

But this does not mean that all 'conservation' is necessarily good for the poor. The environment is an arena of conflict. Environmental protection must be tackled by taking account of people's needs and aspirations first. It should be built on people's knowledge of their own local environment and be suspicious of outsiders' attempts to enforce 'don't touch' rules for people in the name of conservation. The aim must be to marry long-term protection of the environment with sustainable improvements in poor people's livelihoods. In turn this will guard against poverty-induced environmental destruction.

3. Letting the poor have a say

People-first development must aim to empower poor people to become the primary agents in their own development, nurturing the ability to determine their own future. We have seen how development and environmental protection rarely starts with the needs and aspirations of the poor. But even when poor people are supposed to be the beneficiaries, they are often poorly consulted and not allowed to play an active role. The supposed end of development – strengthening people's ability to forge a better future – is frequently undermined by the impositions of powerful outsiders, even where they are 'benign'.

Essential needs are 'delivered' to the poor by government programmes or international aid projects. It takes time to overcome the legacy of distrust towards outsiders who have carried out development and environmental conservation in this way. Real participation does not only consist of local people implementing plans already decided on by outsiders, but also choosing the goals and methods, with outsiders playing a supporting rather than leading role.

Too often programmes to protect the environment assume that poor people are mainly responsible for its destruction because they are ignorant, short-sighted or lazy. Time and money are spent on getting outsiders to 'teach' local people about the value of conserving trees and soil, even though they often know far more about it than their 'educators'. Forest reserves are set up with little consultation with local people who are dependent on them and guards are posted to keep people out by force. Respectful and cooperative support for community methods of environmental management should be favoured over the imposition of environmental policing and 'education' by outsiders – whether from governments or international agencies. Such approaches will challenge national and international power structures (as well as poverty itself and the physical and psychological vulnerability that goes with it), but are likely to be far more successful in achieving sustainability in the long run.

Development must therefore take seriously the need to build up the institutions that will enable people to have a real say:

(1) At the local level via local non-governmental organizations (such as the rubber-tappers' union in the Amazon, or women's groups). The structures of local government should also be strengthened as a medium for wide participation by poor people (which has happened through the panchayat village parliaments in India and Village Development Committees (VIDCOs) in Zimbabwe).

(2) At the national level, through accountable government.

(3) At the international level, by democratizing the international institutions, such as the IMF and World Bank, which have such great influence over poor countries but which are controlled by the rich countries – by right of their large shareholdings.

PEOPLE-FIRST DEVELOPMENT: MAKING IT HAPPEN

At the heart of this different development path, then, is the imperative of enabling poor people to take development and environmental management into their own hands. To some, this means that people in rich countries can do little to help bring about the changes needed. But a major theme of this book has been the way in which people's local environments and their daily battle against poverty are hindered or helped not only by local power-brokers and governments but also by international policies, governments, businesses and institutions in rich countries.

Malaysian environment and development activist Martin Khor Kok Peng describes the experience of his own organization:

We have been working for many years, particularly at the grassroots community level, with fishermen, with farmers, with rubber-tappers and so on. We have found that, when we are trying to solve the problem of a particular community, very often that problem cannot be tackled as a problem of that community alone because it is related to national policies which, for example, result in unequal structures of income and wealth between the urban and rural areas. And when we examine the national situation and national policies, we find that they are very often related to the international system.

For instance if you pour in one million man hours and twenty million dollars to help poor communities who are producing rubber, all that wonderful work which may take years and years may be destroyed in a single day when the world price of rubber collapses. So we have come to see that what happens at the ground level very often has its roots in the international system which is controlled, to a very large extent, by multi-national organizations such as, at the commercial level, the transnational companies and at the intergovernmental level, the UN agencies or the GATT, the World Bank and so on.[8]

PARTNERS IN CHANGE

This book has placed a strong emphasis on the external, international, economic, political and military forces arraigned against sustainable development for two reasons. First, while it is not trying to argue that Third World poverty and environmental destruction are caused only by hostile international forces, there are substantial external causes in the webs of international debt and unfair trade. International factors are crucial in explaining world poverty and environmental destruction, despite the attempts of the rich world to deny a real responsibility, other than a charitable one, for the deepening crisis of the Third World.

The second reason for the emphasis on international causes is a straightforward case of practical politics. It is this aspect for which we have the greatest responsibility and over which we have the greatest influence. It is *our* governments which slap up trade barriers against Third World countries, *our* high-street banks that claw back vast debt repayments, *our* governments which control world financial institutions. Although debt or unfair trade are not the only problems facing the Third World, they are the issues over which the rich countries – and people in them – can have greatest impact. Lloyd Timberlake recounts how, after the publication of his book *Africa in Crisis*, he was invited to speak before a sub-committee of the US Congress:

The politicians wanted to focus on Africa's difficult climate and poor soils, on its rapidly growing population, on its political ideologies – all things over which they had no control. They most decidedly did not want to talk about debt relief, trade barriers, or more effective and increased aid – things over which they do have some control, issues in which they have direct responsibilities.[9]

CHANGING DIRECTION

Dire warnings of impending catastrophe are something of a hall-mark of reports and studies of world poverty and ecological destruction. Although with the millennium not far off it is tempting to take this path, it is not the focus offered here. Not only do the doomsday accounts tend to leave one feeling scared and powerless, the crystal-ball visions they offer can blur more than they clarify. The reality is both more desperate and more hopeful. It is more desperate, because while in the rich countries we may speculate about a future crisis, in the Third World the human and environmental crisis is here and now. It is more hopeful because the forces at work are not inevitable or natural processes, and because they are created by people, they can be solved by people.

For intense – if fairly brief – moments in recent history, public, media and political attention have provided fleeting windows into the lives of particular communities in poor countries who are hidden from Western view – Ethiopian peasants hit by famine, rubber-tappers and Indian peoples threatened by the destruction of the Amazon rainforest, riots in the streets of cities of debt-strapped Latin American countries. In the rich countries reactions to these crises have, of course, varied. Some commentators point to the fickleness of public attention. A particular issue holds centre-stage for a few weeks and months and then drops away again into obscurity. One year the pop concerts and the T-shirts are for Ethiopia, the next for the Amazon.

But these outbursts do indicate a large and more persistent groundswell of feeling that it is no longer acceptable or rational to tolerate such unnecessary suffering and destruction. It shows some capacity to identify, people-to-people, across miles, cultures and continents, with communities in the Third World. What this book has tried to show is that the connections are not simply ones of human empathy, but of political, economic and ecological reality. The challenge now is to deepen and broaden our understanding of the connections, so that action is fuelled not only by passing compassion, but also out of recognition of the global injustice of which the rich world is part. Action is then not only directed towards the raising of charitable funds, but to understand, address and change the underlying causes.

MAKING CHANGE

One priority is to extend understanding of the links between the rich world and the poor world. By keeping ourselves informed of what is happening in the Third World and of policy developments in rich countries that affect the poor and the environment, we can try to bring the issues to light within our own community. One way is to join a group trying to promote better understanding and action on global issues of world poverty and environmental destruction. Increasingly, environmental groups like the Friends of the Earth or the World-wide Fund for Nature are working together, locally and nationally, with groups campaigning on world poverty, like the World Development Movement.

The priority now is not so much to arouse people to the scale of world poverty and global environmental threats. It is to focus on *why* such things are happening, and what links people, governments, banks and businesses in the rich world with the problems – or solutions. The pity, frustration and despair resulting from television images of famines happening far away, which often seem to leave no option but for people to reach guiltily for their purses for the charity collection, can be replaced with a constructive anger which questions and demands change. Poverty can no longer be understood as simply numbers of people without enough.

An exploration of the global causes of poverty and environmental decay shows how the decisions taken by governments, institutions and businesses in the rich countries have enormous impact on the economies and ecologies of the poor countries. Engaging with and seeking to change these institutions is therefore vital. Although they seem remote from ordinary people and difficult to influence, politicians, civil servants or bankers cannot remain invulnerable to concerted public pressure. We have seen examples in this book of how campaigns can bring real change – and often with more far-reaching results than the largest collections for charities.

Involvement can cover the range of activities from strategies of mass public pressure, such as the 'Fight World Poverty' lobby in Britain organized by WDM in 1985, which brought 20,000 people together in the largest-ever mass lobby of Parliament, through to individuals and groups of people persistently pressing their local MP or high-street bank manager for specific action. It can take the form of making clearer connections between the individual choices we make in the workplace and home, as consumers or investors, with people in the Third World. Everyone can do something to keep pushing these global issues up the political agenda.

Deeper understanding of the issues leads to working for change. But working for change also leads to deeper understanding of the issues. You don't have to be an 'expert' before doing something. Action works best when people of every different kind come together behind the issue and contribute different skills and experience. The answer to breaking free from the poverty and ecological destruction which every day threatens the lives of millions of poor people lies ultimately in their own hands. But our practical solidarity and action can play a significant part in removing some of the obstacles which, at present, stand in their way.

Issues of poverty and the planet touch on more than the quality of life, they are a question of survival; today for the world's poor, tomorrow for us all. Individual action and action together can change that. Without it, children in the twenty-first century may well come to ask, 'What were you doing in the 1990s?'

Notes and References

Chapter 1: A Question of Survival

1. Friends of the Earth, *Hydro-electric Dams and Rainforest Destruction in the Amazon Basin*, Briefing Paper (mimeo), 1988.
2. *Financial Times*, 22 February 1989.
3. *Guardian*, 22 February 1989.
4. ibid., 27 February 1989.
5. Rachel Carson, *Silent Spring*, 1962.
6. Jonathan Porritt, *Seeing Green*, Basil Blackwell, Oxford, 1984, p. 4.
7. WCED, *Our Common Future*, Oxford University Press, Oxford, 1987; usually known as 'The Brundtland Report', after its chairperson.
8. These NGOs, with the IIED acting as the secretariat, jointly produced two booklets setting out specific policy measures. The first, *Britain and the Brundtland Report: A Programme of Action for Sustainable Development*, was published (in association with Oxfam) in July 1988 and called on the government to produce its own official response to the Brundtland Report; which it then did, calling it *Our Common Future: A Perspective by the United Kingdom on the Report of the World Commission on Environment and Development*. The group of NGOs welcomed this as a 'positive step', but set out many general and detailed weaknesses in what the official response had (or more often hadn't) said in *Brundtland in the Balance: A Critique of the UK Government's Response to the World Commission on Environment and Development*, published in January 1989. In September 1989 the government produced a further document as its contribution to the international conference to follow up the Brundtland Report, entitled *Sustaining Our Common Future: A Progress Report by the UK on Implementing Sustainable Development*.
9. *Spur*, newspaper of the WDM, November 1988.

10. Anil Agarwal, 'Ecological destruction and the emerging patterns of poverty and people's protests in rural India', *Social Action: A Quarterly Review of Social Trends*, Indian Social Institute, New Delhi, January–March 1985, p. 57.

11. UNEP, 'Sands of Time: Why land becomes desert and what can be done about it', *Environment Brief* No. 2, UNEP, Nairobi, n.d.

12. J. Charney, P. Stone and W. Quirk, 'Drought in the Sahara: A biogeographical feedback mechanism', *Science*, Vol. 187, 1975, p. 434. It is worth noting that other scientists dispute the Charney team's claims, saying that vegetation loss has not occurred on a large enough scale seriously to affect overall rainfall patterns in the region. See E. A. Ripley, 'Drought in the Sahara: Insufficient geophysical feedback?', *Science*, Vol. 191, 1976.

13. UNEP, op cit., n.d.

14. USAID figures, in Nick Cater, *Sudan: The Roots of Famine*, Oxfam, 1986, p. 8.

15. When I was carrying out research in Sudan in 1985 and 1986, a number of Sudanese people told me how rapidly things had deteriorated. The figures are from Jay O'Brien, 'Sowing the seeds of famine: The political economy of food deficits in Sudan', in Peter Lawrence (ed.), *World Recession and the Food Crisis in Africa, Review of African Political Economy*/James Currey, London, 1986, p. 196.

16. UNICEF, *The State of the World's Children 1989*, Oxford University Press, Oxford, 1989, pp. 3 and 48.

17. See Chapter 3.

18. Sudhrinder Sharma, 'Water crisis in east Asia', *Ecoforum*, Vol. 10, No. 5, Environment Liaison Centre, Nairobi, October 1985, p. 13.

19. ibid.

20. Avijit Gupta, *Ecology and Development in the Third World*, Routledge, London, 1988, p. 34.

21. Charles Secrett, 'Greater Carajas: Sustainable development or environmental catastrophe?', in David Treece, *Bound in Misery and Iron*, Survival International, London, 1987, p. 82.

22. WCED, op. cit., 1987, p. 190.

23. UNEP, op. cit., n.d.

24. WCED, op. cit., 1987, p. 190.

25. Ben Jackson, 'The people and the trees', *Spur*, December/January 1989. Much useful information on this topic was kindly supplied by Jo McGregor and Ken Wilson.

26. Irene Dankelman and Joan Davidson, *Women and the Environment in the Third World*, IUCN/Earthscan, London, 1988, p. 69.

27. ibid., p. 147.
28. Martin Haigh, 'Deforestation and flooding in the Ganges Basin', in *Reclaiming the Earth: Development and the Environment*, Third World First, Oxford, 1984.
29. *Financial Times*, 5 September 1988.
30. *Independent*, 5 September 1988.
31. *Guardian*, 5 September 1988.
32. ibid., 7 September 1988.

Chapter 2: Why Are the Forests Disappearing?

1. Based on figures for rates in 1989 in Norman Myers, *Deforestation Rates in Tropical Countries and their Climatic Implications*, Friends of the Earth, London, 1989.
2. François Nectoux and Yoichi Kuroda, *Timber from the South Seas: An Analysis of Japan's Tropical Timber Trade and its Environmental Impact*, WWF International, Gland (Switzerland), 1989, p. 23.
3. Quoted in Robert Repetto, *Economic Policy Reform for Natural Resource Conservation*, World Bank Environment Department Working Paper No. 4, World Bank, Washington DC, May 1988, p. 31.
4. Friends of the Earth, *TRF Times*, Summer 1987, p. 1.
5. 'Sarawak natives fight on', *Utusan Konsumer*, Consumers Association of Penang, December 1988.
6. Michael Cross, 'Spare the tree and spoil the forest', *New Scientist*, 26 November 1988.
7. François Nectoux, *Timber! An Investigation of the UK Tropical Timber Industry*, Friends of the Earth, London, 1985, p. 3.
8. Quoted in Cross, op. cit., 1988.
9. Nectoux, op cit., 1985, p. 5.
10. While the rich countries put tariffs of only 1.8 per cent on semi-manufactured wood, they put 4.1 per cent on wood articles, 6.6 per cent on furniture and 9.2 per cent on wood panels (figures from the World Bank's *World Development Report 1987*, p. 138). The effect of these 'escalating tariffs' is explored further in Chapter 4.
11. Nectoux and Kuroda, op cit., 1989, p. 81.
12. M. C. Howard, *Transnational Corporations and the Island Nations of the South Pacific*, TNC Research Project Paper No. 10, University of Sydney, 1986.
13. Nectoux and Kuroda, op. cit., 1989, p. 83.
14. H. Jeffrey Leonard, *Natural Resources and Economic Development in Central America*, IIED Transaction Books, New Brunswick, N.J., and Oxford, 1987, p. 223.

15. James D. Nations and Daniel I. Komer, 'Rainforests and the hamburger society', *Ecologist*, Vol. 17, No. 4/5, 1987, p. 163.

16. Leonard, op. cit., 1987, p. 88.

17. Nations and Komer, op. cit., 1987, p. 164.

18. This is discussed in greater detail in Chapter 7.

19. David Treece. *Bound in Misery and Iron*, Survival International, London, 1987.

20. *Financial Times*, 7 February 1989.

21. Treece, op. cit., 1987, p. 46.

22. *World Bank Annual Report 1983*, World Bank, Washington DC, 1983, p. 116.

23. ibid.

24. Quoted in Treece, op. cit., 1987.

25. *World Bank Annual Report 1983*, op. cit., p. 116.

26. World Bank, *The Carajas Iron Ore Project: Amerindian and Environmental Protection Measures* (mimeo), 1988.

27. Treece, op. cit., 1987, p. 10.

28. Gradwohl and Greenberg, op. cit., 1988, p. 37.

29. *Daily Telegraph*, 18 July 1988.

30. Gradwohl and Greenberg, op. cit., 1988, p. 38.

31. Susanna Hecht and Alexander Cockburn, *The Fate of the Forest: Developers, Destroyers and Defenders of the Amazon*, Verso, London and New York, 1989, p. 97.

32. Figures from the Instituto Brasileiro de Analises Sociais e Economicas (IBASE), quoted in Frances Moore Lappe and Joseph Collins, *World Hunger: Twelve Myths*, Earthscan, London, 1988, p. 33.

33. Jose Lutzenberger, 'The World Bank's Polonoroeste Project – a social and environmental catastrophe', *Ecologist*, Vol. 15, No. 1/2, 1985. (Written before he became Brazil's environment minister in 1990.)

34. Gradwohl and Greenberg, op. cit., 1988, p. 40.

35. Friends of the Earth *et al.*, *Financing Ecological Destruction*, Friends of the Earth, London, 1988.

36. *World Bank Debt Tables 1989–90*, Vol. 1, World Bank, Washington DC, 1989, Table 2, p. 9. The causes and effects of debt are discussed in greater detail in Chapter 5.

37. 'Rising gold fever', *South*, March 1989.

38. Susanna Hecht, interviewed by Peter Madden, in *New Ground*, Socialist Environment and Resources Association (SERA), London, Spring 1990, p. 14.

39. *South*, op. cit., 1989.

40. *Spur*, WDM, December 1988, p. 3.

41. *World Conservation Strategy*, IUCN/WWF/IIED, 1980, p. 24.
42. WCED, *Our Common Future*, Oxford University Press, Oxford, 1987, p. 156.
43. P. Bunyard, 'World climate and tropical forest destruction', *Ecologist*, Vol. 15, No. 3, 1985.
44. For more detail on the greenhouse effect, see WDM's briefing paper *Global Warming and the Third World*, 1990; and also Martin Holdgate *et al.*, *Climate Change: Meeting the Challenge*, Commonwealth Secretariat, London, 1989.
45. The terms are from N. Shanmugaratnam's excellent article examining the differences between the environmental crisis in the rich North and poor South: 'Development and environment: A view from the South', *Race and Class*, Vol. 30, No. 3 (entitled 'Ungreening the Third World'), Institute of Race Relations, London, January–March 1989, p. 13.
46. Letter to the Shadow Foreign Affairs spokesman, Gerald Kaufman, 30 December 1988.

Chapter 3: Feeding the World

1. There is not enough space here to explore the roots of the national, regional and political conflicts within Ethiopia, but two useful books, even if not right up to date, are: Basil Davidson, Lionel Cliffe and Bereket Habte Selassie, *Behind the War in Eritrea*, Spokesman, Nottingham, 1980, and Fred Halliday and Maxine Molyneux, *The Ethiopian Revolution*, Verso, London and New York, 1981.
2. Barbara E. Harrell-Bond, *Imposing Aid: Emergency Assistance to Refugees*, Oxford University Press, Oxford, 1986, p. 4; Rebecca Francis and Ben Jackson, *Urban Refugees in Sudan: An Overview* (mimeo), 1985.
3. Dessalegn Rahmato, 'Peasant survival strategies in Ethiopia', *UNDRO News*, United Nations Disaster Relief Organisation, July/August 1988, p. 10.
4. World Bank, *Poverty and Hunger: Issues and Options for Food Security in Developing Countries*, World Bank, Washington DC, 1986, p. 26.
5. Rahmato, op. cit., 1988, p. 19.
6. World Bank, op. cit., 1986, p. 5.
7. Figures and Oxfam quote from Peter Gill, *A Year in the Death of Africa: Politics, Bureaucracy and the Famine*, Paladin/Grafton Books, London 1986, p. 46. The WFP figure of 300,000 tonnes of food needed was a severe underestimate anyway. The Ethiopian government's RRC had estimated a need for 900,000 tonnes (shown to be correct by the UN only after the famine hit the headlines), and made a request for half

this amount from donors in March 1984 because they thought – perhaps mistakenly – that this was all they could distribute. Even this request was virtually ignored by Western donors. The underlying causes of this shamefully inadequate response are explored in Peter Gill's book, but include: the WFP's much lower estimate of food imports, which took the wind out of the RRC's request; general Western antipathy towards Ethiopia's Marxist government, and by extension the RRC, stemming in part from superpower rivalry because of Ethiopia's strong links with Moscow; a severe underestimate of the capacity of the Ethiopian ports and distribution system to handle large quantities of food – an assessment that was allowed to cloud the issue of how much food was actually needed.

8. Quoted in ibid., p. 48.
9. Rhiannon Barker and Suzanne Quinney, who carried out an evaluation into the internal purchase of grain in Tigray in 1989, set out these facts in a letter to the *Guardian*, 16 December 1989. In 1984 UNICEF operated a scheme in the Shoa and Gonder regions of Ethiopia under which a certain amount of cash was given each month to poor famine-stricken families, in exchange for work on local projects like road-building, where family members were well enough, so that they could buy food in local markets. The system encouraged local farmers to carry on growing food and was more cost-effective for the relief agencies, since the food did not have to be shipped in and transported cross-country to the affected area. See World Bank, op. cit., 1986, p. 39.
10. Amartya Sen, *Poverty and Famines: An Essay on Entitlement and Deprivation*, Clarendon Press, Oxford, 1981.
11. Keith Griffin, 'The economic crisis in Ethiopia', in his collection of essays, *World Hunger and the World Economy*, Macmillan, London, 1987; the chapter as a whole is a useful examination of the wider economic background to the famine disaster.
12. Paul Harrison, *The Greening of Africa: Breaking Through in the Battle for Land and Food*, Paladin/Grafton Books, London, 1987, p. 125.
13. ibid.
14. Griffin, op. cit., 1987, p. 193.
15. UNICEF, *The State of the World's Children 1989*, Oxford University Press, Oxford, 1989, p. 5.
16. World Bank, op. cit., 1986, p. 1.
17. ibid., following the FAO/WHO estimated requirements for daily food intake.
18. Frances Moore Lappe and Joseph Collins, *World Hunger: Twelve Myths*, Earthscan, London, 1988, p. 7.

19. WCED, *Food 2000: Global Policies for Sustainable Agriculture*, Zed, London and New Jersey, 1987, p. 9.

20. World Bank, op. cit., 1986, p. 4.

21. ibid., Tables 2–3, p. 17.

22. See, for example, the case of El Salvador in Chapter 7, p. 154.

23. For a more detailed look at the differing positions – old and new – in the long-running 'peasant question' debate, see the excellent collection of papers brought together by John Harriss in his *Rural Development: Theories of Peasant Economy and Change*, Hutchinson, London, 1982.

24. Mozambique's initial disastrous stress on the state farm sector (largely consisting of large farms abandoned by Portuguese settlers) has, however, given way to a greater emphasis on the peasant sector. Throughout, of course, its whole agricultural system has had to cope with enormous outside pressures, in the shape of the attacks and sabotage carried out by South African-backed Renamo rebels.

25. Gavin Williams, 'Marketing without and with Marketing Boards: The origins of state marketing boards in Nigeria', *Review of African Political Economy*, No. 34, December 1985.

26. ibid., p. 5.

27. Robert H. Bates, 'The regulation of rural markets in Africa', in Stephen K. Commins, Michael F. Lofchie and Rhys Payne (eds.), *Africa's Agrarian Crisis: The Roots of Famine*, Lynne Rienner, Boulder, Colorado, 1986, p. 39.

28. ibid., p. 42.

29. See Chapter 4, p. 63.

30. In Bates, op. cit., 1986, p. 47.

31. Brooke Grundfest Schoepf, 'Food crisis and class formation in Zaire: Political ecology in Shaba', in Peter Lawrence (ed.), *World Recession and the Food Crisis in Africa*, Review of African Political Economy/James Currey, London, 1986, p. 200.

32. ibid.

33. Philip Raikes, *Modernising Hunger: Famine, Food Surplus and Farm Policy in the EEC and Africa*, Catholic Institute for International Relations/James Currey (London)/Heinemann (Portsmouth, New Hampshire), 1988, p. 6. This book, written in largely non-technical language, is one of the best detailed accounts of the causes of hunger in Africa, and their links with Europe.

34. Christopher Jackson, *EEC Food Policy*, CAP Briefing, Nos. 1–3, Catholic Institute for International Relations, London, October 1987, p. 8.

35. Philip Raikes, *The Common Agricultural Policy and the African Food*

Crisis, CAP Briefing, Nos. 13–14, Catholic Institute for International Relations, London, March 1987, p. 2.

36. Kevin Watkins, *International Agricultural Co-operation and Lomé*, Lomé Briefing, Nos. 5–6, Liaison Committee of development NGOs to the European Communities, Brussels, January/February 1989.

37. Robert Chambers explores this theme in his *Rural Development: Putting the Last First*, Longman, London, 1983, especially in Chapter 4. This book is highly recommended, especially for anyone visiting or going to work in the Third World.

38. In Raikes, op. cit., 1988, p. 3.

39. *World Bank Development Report 1989*, World Bank, Washington DC, 1989, p. 13.

40. Adjustment programmes are discussed more generally in Chapter 5.

41. *World Bank Development Report 1989*, op. cit.

42. For a discussion of this in the context of Nigeria, see Gavin Williams, 'The World Bank in rural Nigeria revisited: A review of the World Bank's Nigeria Agricultural Sector Review 1987', *Review of African Political Economy*, No. 43, 1988, p. 42.

43. Biswapriya Sanyal, 'Rural development and economic stabilization: Can they be attained simultaneously?', in Commins *et al.*, op. cit., 1986 (note 27), p. 189.

44. Michael Lofchie, 'Africa's agricultural crisis: An overview', in ibid.

45. Quoted in Tony Addison and Lionel Demery, 'The economics of rural poverty alleviation', in Simon Commander (ed.), *Structural Adjustment and Agriculture: Theory and Practice in Africa and Latin America*, ODI, (London)/James Currey (London)/Heinemann (Portsmouth, New Hampshire), 1989, p. 75.

46. ibid.

47. 'The people and the trees', *Spur*, WDM, December/January 1989.

48. In Terence Ranger, *Peasant Consciousness and Guerilla War in Zimbabwe*, James Currey, London, 1985, p. 158.

49. Chambers, op. cit., 1983, p. 30.

50. Paul Richards, *Indigenous Agricultural Revolution: Ecology and Food Production in West Africa*, Unwin Hyman, London, 1985, p. 56.

51. ibid., p. 57.

52. ibid., Chapter 4; Chambers, op. cit., 1983, p. 86.

53. World Bank, *Sub-Saharan Africa: From Crisis to Sustainable Growth*, World Bank, Washington DC, 1989, p. 95.

54. Quoted in T. P. Bayliss-Smith, *The Ecology of Agricultural Systems*, Cambridge University Press, Cambridge, 1982, p. 69.

55. World Bank, op. cit., 1986.

56. B. H. Farmer, 'The Green Revolution in South Asia's rice fields: Environment and production', *Journal of Development Studies*, No. 15, 1979.

57. Betsy Hartmann and James K. Boyce, *A Quiet Violence: View from a Bangladesh Village*, Food First (San Francisco)/Zed (London), 1983, p. 256.

58. Garrison Wilkes, 'The endangered genetic base of the world's food supply', *Bulletin of the Atomic Scientist*, February 1977, p. 11.

59. WCED, *Food 2000*, op. cit., 1987, p. 37.

60. Arnold Schwab, *Fighting Pests the Natural Way*, PAN-Europe, Brussels, 1988, p. 5.

61. *Utusan Konsumer*, Penang, June 1988.

62. Schwab, op. cit., 1988, p. 6.

63. ibid., p. 8.

Chapter 4: 1992 and All That: Trade and Self-reliance

1. World Bank, *Sub-Saharan Africa: From Crisis to Sustainable Growth*, World Bank, Washington DC, 1989, calculated from Table 14, p. 244.

2. UN, *Financing Africa's Recovery*, UN Advisory Group on Financial Flows for Africa, New York, 1988, Annex Table 3, p. 54.

3. World Bank, op. cit., 1989, Table 16, p. 249.

4. *World Bank Development Report 1989*, World Bank, Washington DC, 1989, from Table 16, p. 195.

5. As measured by non-oil commodity prices relative to the price of manufactured goods. Figures from ODI, *Commodity Prices: Investing in Decline?*, ODI Briefing Paper, March 1988, p. 1.

6. *Financial Times*, 22 November 1989.

7. D. H. Meadows, D. L. Meadows, J. Randers and W. W. Behrens, *The Limits to Growth*, Pan, London, 1972.

8. See Chapter 7, p. 167.

9. Robin Stainer, 'New fronts in the coffee war', *South*, December 1989, p. 32.

10. *World Financial Markets*, J. P. Morgan, New York, August 1987, Table 3, p. 4.

11. ibid.

12. *World Bank Development Report 1989*, op. cit., Table A.5, p. 148.

13. *Guardian*, 15 January 1990.

14. Henk Hobbelink, *New Hope or False Promise? Biotechnology and Third World Agriculture*, International Coalition for Development Action, Brussels, 1987, p. 23.

15. Belinda Coote, *The Hunger Crop: Poverty and the Sugar Industry*, Oxfam, 1987, p. 78.

16. Hobbelink, op. cit., 1987, p. 23.

17. 'The Asian NICs: Wrestling with success', *World Financial Markets*, J. P. Morgan, New York, 17 April 1989, p. 1.

18. ibid.

19. OECD, *The Newly Industrialising Countries: Challenge and Opportunity for OECD Countries*, OECD, Paris 1988, Table 1.1, p. 11.

20. ibid.

21. Nigel Harris, *The End of the Third World: Newly Industrializing Countries and the Decline of an Ideology*, Penguin, Harmondsworth, 1986. A pithy summary of his argument can be found in Nigel Harris, 'Halfway to liberation', *New Internationalist*, February 1990.

22. OECD, op. cit., 1988, p. 80.

23. ibid., pp. 34ff.

24. Traidcraft, *People-Friendly Clothing*, Campaign Briefing, Traidcraft, Newcastle, February 1990, p. 8.

25. United Nations Centre on Transnational Corporations, *Transnational Corporations in World Development: Trends and Prospects*, UN, New York, 1988, p. 49.

26. ibid., Table V.1, p. 76.

27. World Bank, *World Development Report 1987*, World Bank, Washington DC, 1987, p. 39.

28. *Financial Times*, 'World Industrial Review' (Supplement), 8 January 1990.

29. The effects of the EC's 1992 programme are discussed in greater depth in Edward Mayo, *Beyond 1992: The Effect of the Single European Market on the World's Poor*, WDM, 1989.

30. Figures and quote both from *World Development Report 1987*, op. cit., p. 138.

31. Juan A. de Castro, *Protectionist Pressures in the 1990s and the Coherence of North–South Trade Policies*, UNCTAD Discussion Papers, No. 27, UNCTAD, Geneva, August 1989, Table 3, p. 22.

32. UNCTAD, *Trade and Development Report 1989*, UNCTAD, Geneva, 1989, p. 69.

33. Heerko Dijsterhuis and Udo Sprang, *Nothing Can Beat Cassava*, NIO-Vereniging, Amsterdam, 1988, p. 13.

34. *Financial Times*, 18 January 1990.

35. *Guardian*, 10 October 1987.

36. WDM, *Crisis in the Sugar Industry*, WDM, London, 1987.

37. Joan Robinson, *Aspects of Development and Underdevelopment*,

Cambridge University Press, Cambridge, 1979, p. 132.

38. Frances Stewart, 'Supporting productive employment among vulnerable groups', in Giovanni Andrea Cornia, Richard Jolly and Frances Stewart (eds.), *Adjustment with a Human Face*, Vol. 1, Clarendon Press, Oxford, 1987, p. 217.

39. ibid, p. 208.

40. Tom Ostergaard, *SADCC Beyond Transportation: The Challenge of Industrial Cooperation*, Scandinavian Institute of African Studies, Uppsala, 1989, p. 15.

41. Edward Mayo, op. cit. (note 29 above).

42. WDM, *The Threads of the Issue*, WDM, London, 1985; and WDM, *Textiles and Clothing: Questions and Answers*, WDM, London, 1985.

Chapter 5: Money Makes the World Go Round

1. From a letter reprinted in *IMF Survey*, IMF, Washington DC, 20 March 1989, p. 83.

2. *World Bank Debt Tables 1988–89*, Vol. 1, World Bank, Washington DC, 1988, p. xxxiii.

3. Harry L. Freeman, 'US national security and the LDC debt crisis', in Adrian Hewitt and Bowen Wells, MP (eds.), *Growing Out of Debt*, All-Party Group on Overseas Development/ODI, London, 1989, p. 58.

4. *Spur*, WDM, April 1989.

5. As measured by the fall in average real incomes; see UNICEF, *The State of the World's Children 1990*, Oxford University Press, Oxford, 1990, p. 8. For many, the picture has been much worse than the average: in a number of urban areas in Latin America real minimum incomes have fallen by 50 per cent.

6. Figures calculated for 1987 in UNICEF, *The State of the World's Children 1989*, Oxford University Press, Oxford, 1989, p. 1.

7. ibid.

8. Giovanni Andrea Cornia, Richard Jolly and Frances Stewart, *Adjustment with a Human Face*, Vol. 1, UNICEF/Clarendon Press, Oxford, 1987, p. 30.

9. UNICEF, op. cit., 1989, p. 1.

10. Bruce Fuller, 'Eroding economy and declining school quality: The case of Malawi', *IDS Bulletin*, Vol. 20, No. 1, Institute of Development Studies, University of Sussex, January 1989, p. 12.

11. For more on the effects of debt on women, see *Taking Account of Women*, WDM, London, 1988.

12. From her speech of 15 February 1988, in *Council of Europe Public*

Campaign on North–South Interdependence and Solidarity: Roundtable *on Debt,* WDM, London, 1988, p. 88.

13. Proportions of debt owed to different creditors is calculated on the basis of long-term debt only.

14. As indicated by the ratio of total debt service to the value of exports of goods and services, which was 28.5 per cent in 1988 on average for all countries (but was 40.5 per cent in Latin America); see *World Bank Debt Tables 1989–90,* pp. 78 and 94.

15. World Bank, *World Development Report 1989,* Washington DC, 1989, Table 8, p. 178.

16. *World Bank Debt Tables 1988–89,* op. cit., 1988, p. xi.

17. ibid., p. xii.

18. 1989 figures were 'preliminary estimates' at the time of release (December 1989). Figures may not add up, owing to rounding.

19. Quoted by the former Mexican Ambassador to the United Kingdom, Jorge Eduardo Naverette, in Hewitt and Wells (eds.), op. cit., 1989, p. 28.

20. In John Denham, *Out of their Debts: UK Banks and the Third World Debt Crisis,* War on Want Campaigns, London, 1989, p. 1.

21. Nineteen per cent of Senegal's total export earnings come from fish, while it spends nearly the same amount (17 per cent of its total export earnings) on servicing its long-term debt. For trade earnings figures, see UN, *Financing Africa's Recovery,* UN, New York, 1988, Annex 3.

22. WCED, *Our Common Future,* Oxford University Press, Oxford, 1987, p. 74.

23. ibid., p. 70.

24. In *Roundtable on Debt,* op. cit. (note 12 above), 1988, p. 65.

25. Speech in Hewitt and Wells (eds.), op. cit., 1989, p. 7; made before he resigned as Chancellor.

26. *World Bank Debt Tables 1988–89,* op. cit., p. 2.

27. Lord Lever *et al., The Debt Crisis and the World Economy,* Commonwealth Secretariat, London, 1984, p. 17.

28. *Time* magazine, 10 January 1983, p. 28.

29. UNCTAD, *Trade and Development Report 1989,* UNCTAD, Geneva, 1989, Annex Table 3, p. 234.

30. *Time* magazine, op. cit., p. 10.

31. John Denham, op. cit., 1989.

32. *World Development Report 1989,* op. cit., 1989.

33. In Hewitt and Wells (eds.), op. cit., 1989, p. 24.

34. *Time* magazine, op. cit., p. 8.

35. WDM, *The Financial Famine* (eight-page briefing paper on debt

and economic adjustment), WDM/UNICEF-UK, 1988. For more on the collapse of commodity prices, see Chapter 4, p. 63.

36. *Time* magazine, op. cit., p. 9.
37. ibid., p. 10.
38. Speech to International Herald Tribune conference, February 1988.
39. John Clark with David Keen, *Debt and Poverty: A Case Study in Zambia*, Oxfam, 1988, p. 43.
40. Interview in *Time* magazine, 31 January 1989.
41. *Finance and Development*, IMF/World Bank, Washington DC, December 1988, p. 2.
42. *World Bank Debt Tables 1988–89*, op. cit., p. xvii.
43. *Economist*, 24 September 1988, p. 58.
44. *World Bank Annual Report 1989*, Washington DC, 1989, p. 110.
45. ibid., p. 78.
46. *Africa's Adjustment and Growth*, World Bank/UNDP, Washington DC, 1989.
47. World Bank, *Adjustment Lending: An Evaluation of Ten Years of Experience*, Policy and Research Report 1, Washington DC, March 1989.
48. Cornia *et al.*, op. cit. (note 8 above), 1987.
49. UNICEF, op. cit., 1990, p. 44.
50. See Chapter 3, p. 47.
51. See Chapter 4, p. 83.
52. *World Bank Annual Report 1989*, op. cit., p. 80.
53. *Financial Times*, 6 June 1988.
54. UNICEF, op. cit., 1990, p. 10.
55. ibid.
56. *World Bank Annual Report 1989*, op. cit., p. 81.
57. ECA, *The African Alternative Framework to Structural Adjustment Programmes for Socio-economic Recovery and Transformation*, ECA, Addis Ababa, 1989.
58. ibid., p. 32.
59. Christopher Patten, in *Hansard*, 20 July 1989, col. 250.
60. *Financial Times*, 25 September 1989.
61. ibid.
62. *Financial Times*, 2 February 1990.
63. *Financial Times*, 25 September 1990.
64. John Denham, *In Whose Interest?*, Background Briefing No. 4, Friends of the Earth/Third World First/WDM, London, 1990.
65. Stephany Griffith-Jones, *Debt and Banks' Tax Relief*, paper for the 'In Whose Interest?' campaign, 1990. In his 1990 Budget, John Major in

part conceded this demand of the campaign, by introducing some incentives to banks to write off debt.

66. *World Bank Debt Tables 1988–89*, op. cit., p. xi.
67. Percy Mistry, *Perspectives for Campaigning on Official Debt and on African Debt in Particular*, background paper for FONDAD conference, August 1989, p. 21.
68. *Spur*, WDM, July/August 1988.
69. Mistry, op. cit., 1989, p. 21.
70. ibid.
71. *World Bank Debt Tables 1989–90*, op. cit., Box 6, p. 18.
72. ibid., p. 18.
73. *UN Development Forum*, July–August 1989, p. 12.
74. House of Commons Treasury and Civil Service Committee, *International Debt Strategy*, Third Report (Session 1989–90), HMSO, London, March 1990, p. xxv. For a good summary of the financial impact of the deals, see the briefing document published by the European Campaign on Debt and Development, *Reducing South–North Resource Transfers*, ECDD, The Hague, 1990. (Available from WDM.)
75. UNCTAD, *Trade and Development Report 1988*, UNCTAD, Geneva, 1988.

Chapter 6: Aid in Perspective

1. NAO, *Bilateral Aid to India*, HMSO, London, January 1990, p. 28.
2. ibid., p. 11.
3. ibid., p. 28.
4. teve Percy and Mike Hall, *British Aid to India: What Price?*, Spokesman, Nottingham, 1989, p. 7.
5. In ibid.
6. NAO, op. cit, 1990, p. 15.
7. ibid, p. 10.
8. OECD, *Development Co-operation in the 1990s: Efforts and Policies of the Members of the Development Assistance Committee*, OECD, Paris, 1989, p. 240.
9. ODA, *British Overseas Aid: Anniversary Review 1989*, ODA, London, 1989, p. 7.
10. OECD, op. cit., 1989, p. 26.
11. ibid., Tables 1–3, p. 150. 'New outside finance' refers to the 'net' figure (i.e. discounting lending which simply covers the cost of repaying old debts – as much commercial bank lending now does) of 'total financial flows' which includes bank lending, private investment, bilateral and multilateral aid and government trade credits.

12. 1987–8 average in ibid., Table 1, p. 204; all figures on shares of world aid-giving are from this table.

13. ibid., p. 26, for trends in Arab aid-giving.

14. In reply to a WDM election questionnaire, 31 May 1983.

15. OECD Development Assistance Committee reports, various years.

16. OECD, op. cit., 1989, p. 170.

17. *Financial Times*, 15 June 1988. For a general review, see *Japanese Aid*, ODI briefing paper, Overseas Development Institute, March 1990.

18. *New York Times*, 20 August 1989.

19. OECD, op. cit., 1989, pp. 166 and 170–71.

20. *Guardian*, 7 April 1989.

21. *Financial Times*, 10 November 1988.

22. ODA, op. cit., 1989, p. 7.

23. UNICEF, *The State of the World's Children 1989*, Oxford University Press, Oxford, 1989, p. 32.

24. The ODA, for example, has responded to this need by producing a *Manual of Environmental Appraisal* (1989) as an 'operational guide for the use of aid practitioners'.

25. *Observations by the Government on Second Report from the Foreign Affairs Committee (Session 1986–87)*, HMSO, London, October 1987, para. 3 p. 1.

26. House of Commons Foreign Affairs Committee, *Bilateral Aid: Country Programmes*, Second Report (Session 1986–87), HMSO, London, June 1987, para. 16, p. viii.

27. *Observations by the Government . . .*, op. cit., 1987, para. 4, p. 1.

28. Don Holland, 'The Importance of Aid to British Industry', speech to a conference held on 17 January 1989 in London. Conference proceedings reprinted in DTI, *Africa: Aid-Trade*, Rooster Books, Stanstead Abbotts, 1989, p. 73.

29. Lynda Chalker, speech to the London Business School, 24 May 1990.

30. ODA, op. cit., 1989, p. 40.

31. In DTI, op. cit., 1989, p. 17.

32. ibid, p. 18.

33. ODA, op. cit., 1989, p. 104.

34. *Financial Times*, 23 February 1990.

35. ibid.; also *Financial Times*, 15 February 1990.

36. *Financial Times*, 24 May 1989.

37. *Financial Times*, 24 February 1990.

38. Paul Mosley, *Poverty-Focussed Aid: The Lessons of Experience*, Action Aid, London, 1987, p. 17.

39. NAO, op. cit., 1990, p. 12.

40. Percy and Hall, op. cit., 1989, p. 9.
41. The question of growth is examined in greater detail in Chapter 8.
42. Jeremy Warford and Zeinab Partow, 'Evolution of the World Bank's environmental policy', in *Finance and Development*, IMF/World Bank, Washington DC, December 1989, p. 6.
43. Speech of Barber Conable (President of the World Bank) in Tokyo in 1989, reprinted in ibid., p. 4.
44. Quoted in WDM *et al.*, *Britain and the Brundtland Report*, 1988, p. 7.
45. Conable, op. cit., 1989, p. 4.
46. OECD, op. cit., 1990, p. 44.
47. UNICEF, op. cit., 1990, p. 59.
48. Dr Miriam K. Were, 'Women's Participation: at the heart of recovery and development', Speech to UN symposium on 'Women's Participation: the critical element in food security', 12 October 1989.
49. Idriss Jazairy, 'Foreword' President of IFAD, in William P. Lineberry (ed.), *Assessing Participatory Development: Rhetoric Versus Reality*, IFAD (Rome)/Westview (San Francisco and London), 1989.
50. ibid., p. 4.
51. Mosley, op. cit., 1987, p. 14.
52. Aga Khan Foundation, *The Aga Khan Rural Support Programme* (mimeo), 1990.
53. Mosley, op. cit., 1987, p. 9.
54. Lynda Chalker, speech to the All-Party Group on Overseas Development, 8 November 1989.

Chapter 7: War of the Worlds

1. Chico Mendes, *Fight for the Forest: Chico Mendes in his own Words*, Latin America Bureau, London, 1989, p. 66.
2. ibid., p. 84.
3. ibid., p. 41.
4. ibid., p. 6.
5. ibid., p. 66.
6. ibid., p. 67.
7. Susanna Hecht and Alexander Cockburn, *The Fate of the Forest: Developers, Destroyers and Defenders of the Amazon*, Verso, London and New York, 1989, p. 95. The whole of their Chapter 6 provides a well-documented account of the central role of the military in Amazonian destruction.
8. In Noam Chomsky, *Turning the Tide*, Pluto, London, 1985, p. 159.

9. CIIR, *Central America* ('Comment' series), CIIR, London, May 1989, p. 1.

10. ibid.

11. H. Jeffrey Leonard, *Natural Resources and Economic Development in Central America*, IIED/Transaction Books, New Brunswick, N.J., and Oxford, 1987, p. 106.

12. See Chapter 2, p. 21.

13. Leonard, op. cit., 1987, p. 127.

14. ibid., p. 129.

15. Bill Hall and Daniel Faber, *El Salvador: Ecology of Conflict*, Green Paper No. 4, Environmental Project on Central America, San Francisco, March 1989, p. 1. Because of escalating repression in El Salvador, the name had to be omitted in the original text, out of fear for his safety.

16. ibid., p. 3.

17. ibid., p. 4.

18. Leonard, op. cit., 1987, p. 107.

19. Hall and Faber, op. cit., 1989, p. 5.

20. Policy Alternatives for the Caribbean and Central America, *Changing Course: Blueprint for Peace in Central America and the Caribbean*, Institute for Policy Studies, New York and Amsterdam, 1984, p. 18.

21. CIIR, *El Salvador* ('Comment' series), CIIR, London, February 1988, p. 16.

22. Interview from 'The World This Week', Channel 4, 17 March 1990.

23. Hall and Faber, op. cit., 1989, p. 7.

24. In ibid., p. 8.

25. CIIR, op, cit., 1988.

26. Hall and Faber, op. cit., 1989.

27. CIIR, op. cit., 1988, p. 24.

28. ibid., p. 13.

29. Morris J. Blachman and Kenneth Sharpe, 'De-democratising American foreign policy: Dismantling the post-Vietnam formula', *Third World Quarterly*, Vol. 8, No. 4, October 1986, p. 1283.

30. James Fergusen, James Painter and Jenny Pearce, 'Under attack: Central America and the Caribbean', in *The Thatcher Years: Britain and Latin America*, Latin America Bureau, London, 1988, p. 37.

31. Interview in Joyce Hollyday (ed.), *Crucible of Hope*, Sojourners, Washington DC, 1984, p. 42.

32. ibid., p. 45.

33. Blachman and Sharpe, op. cit., 1986, p. 1281.

34. In Appendix 2 of Fred Halliday, *Cold War – Third World*, Hutchinson Radius, London, 1989, p. 170.

35. *Jane's Defence Weekly*, 30 September 1989, p. 629.
36. *Guardian*, 27 June 1987.
37. WDM, *Disarm to Develop*, Briefing Paper, WDM, London, March 1990. The wider implications of East–West change for the Third World are discussed in Geoff Tansey, *Real Security* WDM Occasional Paper 2, 1990.
38. *Financial Times*, 16 March 1990.
39. *Guardian*, 14 February 1990.
40. *The Times*, 20 February 1990 (my emphasis).
41. *Financial Times*, 5 January 1990.
42. Official US figures at the time of the invasion put the death toll at about 400. However, independent investigation since has established the real figure to be many times higher. Many of those who died were poor people living in the slums of Panama City, bombed by the Americans. See *Guardian*, 30 June 1990.
43. *The Times*, 5 January 1990.
44. *Guardian*, 31 January 1990.
45. Jonathan Marshall, Peter Dale Scott and Jane Hunter, *The Iran Contra Connection: Secret Teams and Operations in the Reagan Era*, South End Press, Boston, Mass., 1987, p. 158.
46. WCED, *Our Common Future*, Oxford University Press, Oxford, 1987, p. 290.
47. In Michael Klare, *Beyond the 'Vietnam Syndrome'*, Institute for Policy Studies, New York and Amsterdam, 1982.
48. ibid., p. 51.
49. Halliday, op. cit., 1989, p. 168.
50. Helen Collinson, *Death on Delivery: The Impact of the Arms Trade on the Third World*, Campaign Against the Arms Trade (CAAT), London, 1989, p. 93.
51. ibid., p. 91.
52. In *Daily Telegraph*, 8 August 1987.
53. *Jane's Defence Weekly*, 25 March 1989; *International Herald Tribune*, 18 October 1987.
54. Nader Entessar, 'Superpowers and Persian Gulf security', *Third World Quarterly*, Vol. 10, No. 4, October 1988, p. 1444.
55. *Sunday Times*, 27 December 1987.
56. In *Financial Times*, 16 March 1990.
57. *Jane's Defence Weekly*, 25 March 1989.
58. *Christian Science Monitor*, 2 May 1988.
59. *International Herald Tribune*, 18 November 1987.
60. ibid.

61. *Jane's Defence Review*, 11 January 1986. I am grateful to Milan Rai for making his research on the JFHQ available to me.
62. *Sunday Times*, 16 September 1984.
63. 'Desert Sword', *Soldier*, 12 January 1987.
64. *Asian Defence Journal*, June 1988.
65. WDM, *Disarm to Develop*, op cit., 1990.
66. WCED, op. cit, 1987, p. 299.
67. UNICEF, *The State of the World's Children 1990*, Oxford University Press, Oxford, 1990.
68. WDM, *Disarm to Develop*, op. cit., 1990.

Chapter 8: Putting People First

1. Keith Griffin, *World Hunger and the World Economy*, Macmillan, London, 1987, p. 6.
2. David Pearce, Anil Markandya and Edward Barbier, *Blueprint for a Green Economy*, Report to the UK Department of the Environment, Earthscan, London, 1989, p. 5.
3. Jonathan Porritt, for example, complains that Greens are always seen as '"zero-growthers", though such a position is obviously just as absurd as that adopted by the "infinite-growthers". It is our contention that there will always continue to be *some* growth: in the developed world, there will be limited growth in some sectors of the economy . . . in the Third World, there will have to be substantial economic growth for some time, though with much greater discrimination as regards the nature and quality of that growth.' In *Seeing Green*, Basil Blackwell, Oxford, 1984. For a recent popular restatement of anti-growth development economics, see Ted Trainer, *Developed to Death*, GreenPrint, London, 1989.
4. Interviewed in Sten E. Berg, Arun Gandhi and Sunanda Gandhi, *Experiments in Self-help: Voices from Indian Villages*, HIDCA/Almqvist & Wiksell, Stockholm, 1984, p. 148.
5. Robert Chambers, *Sustainable Livelihoods, Environment and Development: Putting Poor Rural People First*, IDS Discussion Paper 240, Institute of Development Studies, University of Sussex, p. 12.
6. ibid., p. 15.
7. Quoted in Berg *et al.*, op. cit., 1984, p. 152.
8. Martin Khor Kok Peng, speaking at a UNCTAD/UN Non-governmental Liaison Service conference, 1989.
9. Lloyd Timberlake, *Africa in Crisis*, Earthscan, London, 1988, p. xii.

Index

FOR THE BEST IN PAPERBACKS, LOOK FOR THE

In every corner of the world, on every subject under the sun, Penguin represents quality and variety – the very best in publishing today.

For complete information about books available from Penguin – including Puffins, Penguin Classics and Arkana – and how to order them, write to us at the appropriate address below. Please note that for copyright reasons the selection of books varies from country to country.

In the United Kingdom: Please write to *Dept E.P., Penguin Books Ltd, Harmondsworth, Middlesex, UB7 0DA.*

If you have any difficulty in obtaining a title, please send your order with the correct money, plus ten per cent for postage and packaging, to *PO Box No 11, West Drayton, Middlesex*

In the United States: Please write to *Dept BA, Penguin, 299 Murray Hill Parkway, East Rutherford, New Jersey 07073*

In Canada: Please write to *Penguin Books Canada Ltd, 2801 John Street, Markham, Ontario L3R 1B4*

In Australia: Please write to the *Marketing Department, Penguin Books Australia Ltd, P.O. Box 257, Ringwood, Victoria 3134*

In New Zealand: Please write to the *Marketing Department, Penguin Books (NZ) Ltd, Private Bag, Takapuna, Auckland 9*

In India: Please write to *Penguin Overseas Ltd, 706 Eros Apartments, 56 Nehru Place, New Delhi, 110019*

In the Netherlands: Please write to *Penguin Books Netherlands B.V., Postbus 195, NL–1380AD Weesp*

In West Germany: Please write to *Penguin Books Ltd, Friedrichstrasse 10–12, D–6000 Frankfurt/Main 1*

In Spain: Please write to *Longman Penguin España, Calle San Nicolas 15, E–28013 Madrid*

In Italy: Please write to *Penguin Italia s.r.l., Via Como 4, I-20096 Pioltello (Milano)*

In France: Please write to *Penguin Books Ltd, 39 Rue de Montmorency, F-75003 Paris*

In Japan: Please write to *Longman Penguin Japan Co Ltd, Yamaguchi Building, 2–12–9 Kanda Jimbocho, Chiyoda-Ku, Tokyo 101*

PENGUIN POLITICS AND SOCIAL SCIENCES

Political Ideas David Thomson (ed.)

From Machiavelli to Marx – a stimulating and informative introduction to the last 500 years of European political thinkers and political thought.

On Revolution Hannah Arendt

Arendt's classic analysis of a relatively recent political phenomenon examines the underlying principles common to all revolutions, and the evolution of revolutionary theory and practice. 'Never dull, enormously erudite, always imaginative' – *Sunday Times*

The Apartheid Handbook Roger Omond

The facts behind the headlines: the essential hard information about how apartheid actually works from day to day.

The Social Construction of Reality Peter Berger and Thomas Luckmann

Concerned with the sociology of 'everything that passes for knowledge in society' and particularly with that which passes for common sense, this is 'a serious, open-minded book, upon a serious subject' – *Listener*

The Care of the Self Michel Foucault
The History of Sexuality Vol 3

Foucault examines the transformation of sexual discourse from the Hellenistic to the Roman world in an inquiry which 'bristles with provocative insights into the tangled liaison of sex and self' – *The Times Higher Educational Supplement*

A Fate Worse than Debt Susan George

How did Third World countries accumulate a staggering trillion dollars' worth of debt? Who really shoulders the burden of reimbursement? How should we deal with the debt crisis? Susan George answers these questions with the solid evidence and verve familiar to readers of *How the Other Half Dies*.

Comparative Government S. E. Finer

'A considerable *tour de force* … few teachers of politics in Britain would fail to learn a great deal from it … Above all, it is the work of a great teacher who breathes into every page his own enthusiasm for the discipline' – Anthony King in *New Society*

Karl Marx: Selected Writings in Sociology and Social Philosophy
T. B. Bottomore and Maximilien Rubel (eds.)

'It makes available, in coherent form and lucid English, some of Marx's most important ideas. As an introduction to Marx's thought, it has very few rivals indeed' – *British Journal of Sociology*

Post-War Britain A Political History Alan Sked and Chris Cook

Major political figures from Attlee to Thatcher, the aims and achievements of governments and the changing fortunes of Britain in the period since 1945 are thoroughly scrutinized in this readable history.

Inside the Third World Paul Harrison

From climate and colonialism to land hunger, exploding cities and illiteracy, this comprehensive book brings home a wealth of facts and analysis on the often tragic realities of life for the poor people and communities of Asia, Africa and Latin America.

Housewife Ann Oakley

'A fresh and challenging account' – *Economist*. 'Informative and rational enough to deserve a serious place in any discussion on the position of women in modern society' – *The Times Educational Supplement*

The Raw and the Cooked Claude Lévi-Strauss

Deliberately, brilliantly and inimitably challenging, Lévi-Strauss's seminal work of structural anthropology cuts wide and deep into the mind of mankind, as he finds in the myths of the South American Indians a comprehensible psychological pattern.

PENGUIN SCIENCE AND MATHEMATICS

Facts from Figures M. J. Moroney

Starting from the very first principles of the laws of chance, this authoritative 'conducted tour of the statistician's workshop' provides an essential introduction to the major techniques and concepts used in statistics today.

God and the New Physics Paul Davies

Can science, now come of age, offer a surer path to God than religion? This 'very interesting' (*New Scientist*) book suggests it can.

Descartes' Dream Philip J. Davis and Reuben Hersh

All of us are 'drowning in digits' and depend constantly on mathematics for our high-tech lifestyle. But is so much mathematics really good for us? This major book takes a sharp look at the ethical issues raised by our computerized society.

The Blind Watchmaker Richard Dawkins

'An enchantingly witty and persuasive neo-Darwinist attack on the anti-evolutionists, pleasurably intelligible to the scientifically illiterate' – Hermione Lee in the *Observer* Books of the Year

Microbes and Man John Postgate

From mining to wine-making, microbes play a crucial role in human life. This clear, non-specialist book introduces us to microbes in all their astounding versatility – and to the latest and most exciting developments in microbiology and immunology.

Asimov's New Guide to Science Isaac Asimov

A classic work brought up to date – far and away the best one-volume survey of all the physical and biological sciences.

PENGUIN SCIENCE AND MATHEMATICS

The Panda's Thumb Stephen Jay Gould

More reflections on natural history from the author of *Ever Since Darwin*. 'A quirky and provocative exploration of the nature of evolution ... wonderfully entertaining' – *Sunday Telegraph*

Genetic Engineering for Almost Everybody William Bains

Now that the genetic engineering revolution has most certainly arrived, we all need to understand its ethical and practical implications. This book sets them out in accessible language.

The Double Helix James D. Watson

Watson's vivid and outspoken account of how he and Crick discovered the structure of DNA (and won themselves a Nobel Prize) – one of the greatest scientific achievements of the century.

The Quantum World J. C. Polkinghorne

Quantum mechanics has revolutionized our views about the structure of the physical world – yet after more than fifty years it remains controversial. This 'delightful book' (*The Times Educational Supplement*) succeeds superbly in rendering an important and complex debate both clear and fascinating.

Einstein's Universe Nigel Calder

'A valuable contribution to the demystification of relativity' – *Nature*

Mathematical Circus Martin Gardner

A mind-bending collection of puzzles and paradoxes, games and diversions from the undisputed master of recreational mathematics.

A CHOICE OF PENGUINS

The Russian Album   Michael Ignatieff

Michael Ignatieff movingly comes to terms with the meaning of his own family's memories and histories, in a book that is both an extraordinary account of the search for roots and a dramatic and poignant chronicle of four generations of a Russian family.

Beyond the Blue Horizon   Alexander Frater

The romance and excitement of the legendary Imperial Airways Eastbound Empire service – the world's longest and most adventurous scheduled air route – relived fifty years later in one of the most original travel books of the decade. 'The find of the year' – *Today*

Getting to Know the General   Graham Greene

'In August 1981 my bag was packed for my fifth visit to Panama when the news came to me over the telephone of the death of General Omar Torrijos Herrera, my friend and host...' 'Vigorous, deeply felt, at times funny, and for Greene surprisingly frank' – *Sunday Times*

The Search for the Virus   Steve Connor and Sharon Kingman

In this gripping book, two leading *New Scientist* journalists tell the remarkable story of how researchers discovered the AIDS virus and examine the links between AIDS and lifestyles. They also look at the progress being made in isolating the virus and finding a cure.

Arabian Sands   Wilfred Thesiger

'In the tradition of Burton, Doughty, Lawrence, Philby and Thomas, it is, very likely, the book about Arabia to end all books about Arabia'.– *Daily Telegraph*

Adieux: A Farewell to Sartre   Simone de Beauvoir

A devastatingly frank account of the last years of Sartre's life, and his death, by the woman who for more than half a century shared that life. 'A true labour of love, there is about it a touching sadness, a mingling of the personal with the impersonal and timeless which Sartre himself would surely have liked and understood' – *Listener*

A CHOICE OF PENGUINS

The Secret Lives of Trebitsch Lincoln   Bernard Wasserstein

Trebitsch Lincoln was Member of Parliament, international spy, right-wing revolutionary, Buddhist monk – and this century's most extraordinary conman. 'Surely the final work on a truly extraordinary career' – Hugh Trevor-Roper. 'An utterly improbable story ... a biographical coup' – *Guardian*

Out of Africa   Karen Blixen (Isak Dinesen)

After the failure of her coffee-farm in Kenya, where she lived from 1913 to 1931, Karen Blixen went home to Denmark and wrote this unforgettable account of her experiences. 'No reader can put the book down without some share in the author's poignant farewell to her farm' – *Observer*

In My Wildest Dreams   Leslie Thomas

The autobiography of Leslie Thomas, author of *The Magic Army* and *The Dearest and the Best*. From Barnardo boy to original virgin soldier, from apprentice journalist to famous novelist, it is an amazing story. 'Hugely enjoyable' – *Daily Express*

The Winning Streak   Walter Goldsmith and David Clutterbuck

Marks and Spencer, Saatchi and Saatchi, United Biscuits, GEC ... The UK's top companies reveal their formulas for success, in an important and stimulating book that no British manager can afford to ignore.

Bird of Life, Bird of Death   Jonathan Evan Maslow

In the summer of 1983 Jonathan Maslow set out to find the quetzal. In doing so, he placed himself between the natural and unnatural histories of Central America, between the vulnerable magnificence of nature and the terrible destructiveness of man. 'A wonderful book' – *The New York Times Book Review*

Mob Star   Gene Mustain and Jerry Capeci

Handsome, charming, deadly, John Gotti is the real-life Mafia boss at the head of New York's most feared criminal family. *Mob Star* tells the chilling and compelling story of the rise to power of the most powerful criminal in America.

A CHOICE OF PENGUINS

Return to the Marshes   Gavin Young

His remarkable portrait of the remote and beautiful world of the Marsh Arabs, whose centuries-old existence is now threatened with extinction by twentieth-century warfare. 'A talent for vivid description rarely found outside good fiction' – Jonathan Raban in the *Sunday Times*

Manhattan '45   Jan Morris

Disembarking with the victorious GIs returning after the war, Jan Morris takes us on a wonderfully nostalgic exploration of Manhattan in 1945; an affectionate portrait of an unrepeatable moment in history.

Britain's Poisoned Water   Frances and Phil Craig

Every day millions of British families drink water containing toxic chemicals. But what are we doing about it? This startling investigation is essential and shocking reading for anyone concerned about our environment, our health, and the health of our children.

How I Grew   Mary McCarthy

Mary McCarthy's account of her formative years possesses all the insight, wit and intelligence of her classic *Memories of a Catholic Girlhood* and her international bestseller *The Group*. 'Rich, generous stuff … it leaves one licking one's lips for what is yet to come' – Penelope Lively

Who Should be Sleeping in Your Bed – and Why   James Oliver

Should a Little Princess be faithful to a Wimp? This series of simple quizzes and personality profiles devised by clinical psychologist James Oliver will show you why infidelity happens – and how to make sure it doesn't happen to you.

The Big Red Train Ride   Eric Newby

From Moscow to the Pacific on the Trans-Siberian Railway is an eight-day journey of nearly six thousand miles through seven time zones. In 1977 Eric Newby set out with his wife, an official guide and a photographer on this journey. 'The best kind of travel book' – Paul Theroux

A CHOICE OF PENGUINS

Trail of Havoc Patrick Marnham

In this brilliant piece of detective work, Patrick Marnham has traced the steps of Lord Lucan from the fateful night of 7 November 1974 when he murdered his children's nanny and attempted to kill his ex-wife. As well as being a fascinating investigation, the book is also a brilliant portrayal of a privileged section of society living under great stress.

Light Years Gary Kinder

Eduard Meier, an uneducated Swiss farmer, claims since 1975 to have had over 100 UFO sightings and encounters with 'beamships' from the Pleiades. His evidence is such that even the most die-hard sceptics have been unable to explain away the phenomenon.

And the Band Played On Politics, People and the AIDS Epidemic
Randy Shilts

Written after years of extensive research by the only American journalist to cover the epidemic full-time, *And the Band Played On* is a masterpiece of reportage and a tragic record of mismanaged institutions and scientific vendettas, of sexual politics and personal suffering.

The Return of a Native Reporter Robert Chesshyre

Robert Chesshyre returned to Britain in 1985 from the United States, where he had spent four years as the *Observer*'s correspondent. This is his devastating account of the country he came home to: intolerant, brutal, grasping and politically and economically divided. It is a nation, he asserts, struggling to find a role.

Women and Love Shere Hite

In this culmination of *The Hite Report* trilogy, 4,500 women provide an eloquent testimony to the disturbingly unsatisfying nature of their emotional relationships and point to what they see as the causes. *Women and Love* reveals a new cultural perspective in formation: as women change the emotional structure of their lives, they are defining a fundamental debate over the future of our society.

Justice for
the world's poor

WORLD
DEVELOPMENT
MOVEMENT

The World Development Movement (WDM) is Britain's leading pressure group on Third World issues. Unlike aid charities, WDM exists solely to campaign for political change. The poor in the Third World have benefited from consistent changes WDM has won on issues such as aid, trade and debt. In recent years WDM has successfully influenced decisions taken by the World Bank, the British Government and the European Community.

WDM is cross-party and backed by the major aid agencies and the churches. It links together people who want to campaign either as an individual or as part of a local group to change the unjust structures that perpetuate poverty.

You can join as a member or support our work as a friend. Members receive a monthly newspaper and campaign leaflets.

By becoming a member or a friend you can support WDM's current campaign, 'A Question of Survival'.

Please return to:
World Development, 25 Beehive Place, London SW9 7QR   £   p

£10 for a year's membership in WDM   . . . .

£10 to support WDM as a friend   . . . .

Please supply *Poverty and the Planet* . . . copies at £5.99   . . . .

Contribution towards postage & packing   . . . .

Free information on WDM's 'A Question of Survival' Campaign   ☐

Donation to WDM's 'A Question of Survival' Campaign   . . . .

                                   TOTAL ENCLOSED   . . . .

Name   ....

Address ....

.... Postcode ....